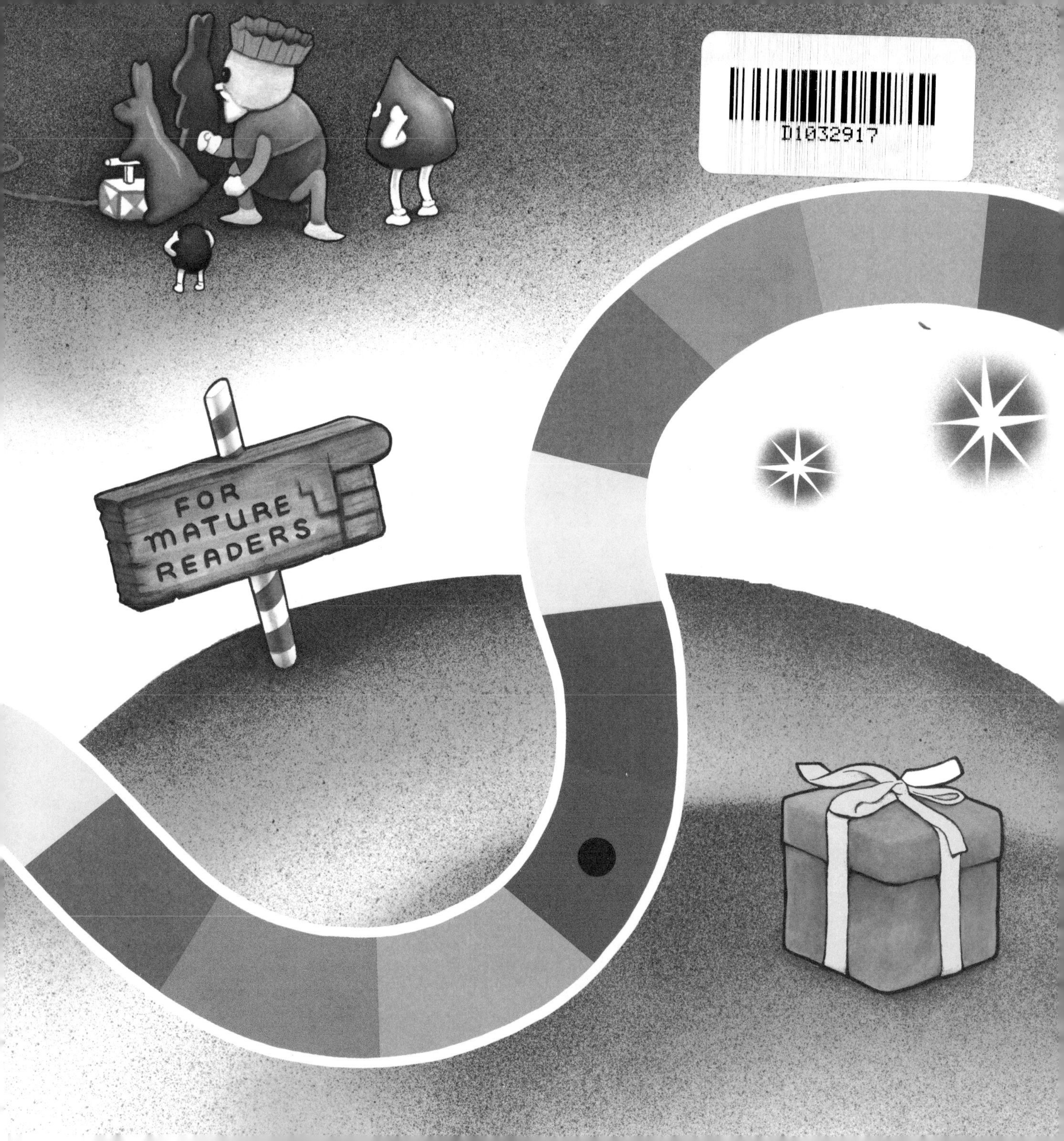
FOR
MATURE
READERS

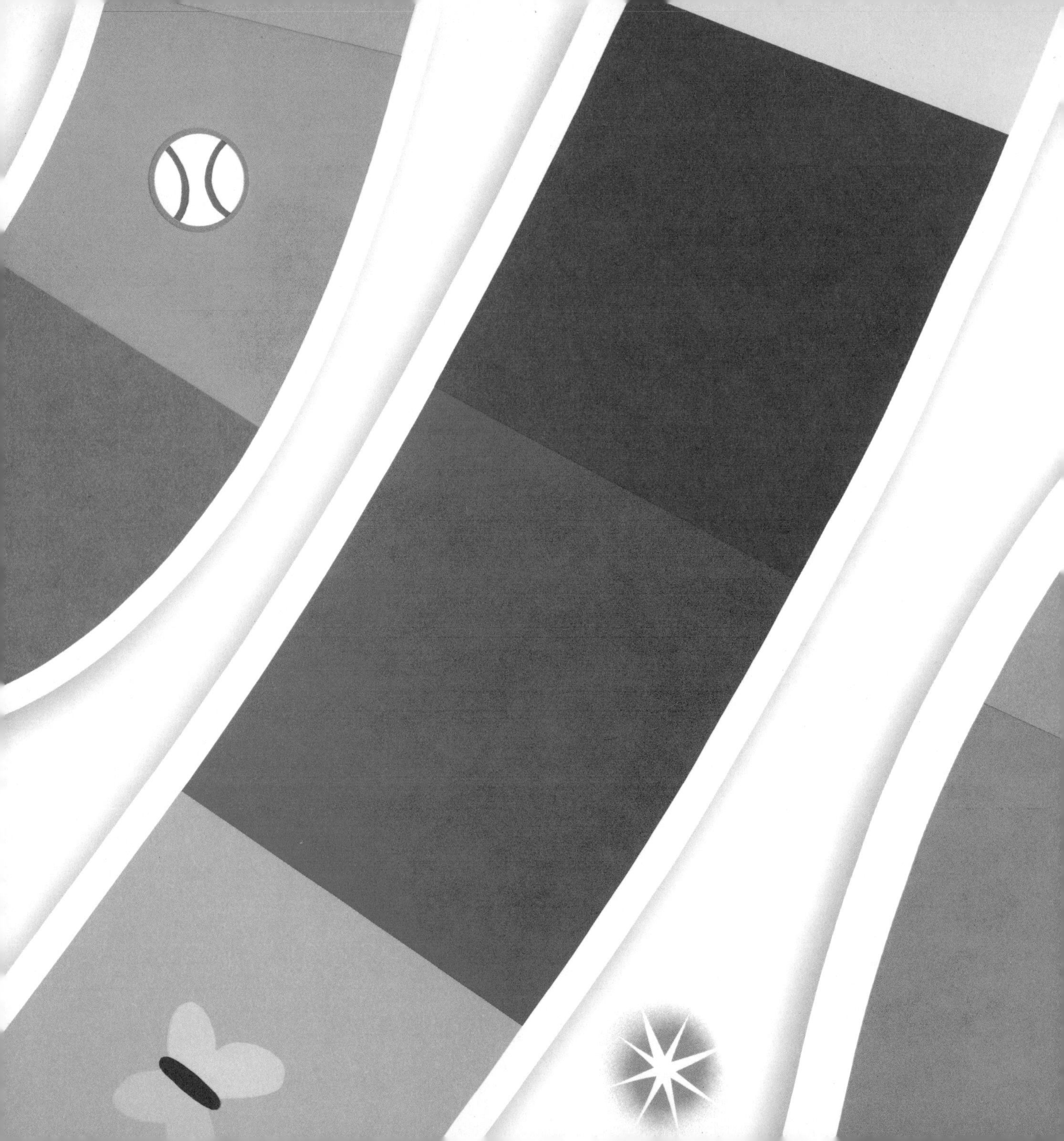

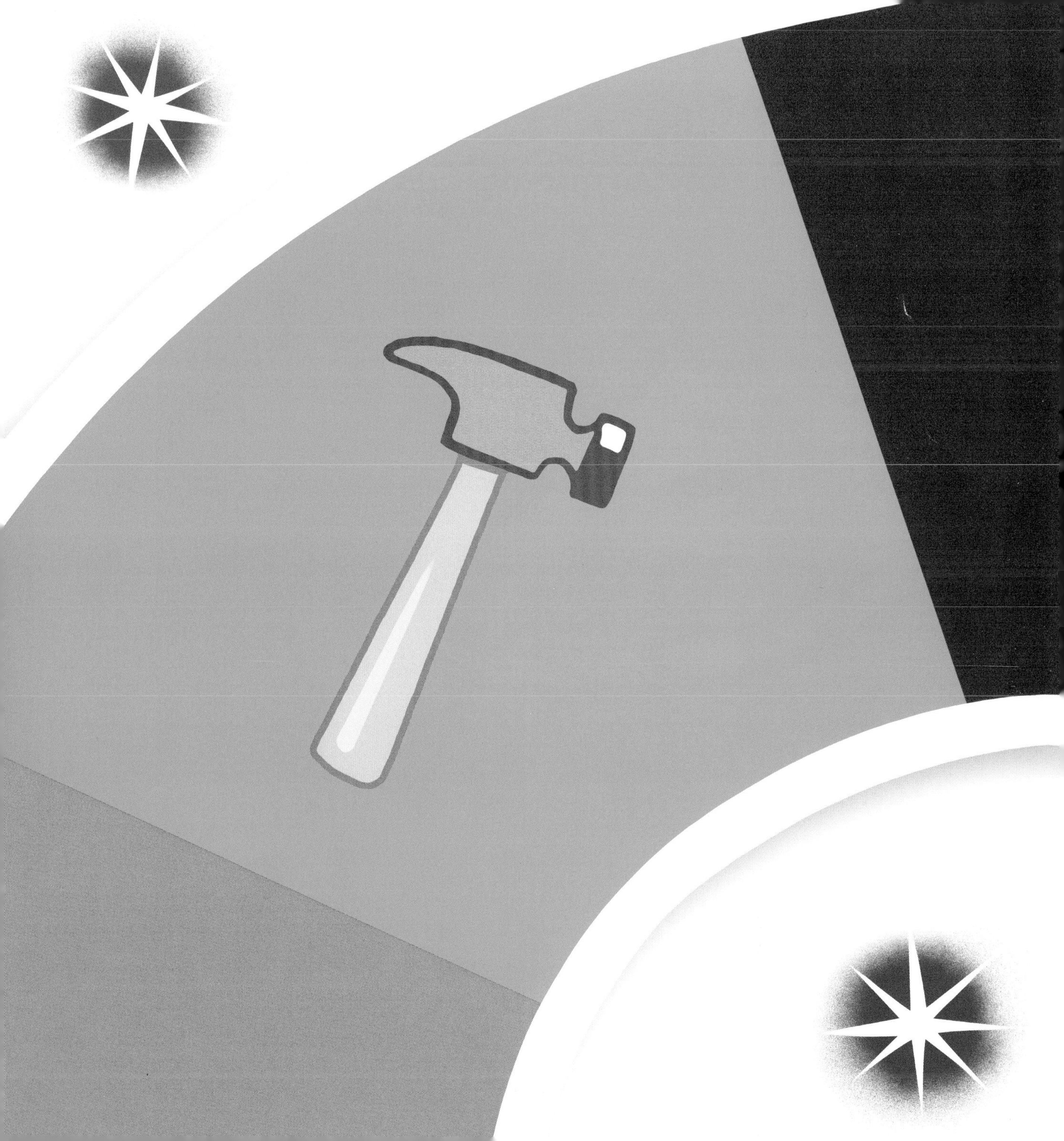

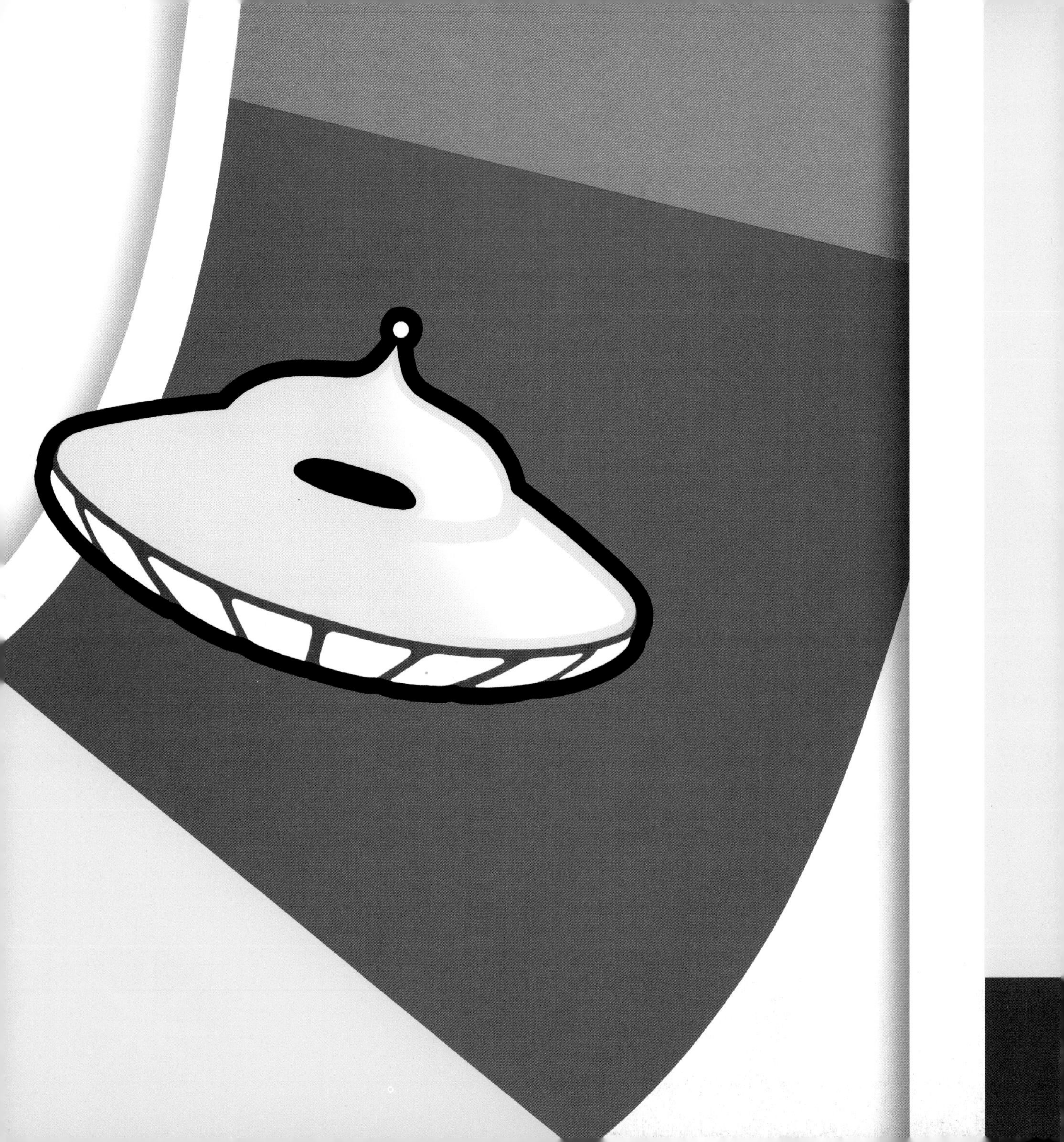

The Trial of
COLONEL
SWEETO
and Other Stories

A Collection of the Comic Strips of *The Perry Bible Fellowship*

by Nicholas Gurewitch

Publisher Mike Richardson
Art Director Lia Ribacchi
Designers Nicholas Gurewitch and Scott Cook
Assistant Editor Katie Moody
Editor Dave Land

THE PERRY BIBLE FELLOWSHIP: THE TRIAL OF COLONEL SWEETO AND OTHER STORIES™

Published by
Dark Horse Books
A division of Dark Horse Comics, Inc.
10956 SE Main Street
Milwaukie, OR 97222

Dark Horse Comics, Inc.
10956 SE Main Street
Milwaukie, OR 97222

darkhorse.com
pbfcomics.com

First edition: September 2007
ISBN-10: 1-59307-844-7
ISBN-13: 978-1-59307-844-7

10 9 8 7 6 5 4 3 2
Printed in the United States of America

CONTENTS

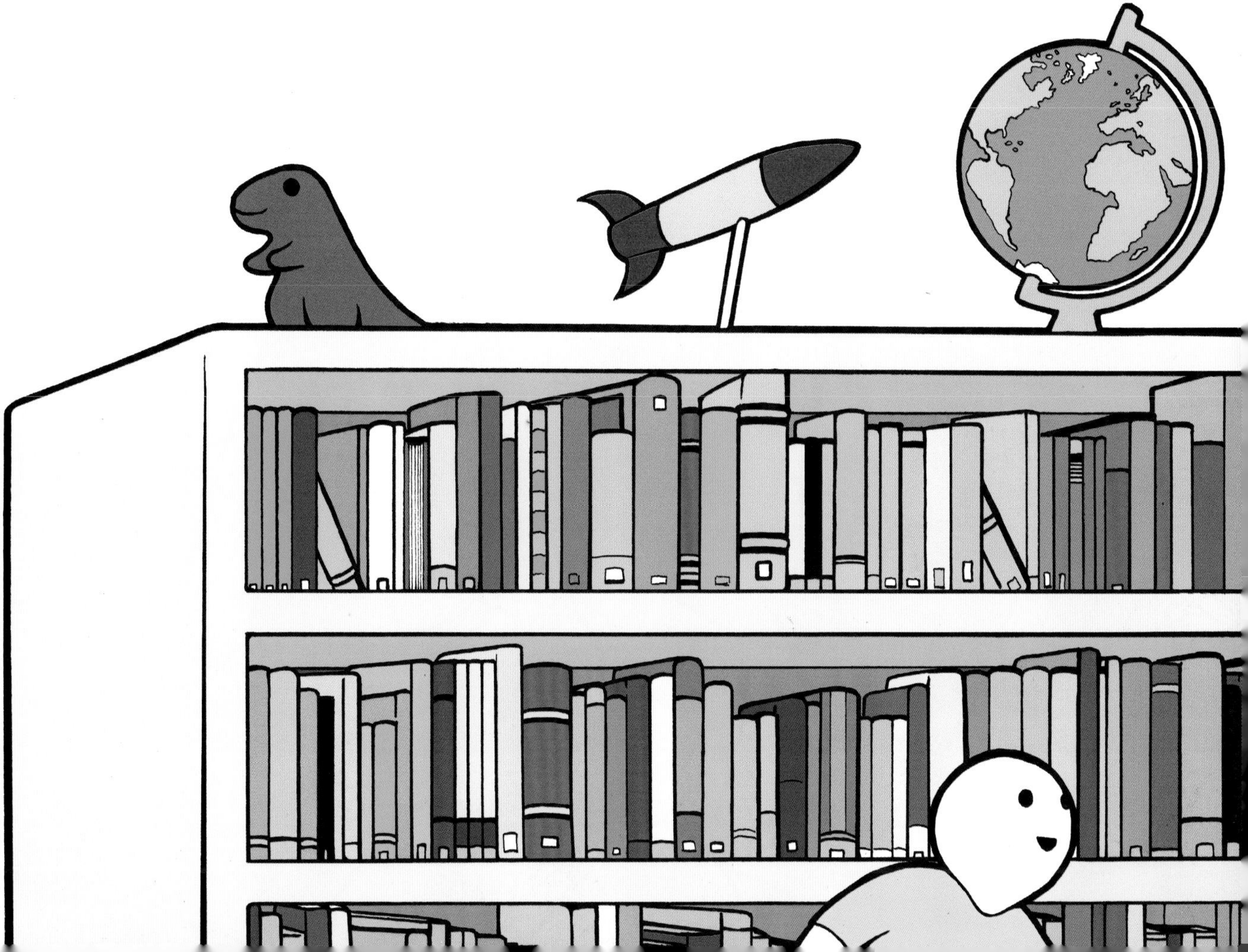

The Perry Bible Fellowship . . . what in the name of all that's confounding does *that* mean? Wait, I take that question back. If that mellifluous phrase has a logical genesis, I don't want to know about it. It has settled down in my mind as the only possible name for Nick Gurewitch's comic strip, and like the comics themselves it is both concrete and ghostly. It rings in the imaginary night like a flat paper gong, and I for one don't want it to stop. I'll bet you don't want it to stop, either. I'll bet you hope Mr. Gurewitch will keep on making these terrifyingly funny cartoons forever so that you can keep having your mind wedgied. Well, he won't, so love 'em while you can.

—Jim Woodring

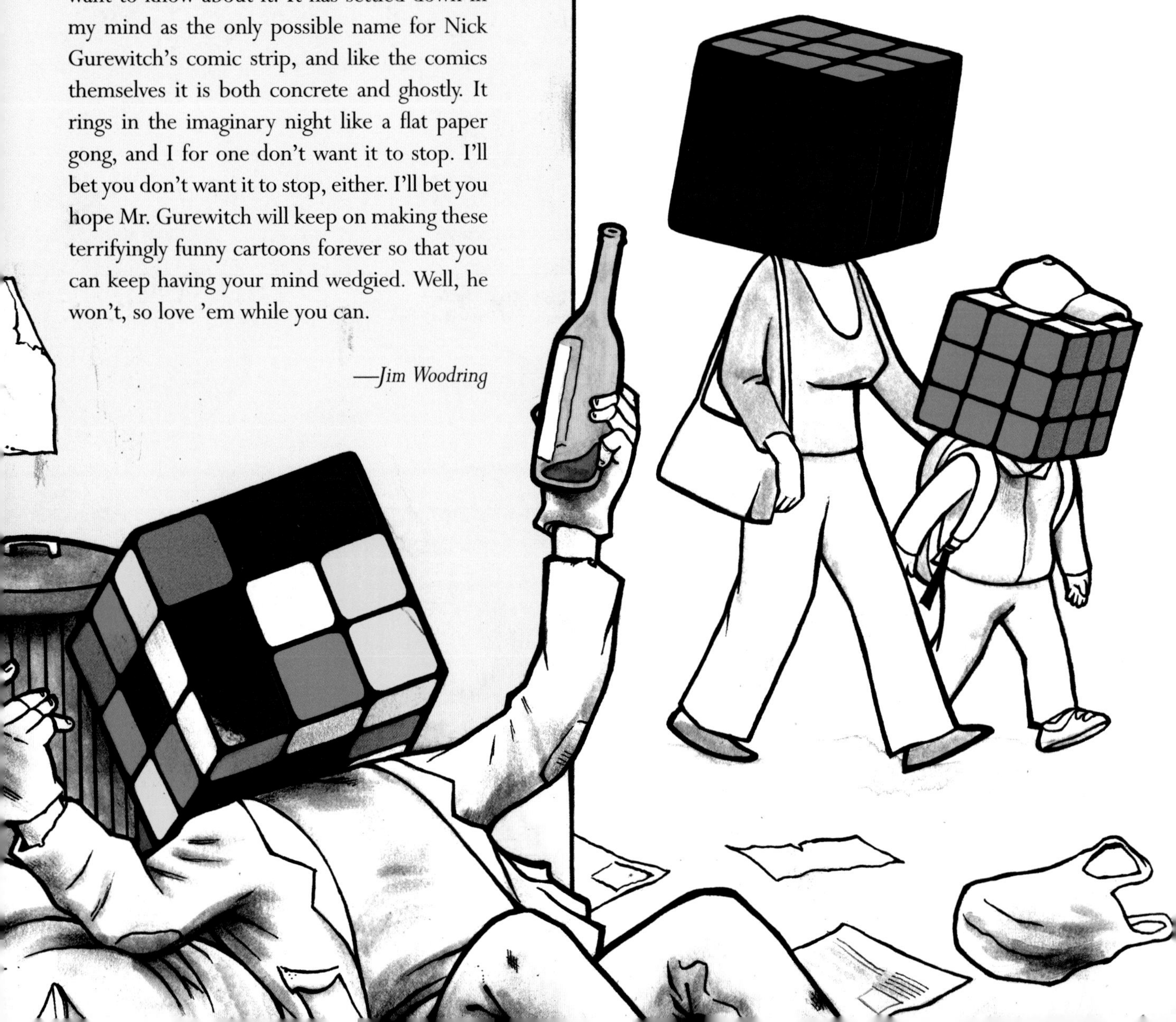

Colonel Sweeto

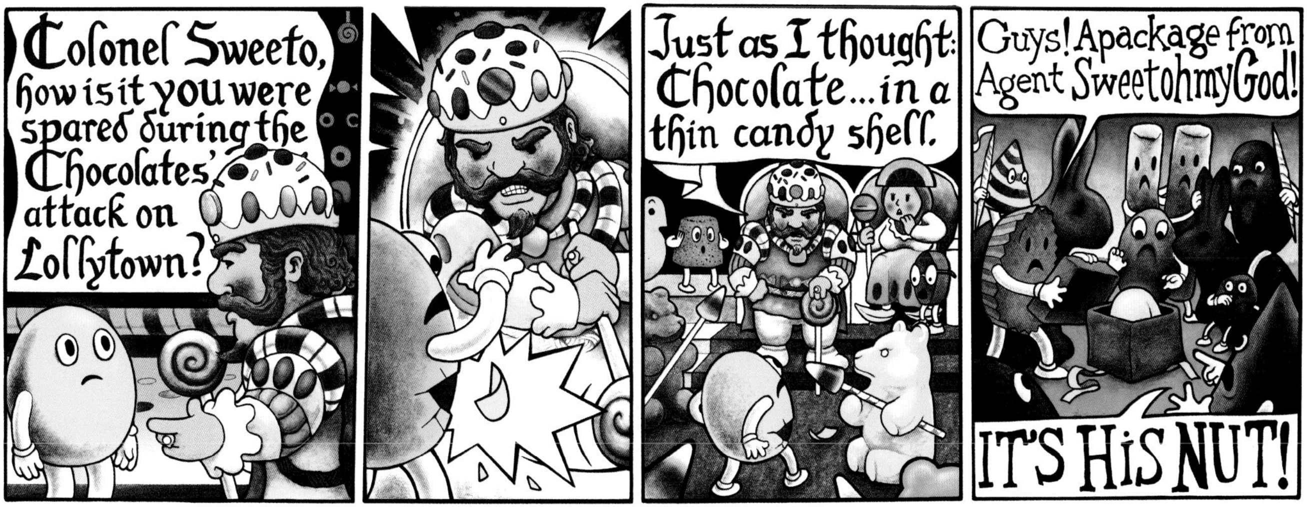
Colonel Sweeto, how is it you were spared during the Chocolates' attack on Lollytown?
Just as I thought: Chocolate...in a thin candy shell.
Guys! A package from Agent Sweetohmygod!
IT'S HIS NUT!

Nice Shirt

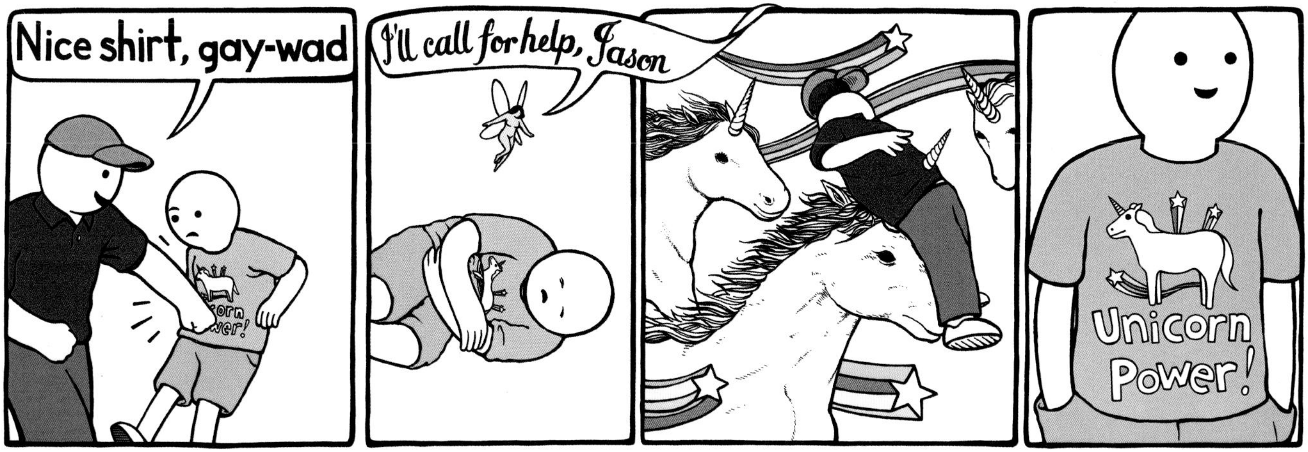
Nice shirt, gay-wad
I'll call for help, Jason
Unicorn Power!

Dinner Time Machine

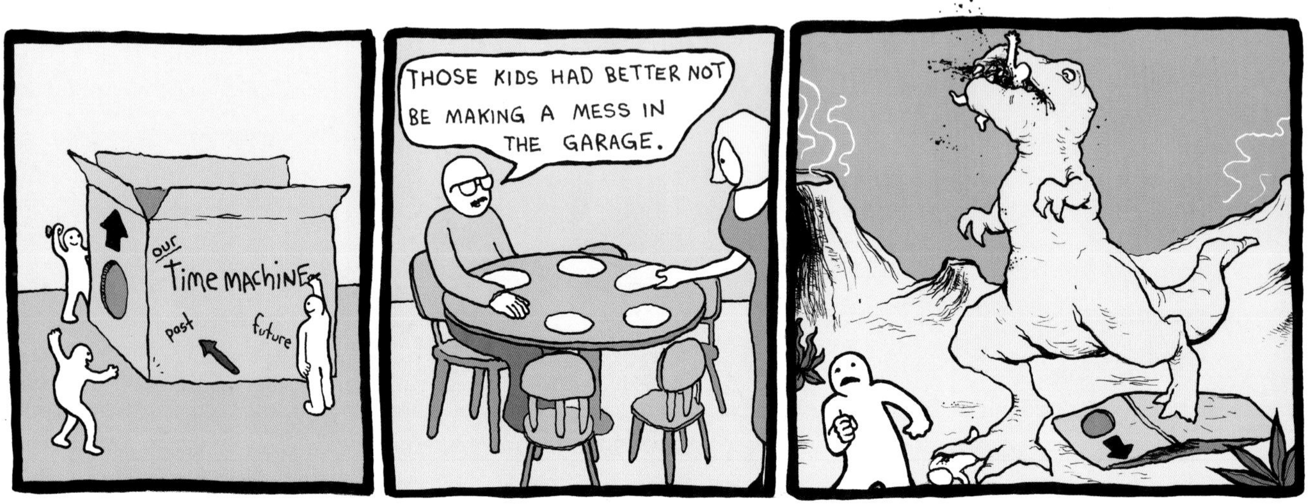
our
Time MACHINE
past
future
THOSE KIDS HAD BETTER NOT BE MAKING A MESS IN THE GARAGE.

Volcano Snails

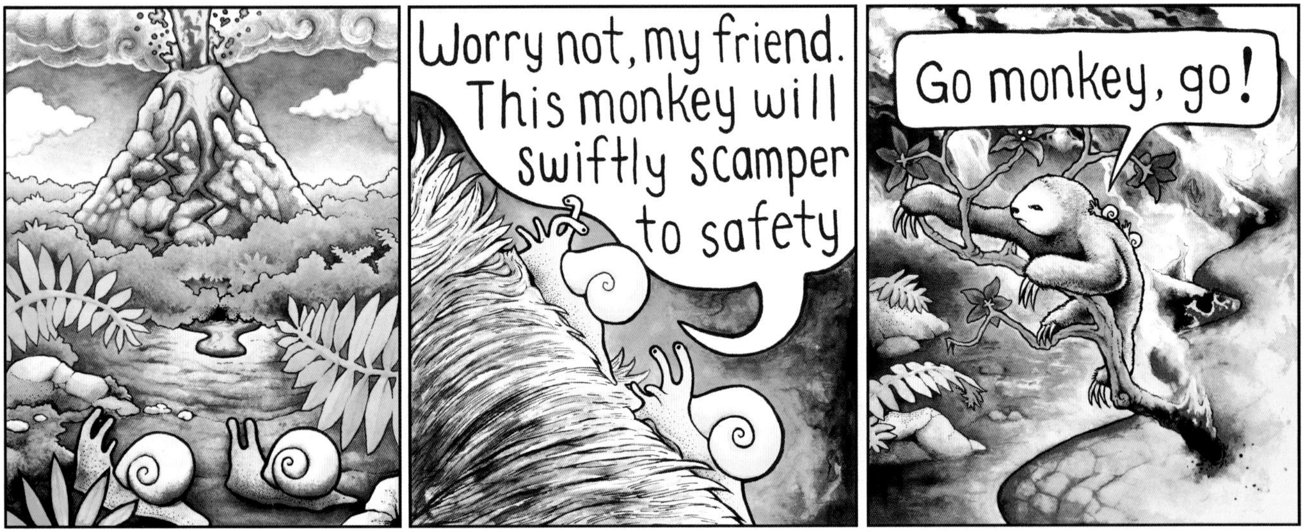
Worry not, my friend. This monkey will swiftly scamper to safety
Go monkey, go!

Instant Bacon

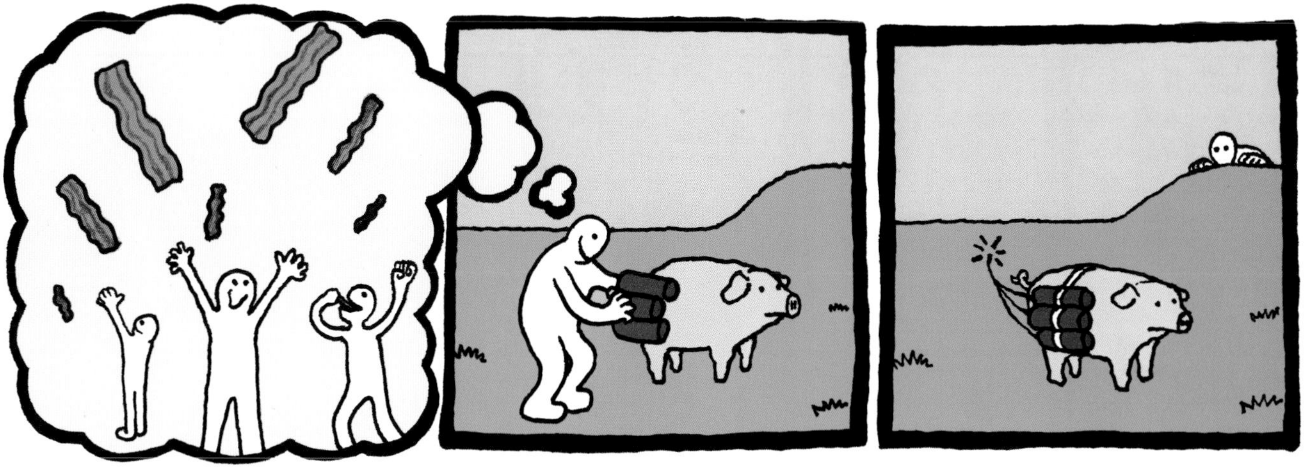

Bunny Pit

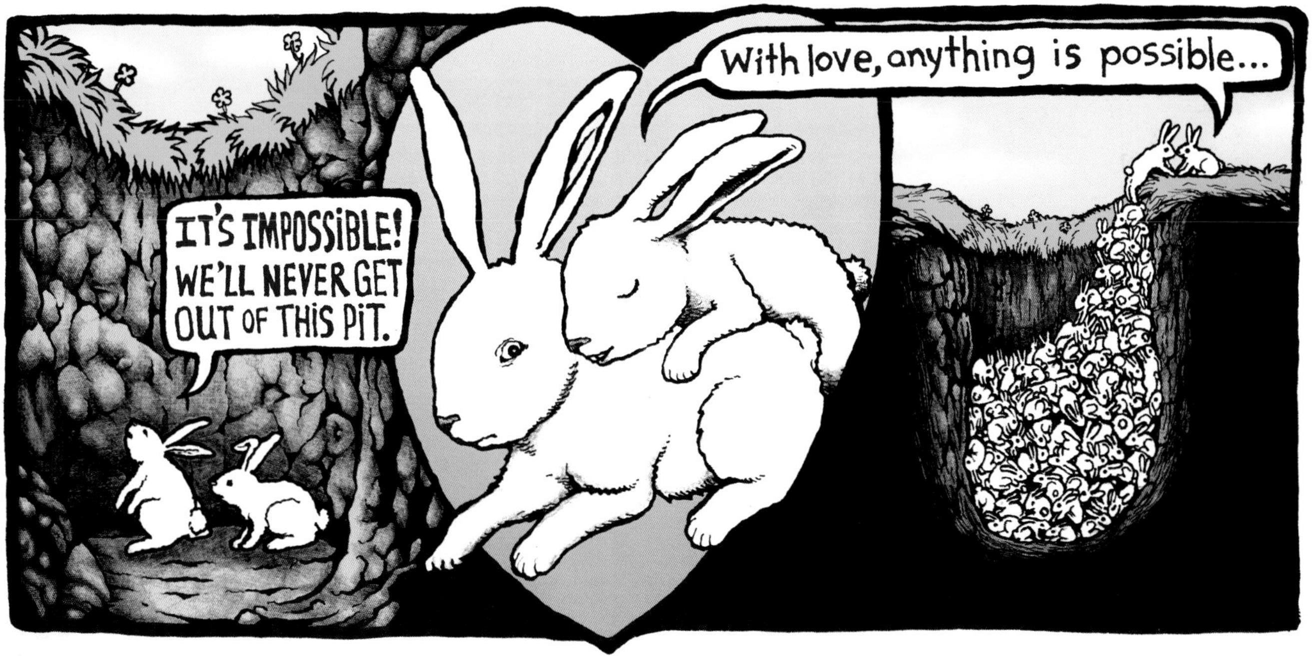
IT'S IMPOSSIBLE! WE'LL NEVER GET OUT OF THIS PIT.
With love, anything is possible...

Puppy Wish

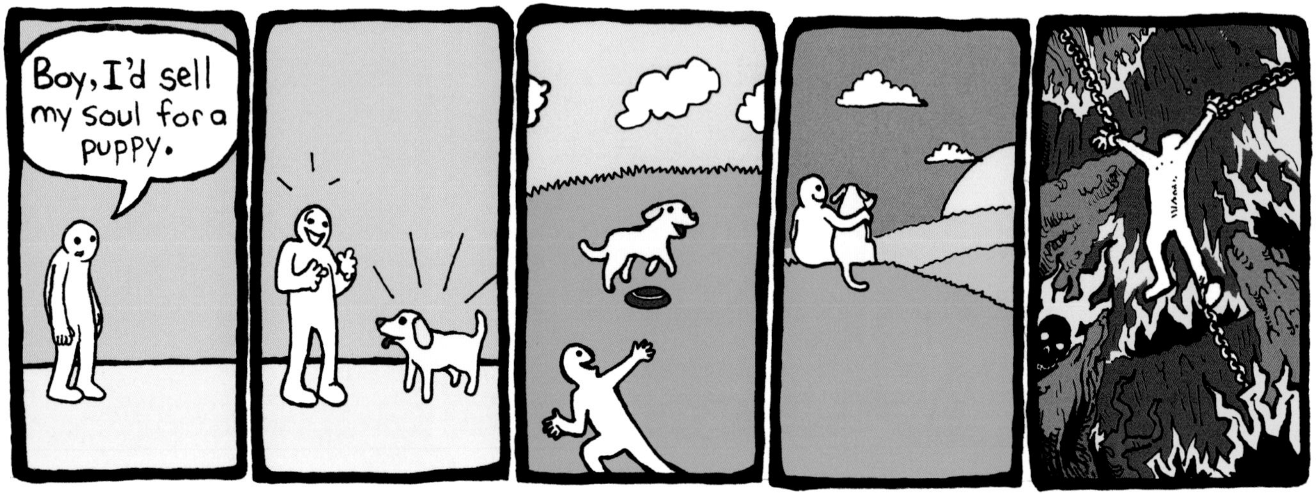
Boy, I'd sell my soul for a puppy.

Zarflax

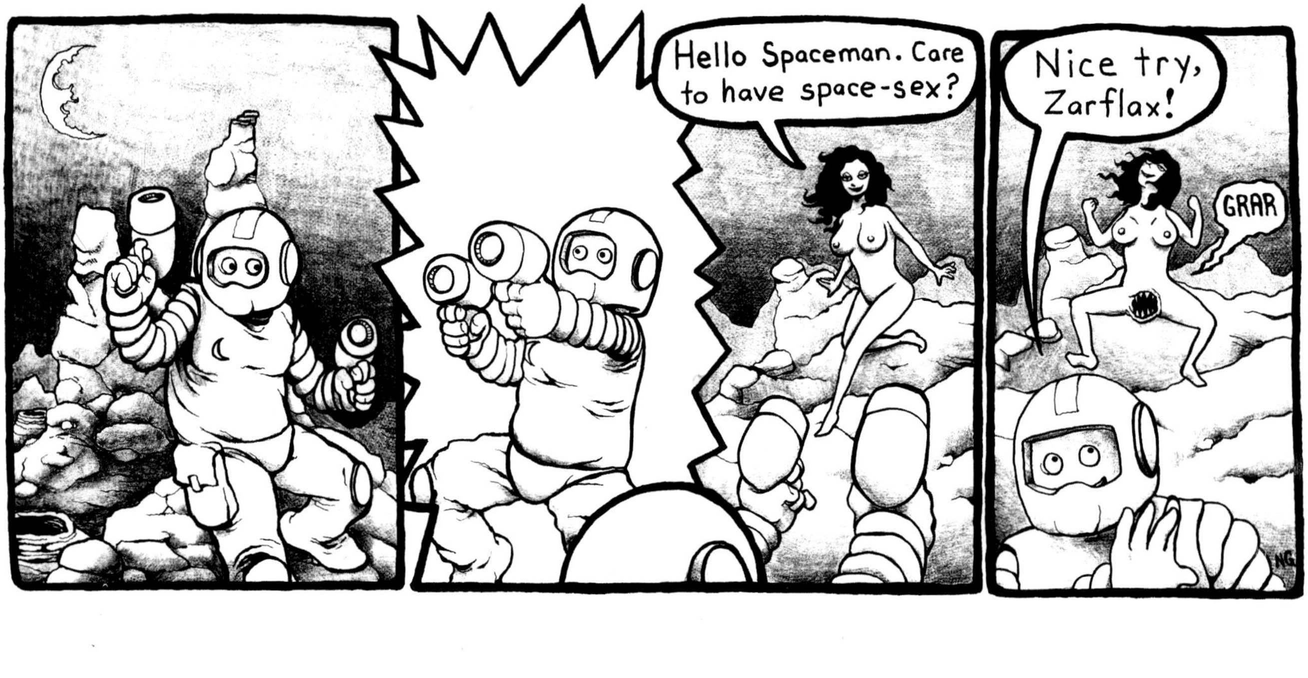
Hello Spaceman. Care to have space-sex?
Nice try, Zarflax!
GRAR
NG

Gotcha the Clown

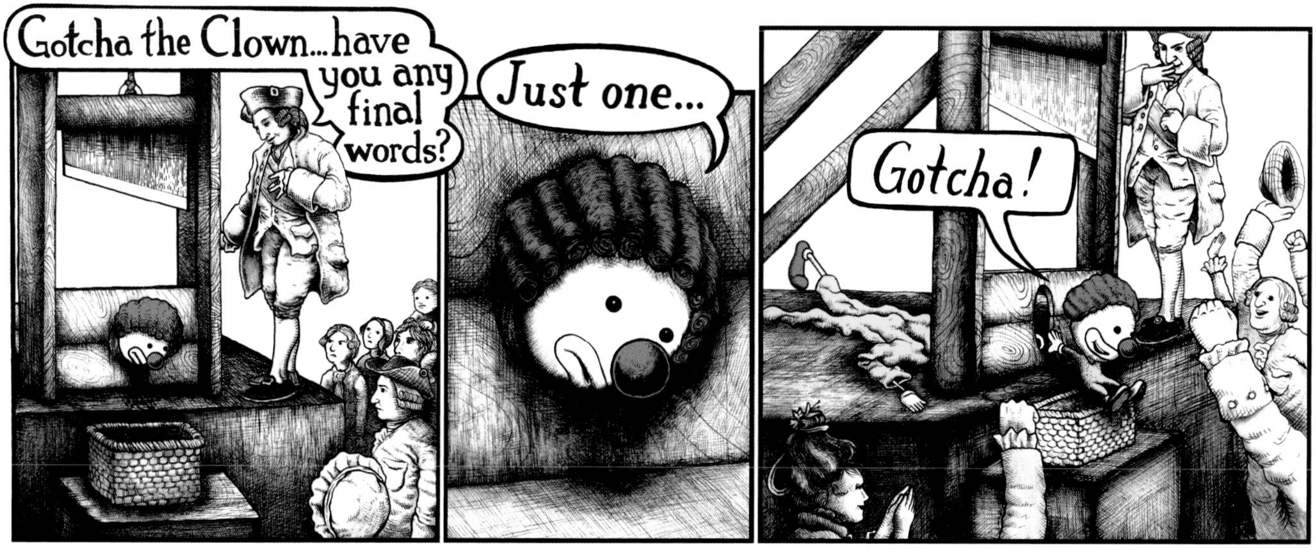
Gotcha the Clown...have you any final words?
Just one...
Gotcha!

Bear Boy

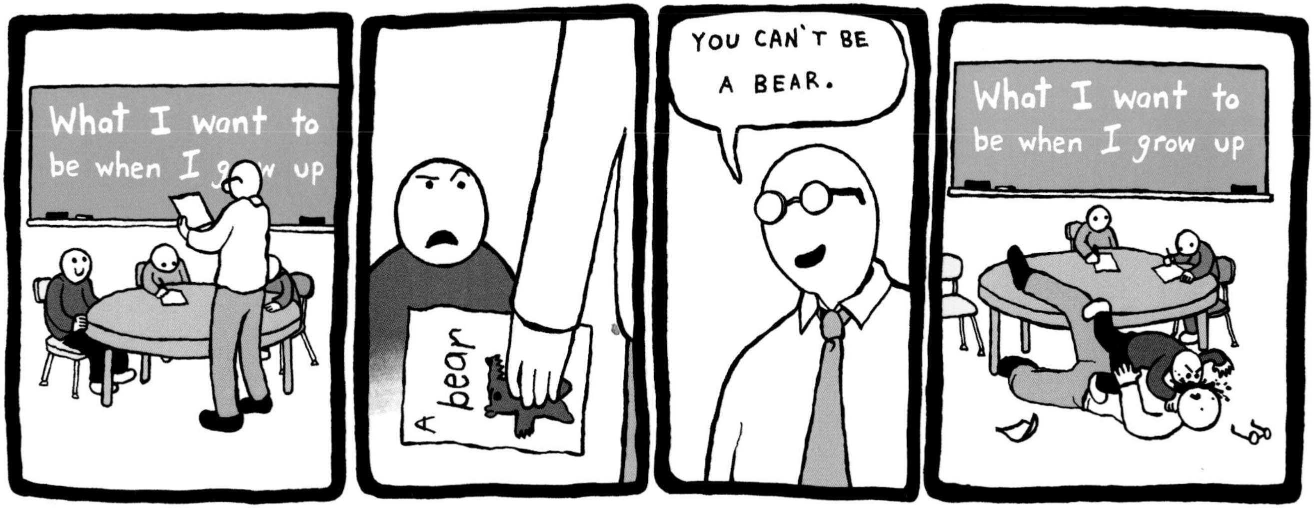
What I want to be when I grow up
A bear
YOU CAN'T BE A BEAR.
What I want to be when I grow up

New Specs for Ken

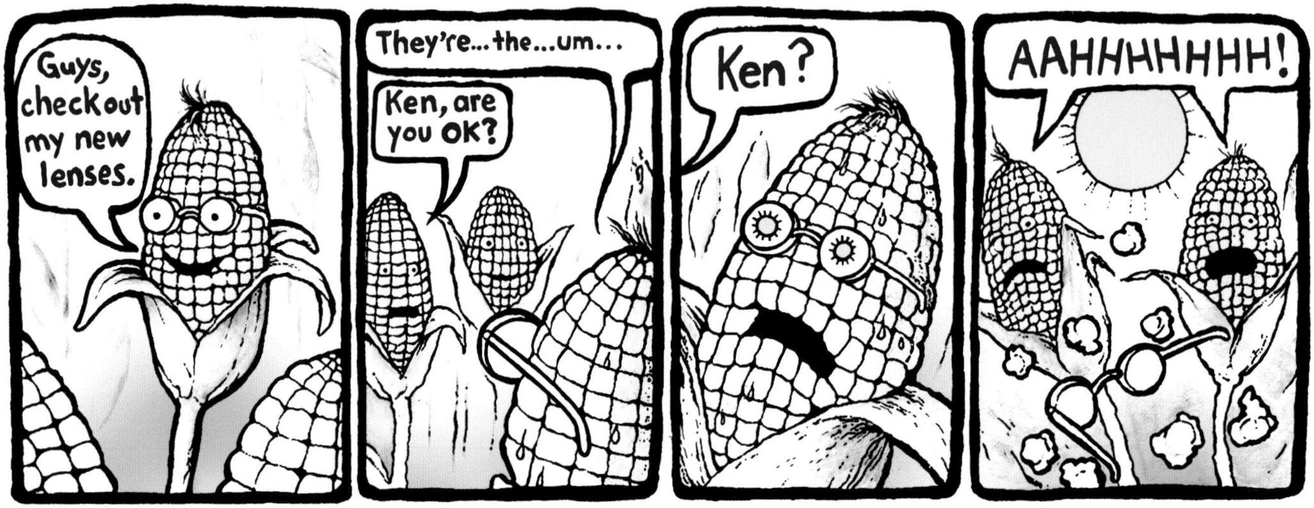
Guys, check out my new lenses.
They're... the... um...
Ken, are you OK?
Ken?
AAHHHHHHH!

Dinosaur Sheriff

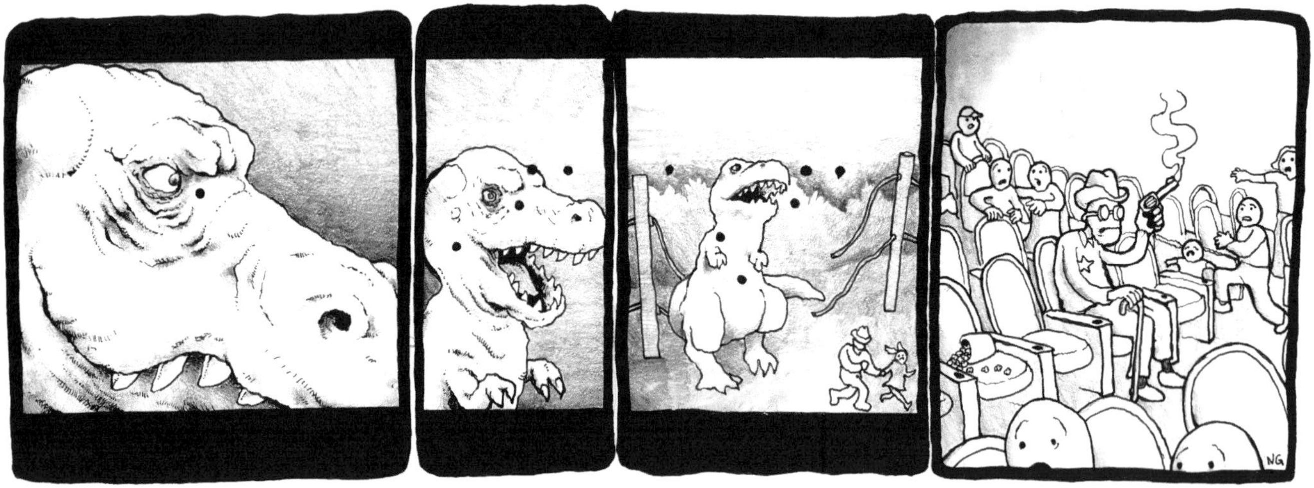
NG

Yarteries

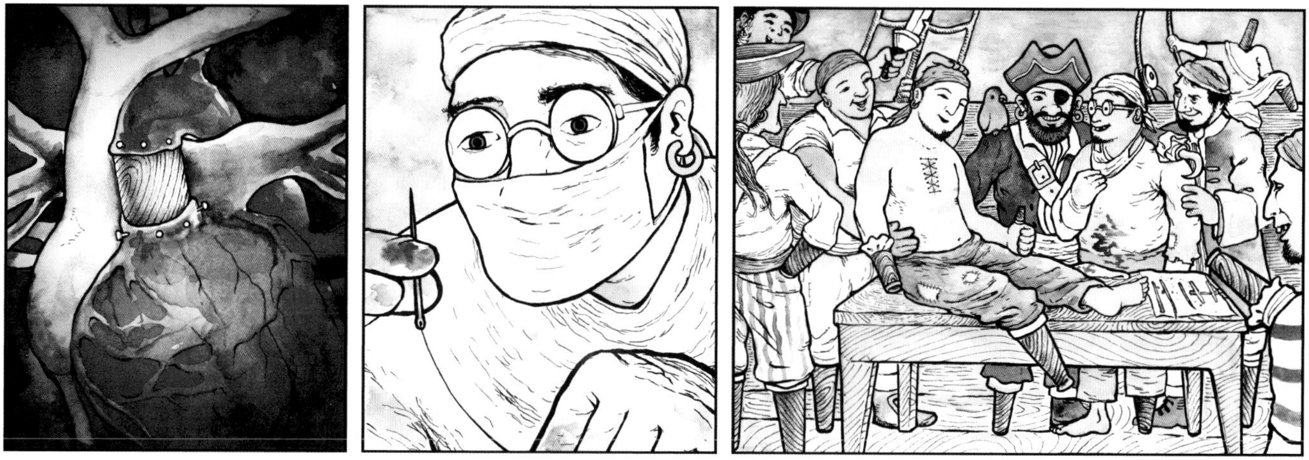

Goodnight Full Moon

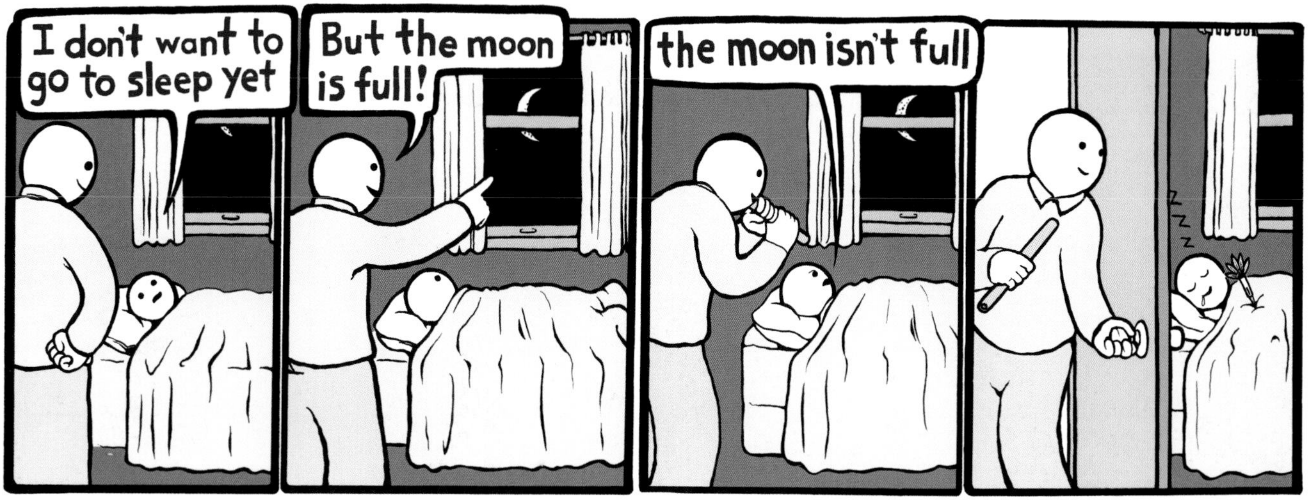
I don't want to go to sleep yet
But the moon is full!
the moon isn't full
Z
Z
Z

Today's My Birthday

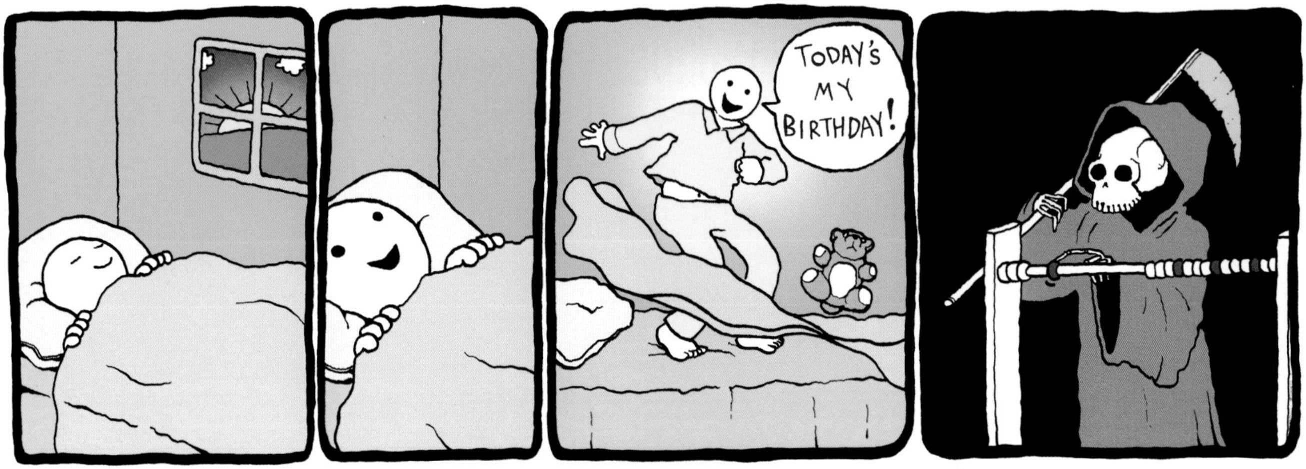
TODAY'S MY BIRTHDAY!

Genius Sir

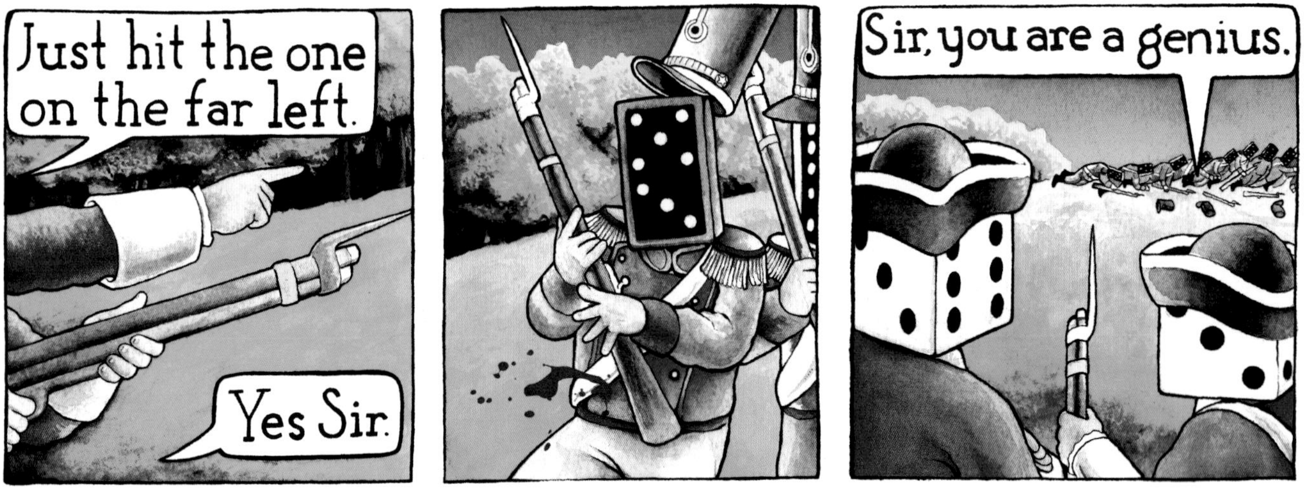
Just hit the one on the far left.
Yes Sir.
Sir, you are a genius.

Sgt. Grumbles

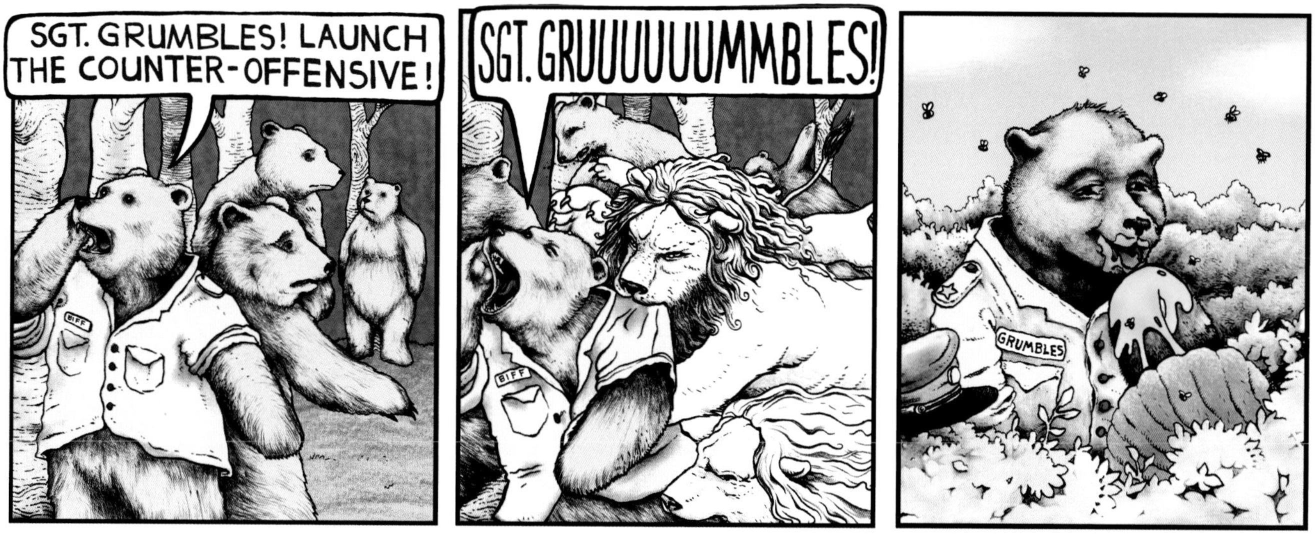
SGT. GRUMBLES! LAUNCH THE COUNTER-OFFENSIVE!
BIFF
SGT. GRUUUUUUMMBLES!
BIFF
GRUMBLES

Kinder-Interview

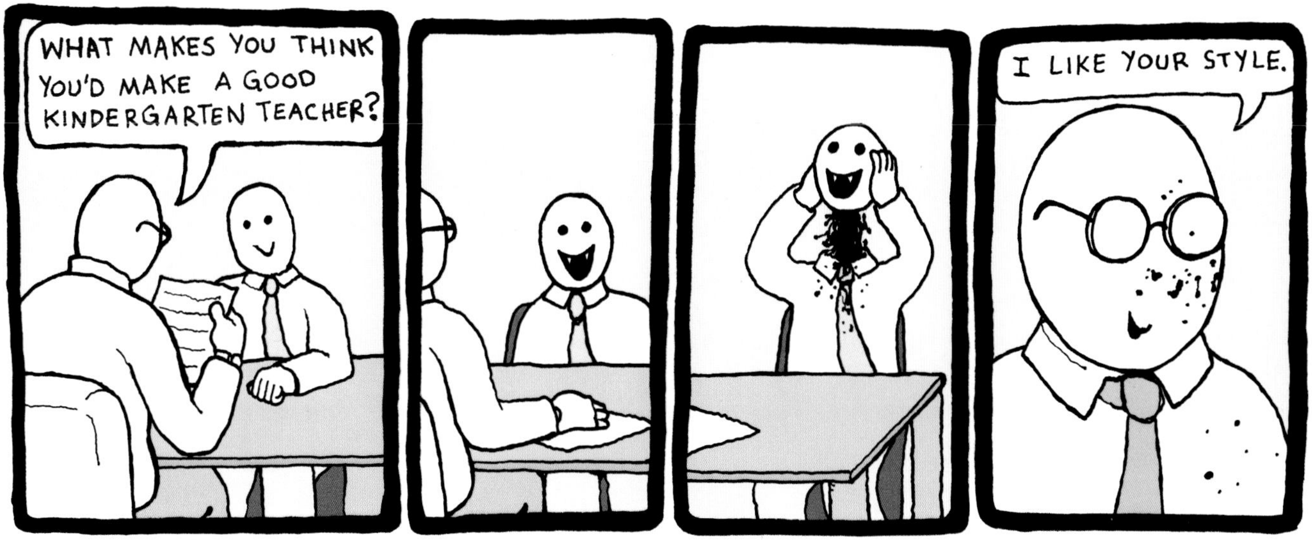
WHAT MAKES YOU THINK YOU'D MAKE A GOOD KINDERGARTEN TEACHER?
I LIKE YOUR STYLE.

Gopher Girlfriend

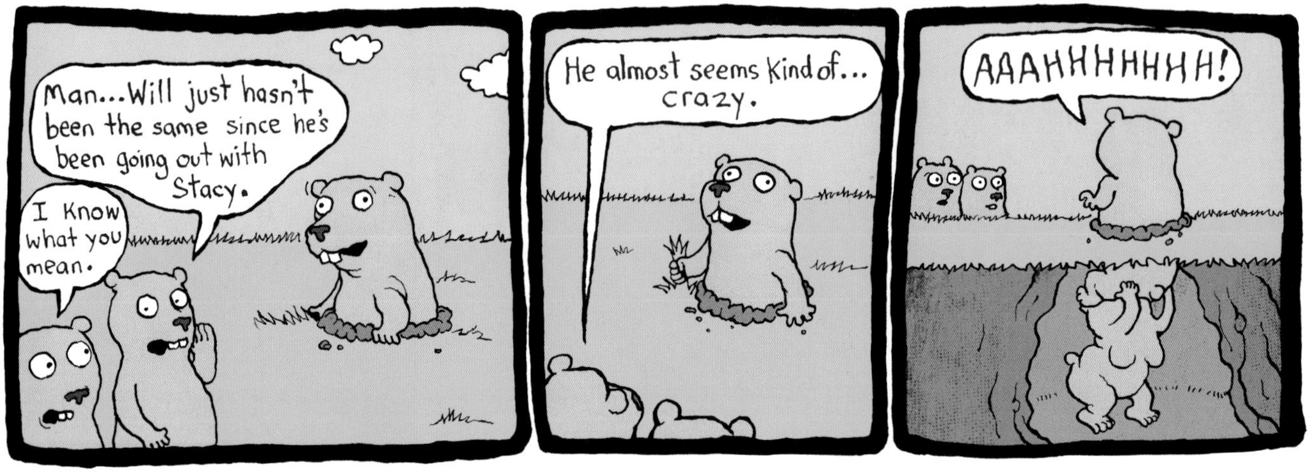
Man...Will just hasn't been the same since he's been going out with Stacy.
I know what you mean.
He almost seems kind of... crazy.
AAAHHHHHHH!

Penguin Enemy

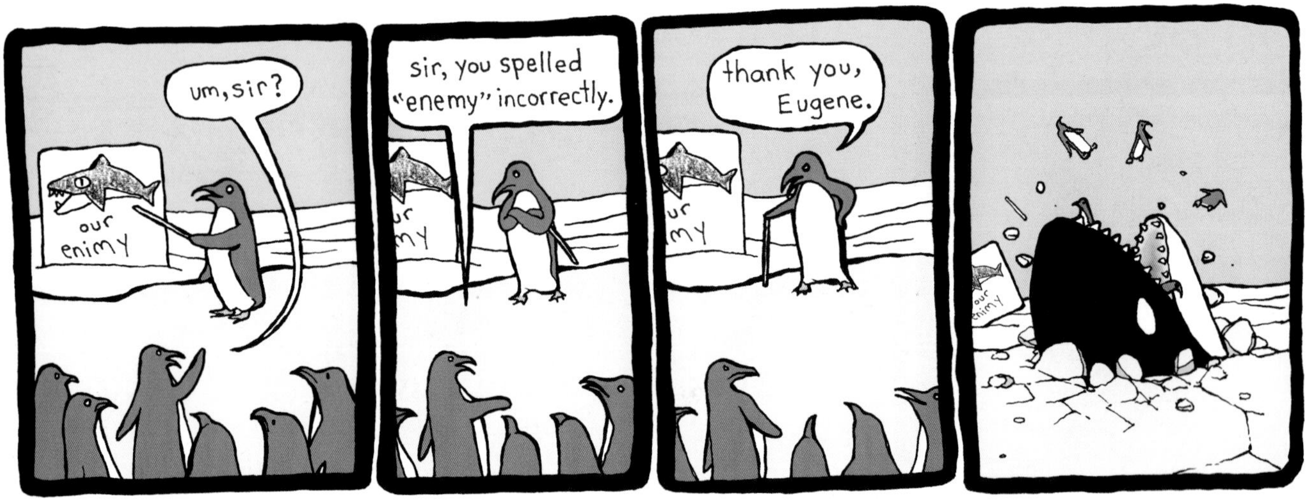
our enimy
um, sir?
sir, you spelled "enemy" incorrectly.
thank you, Eugene.

Annihilation

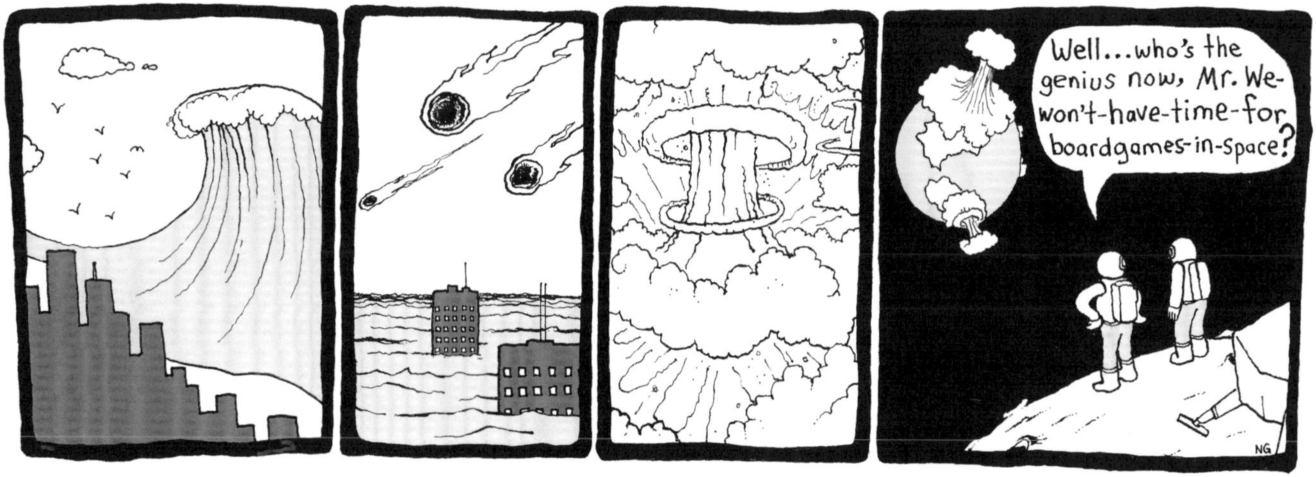
Well...who's the genius now, Mr. We-won't-have-time-for boardgames-in-space?
NG

Suicide Train

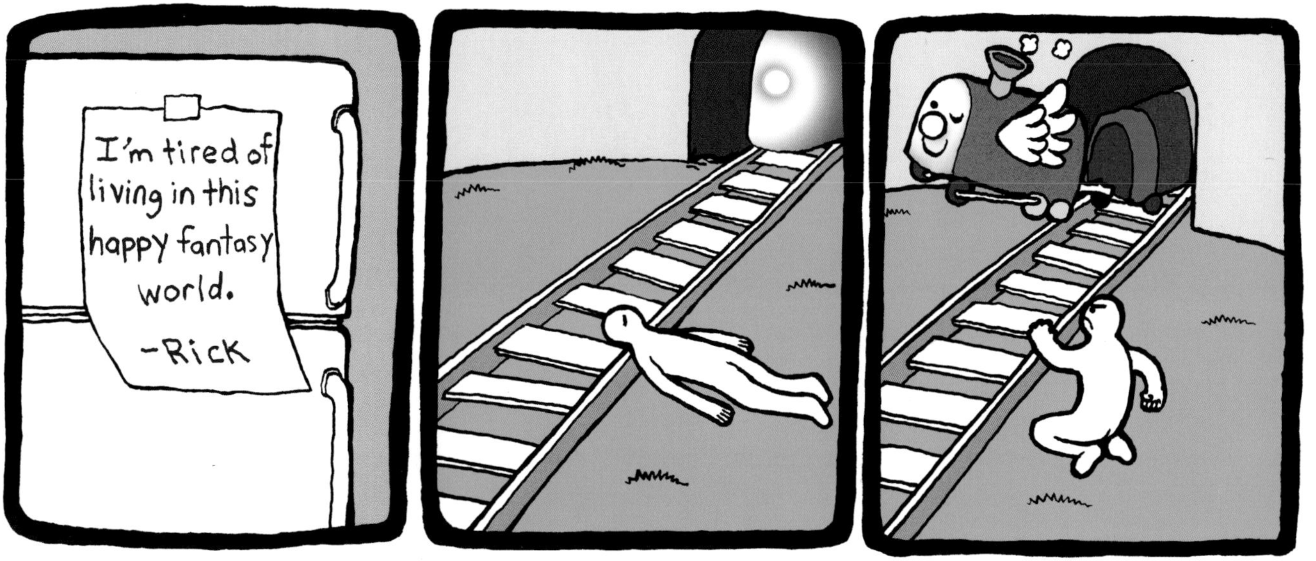
I'm tired of living in this happy fantasy world. -Rick

Raft Friends

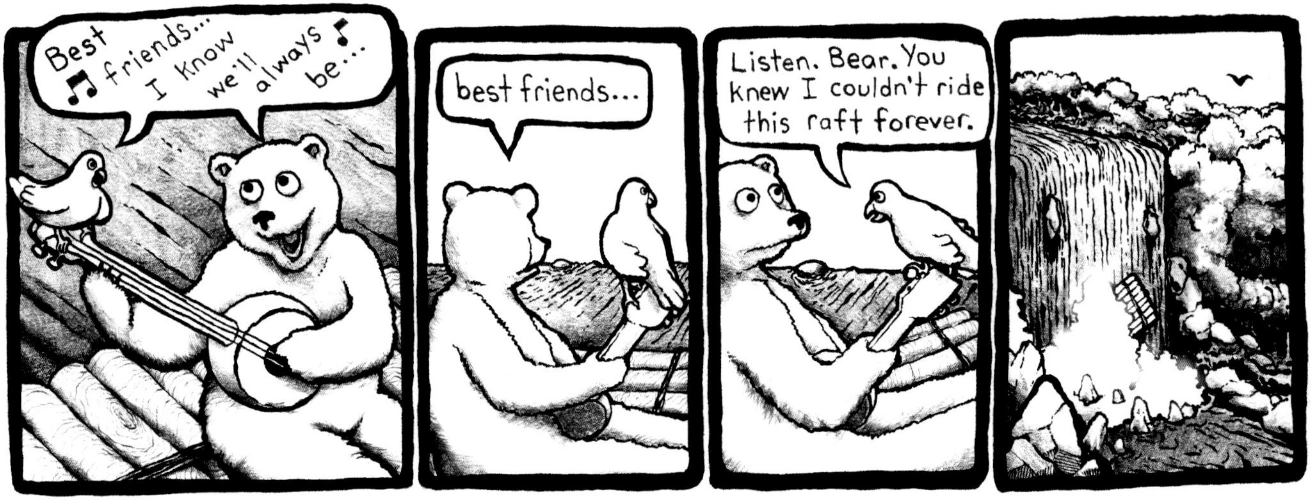
Best friends... I know we'll always be...
best friends...
Listen. Bear. You knew I couldn't ride this raft forever.

Cover Blown

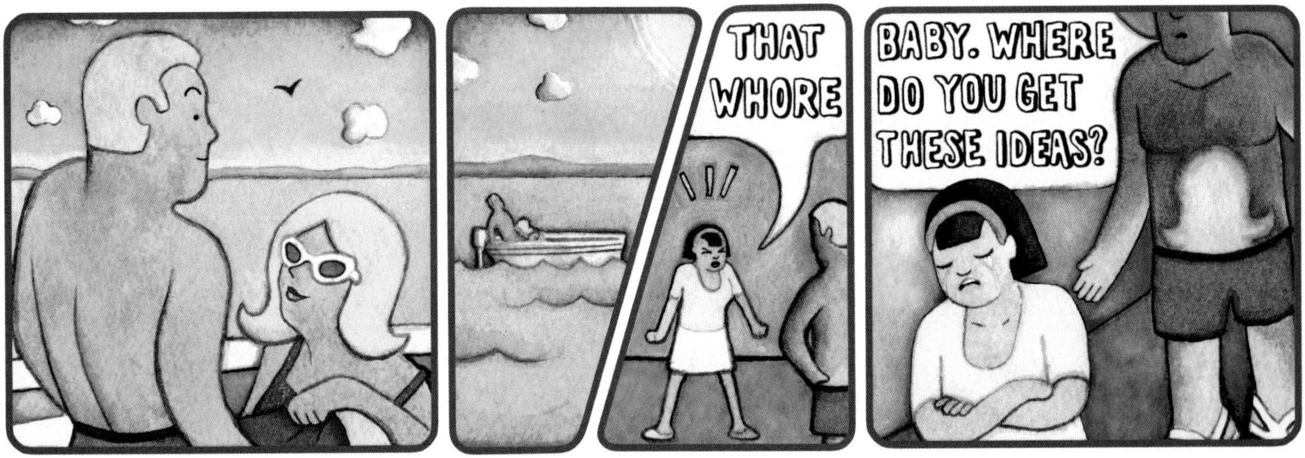
THAT WHORE
BABY. WHERE DO YOU GET THESE IDEAS?

Gnome Bubbles

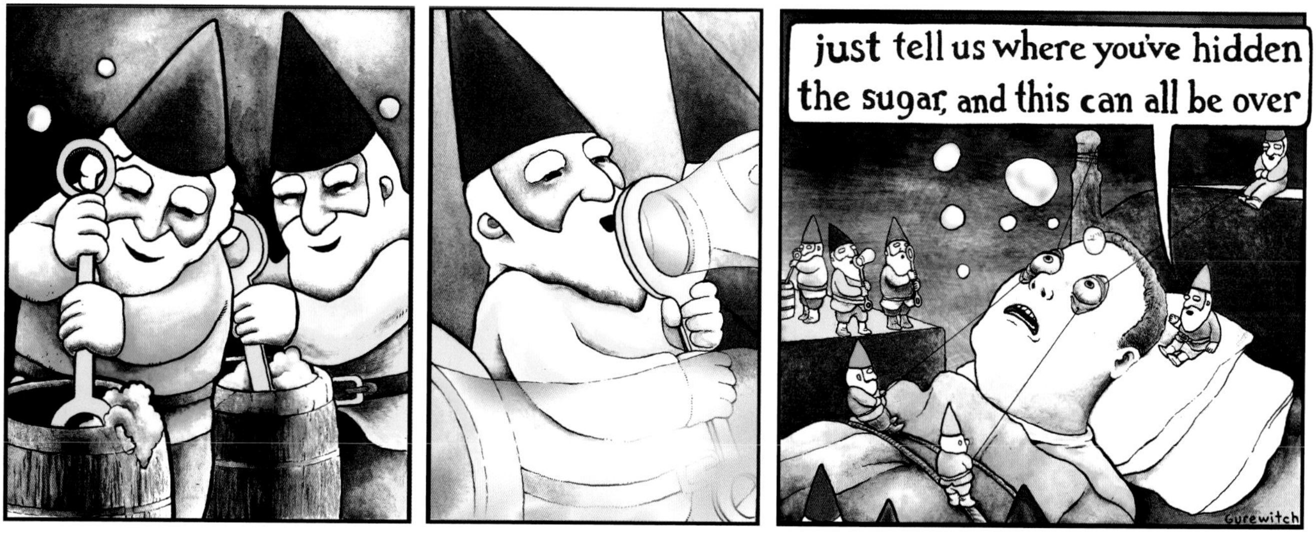
just tell us where you've hidden the sugar, and this can all be over
Gurewitch

Angels Caught

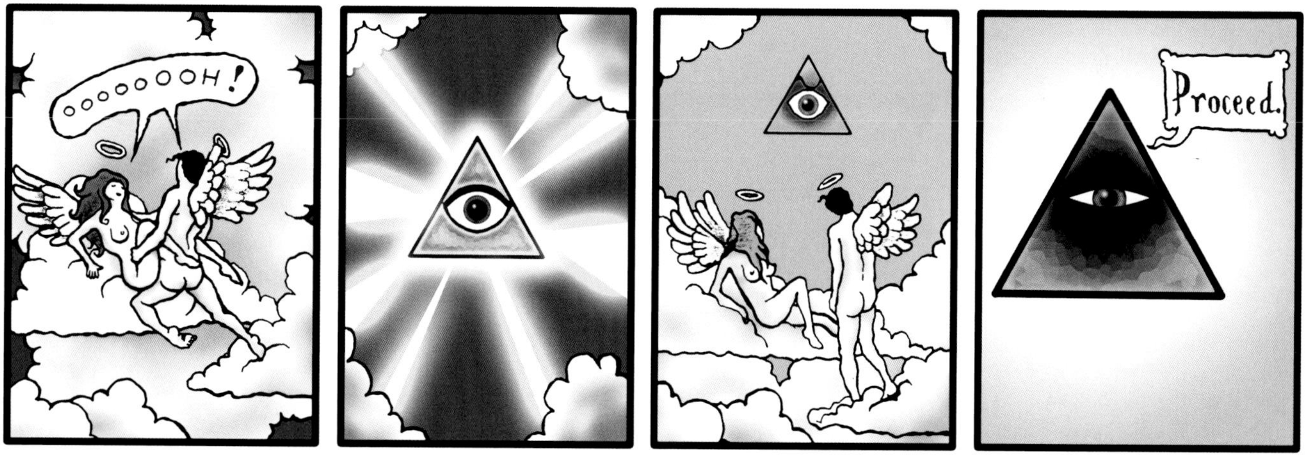
OOOOOOOH!
Proceed.

Shotgun

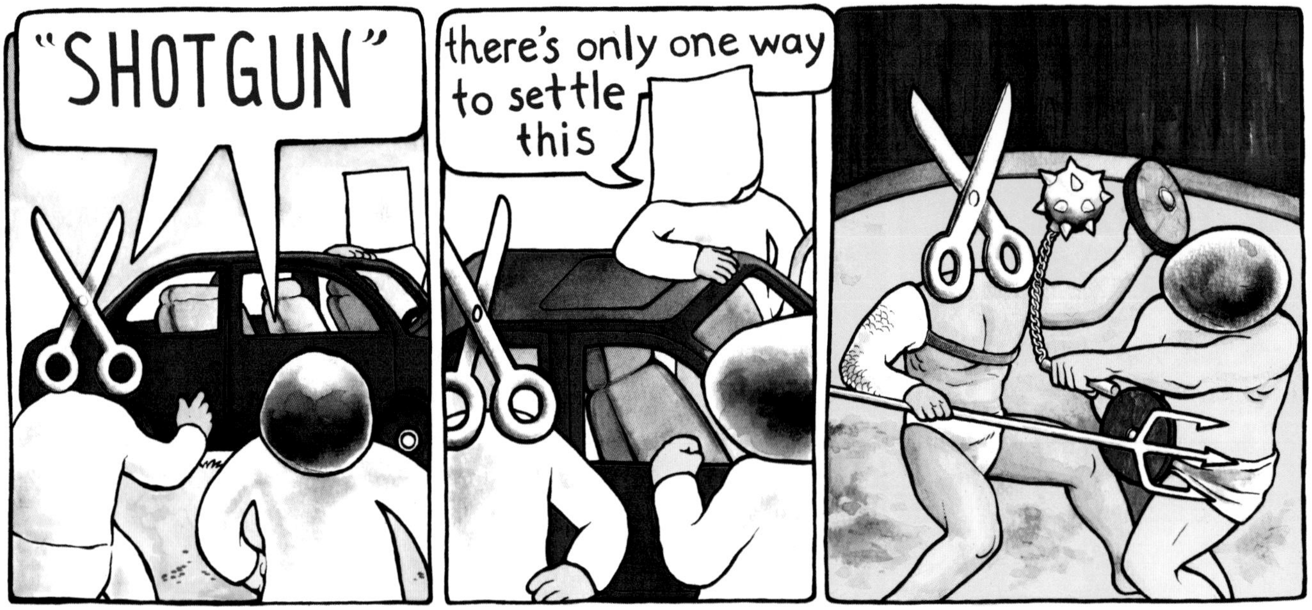
"SHOTGUN"
there's only one way to settle this

Billiards in Heaven

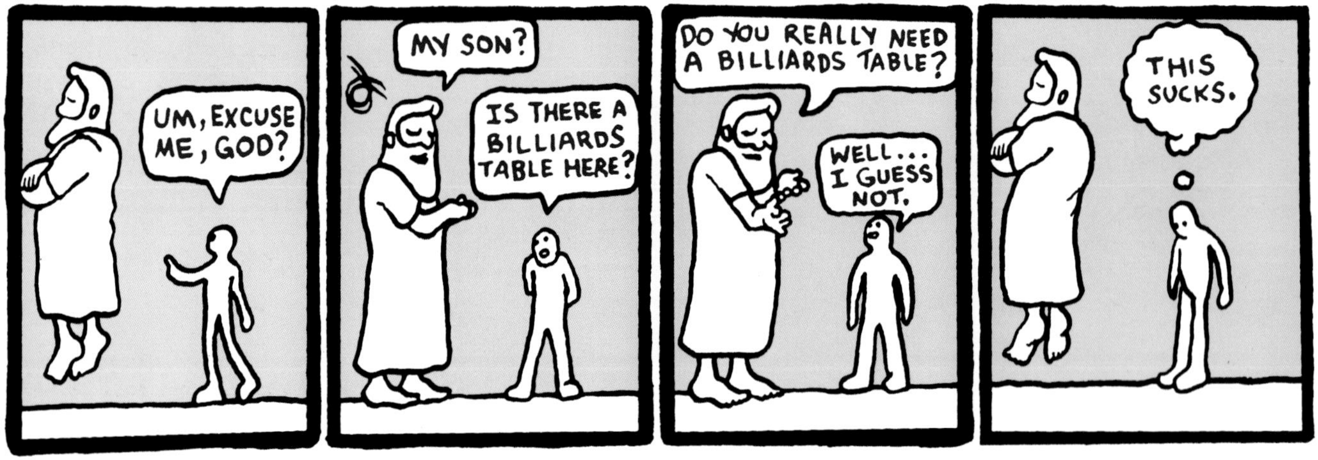
UM, EXCUSE ME, GOD?
MY SON?
IS THERE A BILLIARDS TABLE HERE?
DO YOU REALLY NEED A BILLIARDS TABLE?
WELL... I GUESS NOT.
THIS SUCKS.

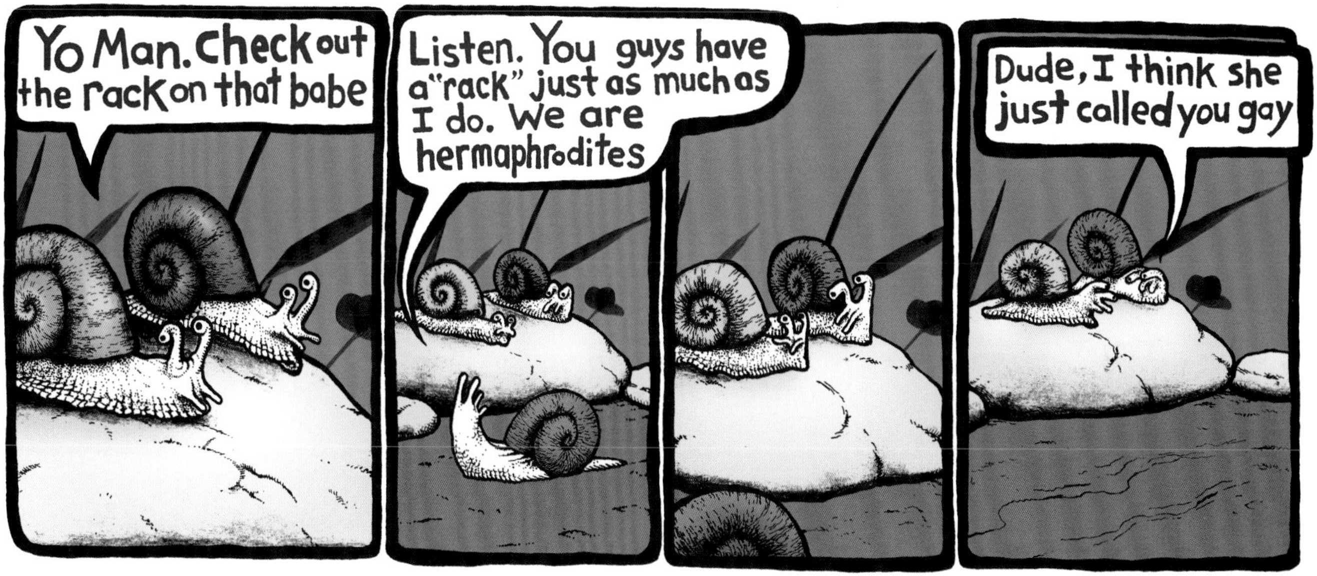
Yo Man. Check out the rack on that babe
Listen. You guys have a "rack" just as much as I do. We are hermaphrodites
Dude, I think she just called you gay

惡作劇龍

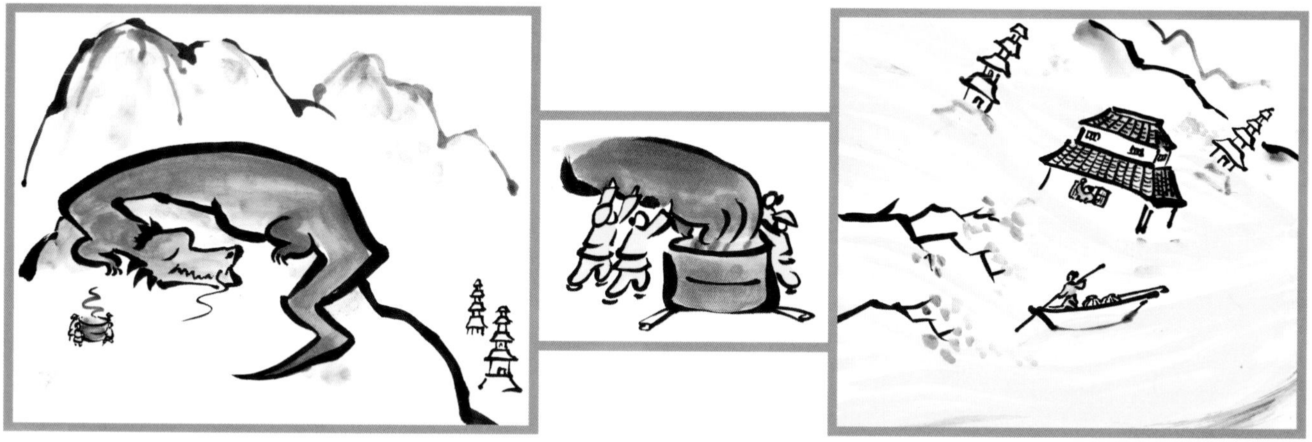

Nautical Awards

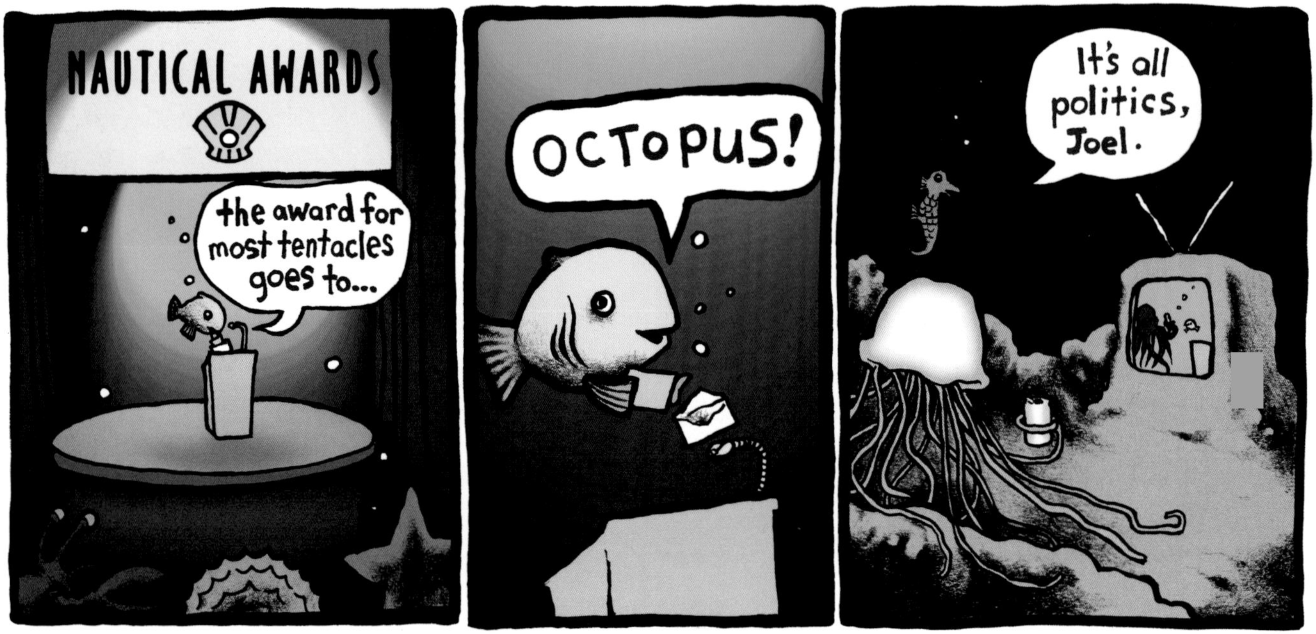
NAUTICAL AWARDS
the award for most tentacles goes to...
OCTOPUS!
It's all politics, Joel.

The Adventures of the Man with No Penis

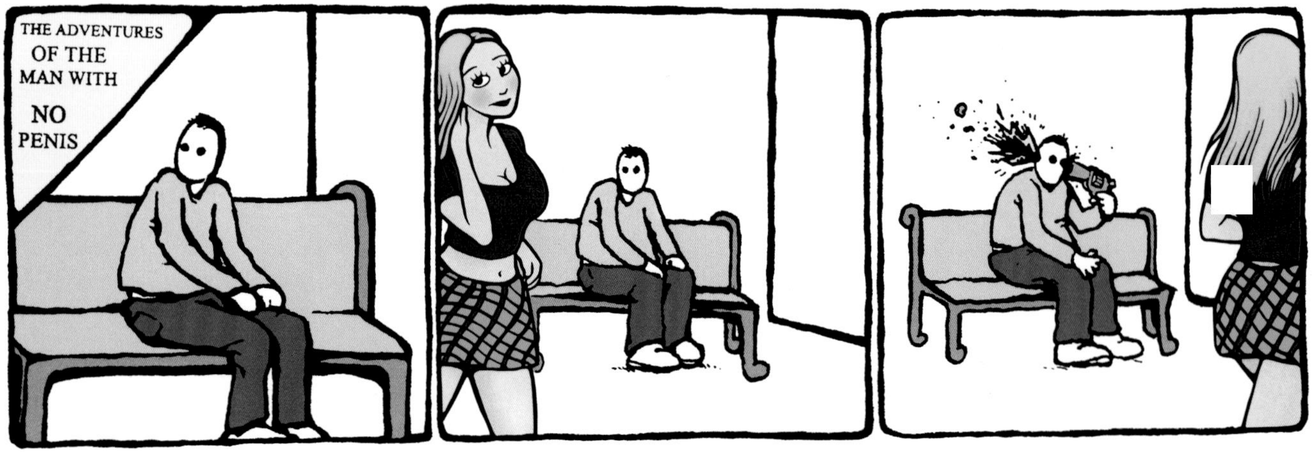
THE ADVENTURES OF THE MAN WITH NO PENIS

Cars

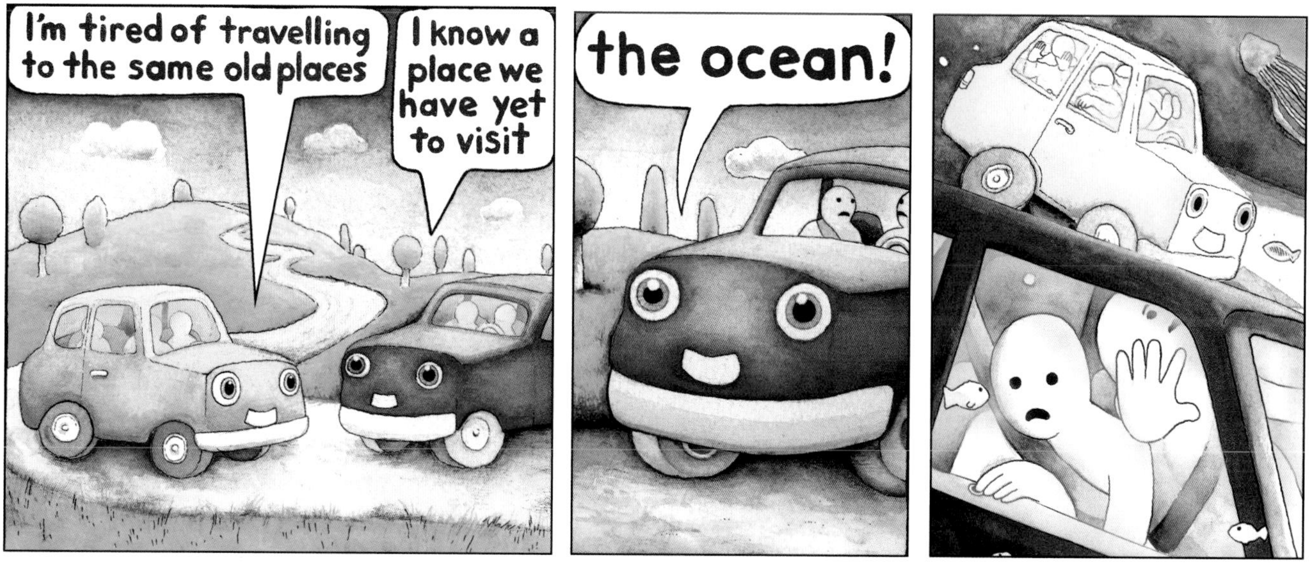
I'm tired of travelling to the same old places
I know a place we have yet to visit
the ocean!

Satan's Hell

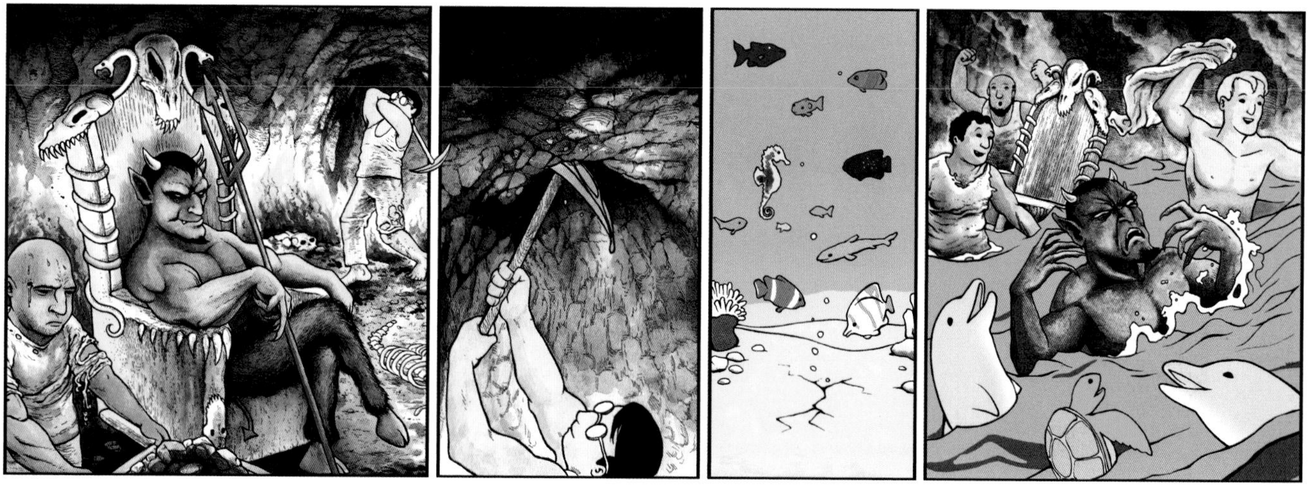

Astronaut Fall

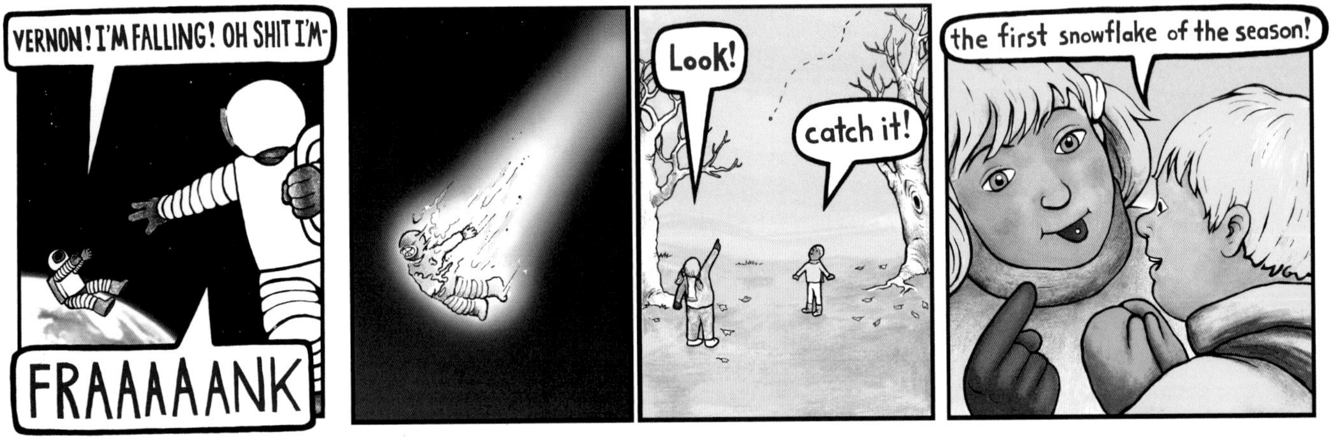
VERNON! I'M FALLING! OH SHIT I'M-
FRAAAAANK
Look!
catch it!
the first snowflake of the season!

Barb and Rudy

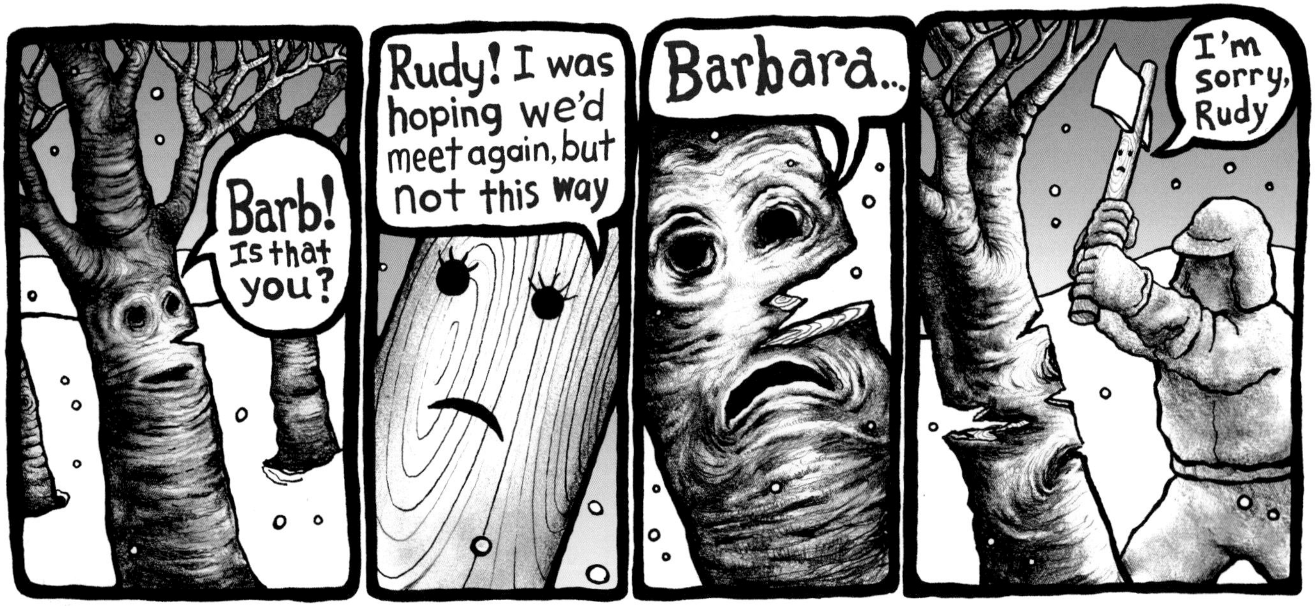
Barb! Is that you?
Rudy! I was hoping we'd meet again, but not this way
Barbara...
I'm sorry, Rudy

Monkey Photographer

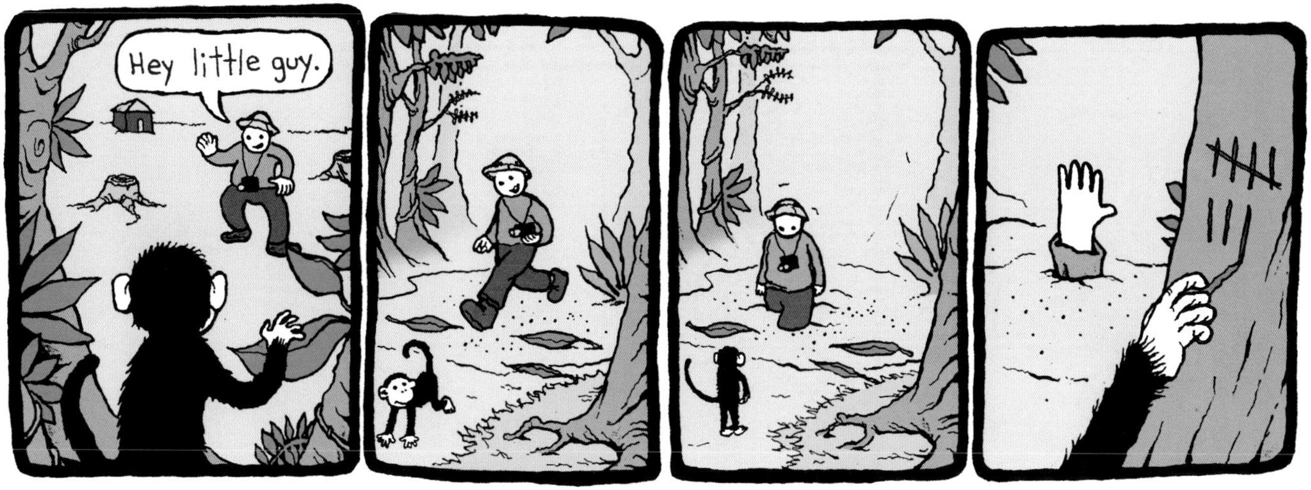
Hey little guy.

Love Lizard

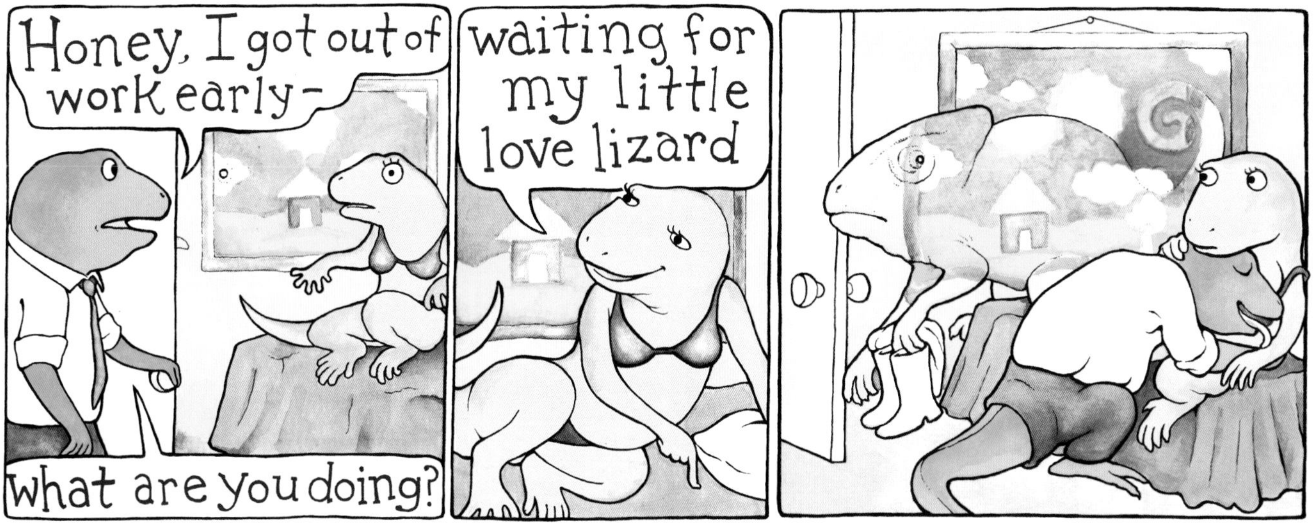
Honey, I got out of work early-
What are you doing?
waiting for my little love lizard

Caring for Your Turtle

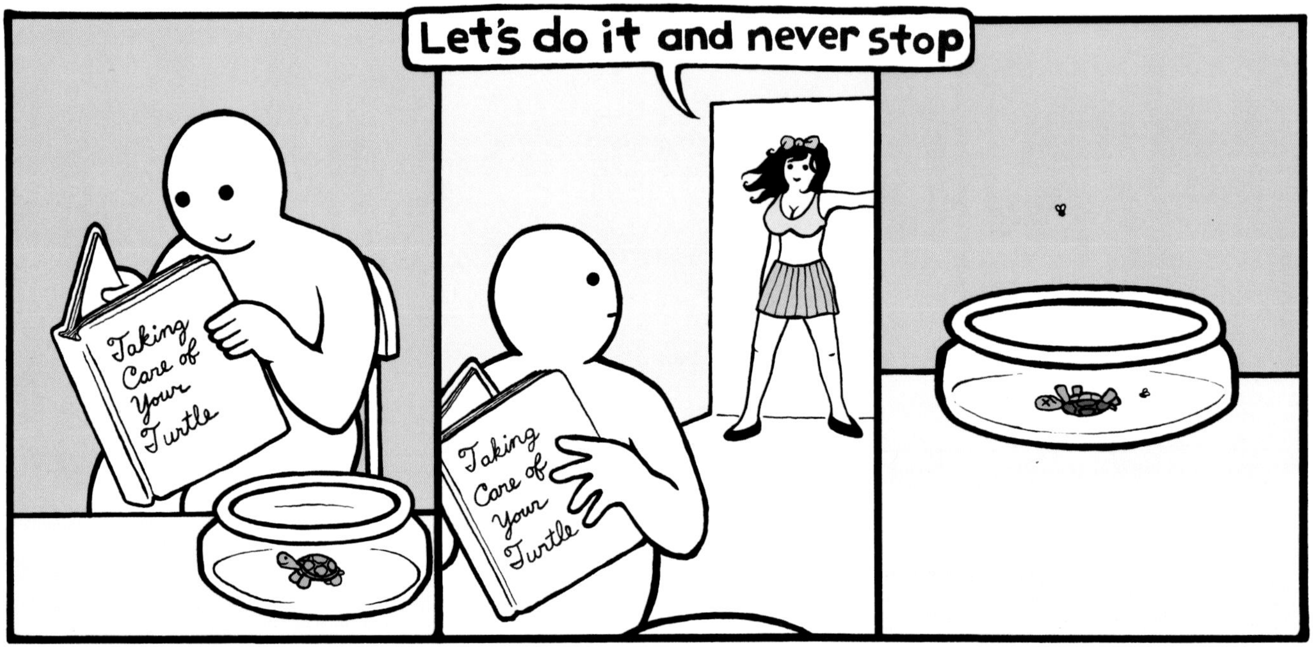
Taking Care of Your Turtle
Let's do it and never stop
Taking Care of Your Turtle

Secret Mutant Hero Team

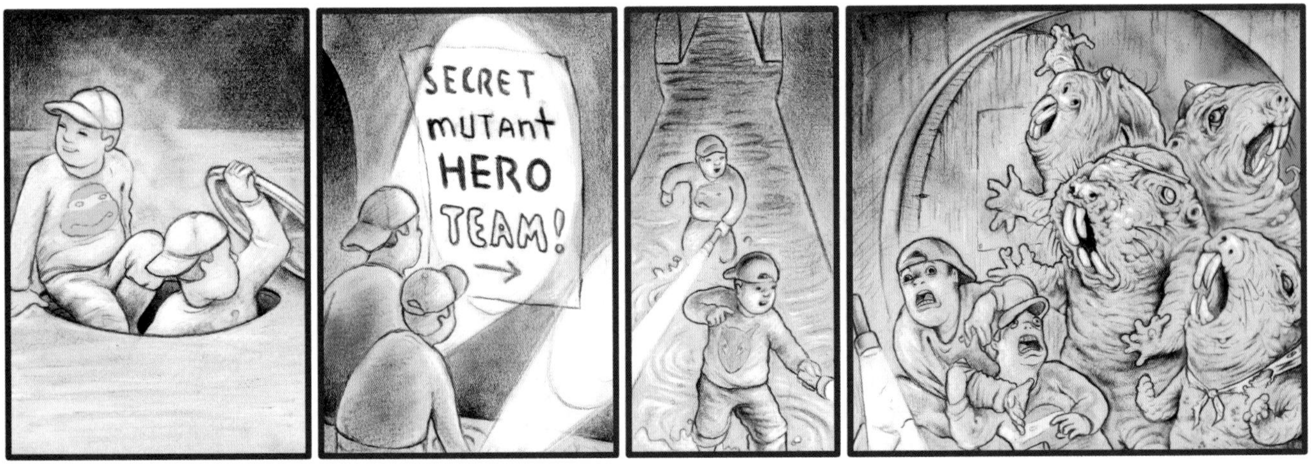
SECRET mutant HERO TEAM! →

Eden

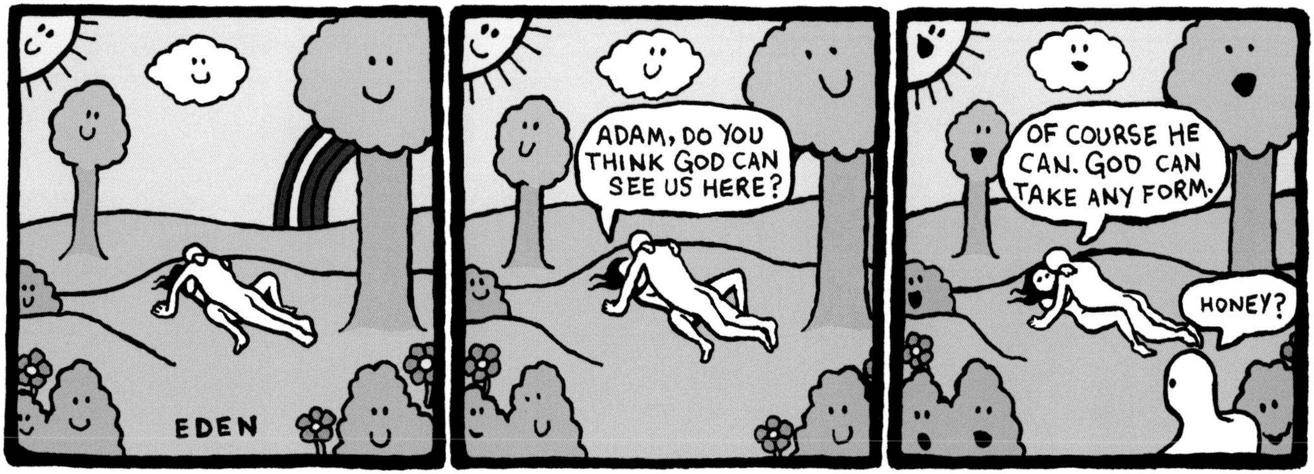
EDEN
ADAM, DO YOU THINK GOD CAN SEE US HERE?
OF COURSE HE CAN. GOD CAN TAKE ANY FORM.
HONEY?

Executive Decision

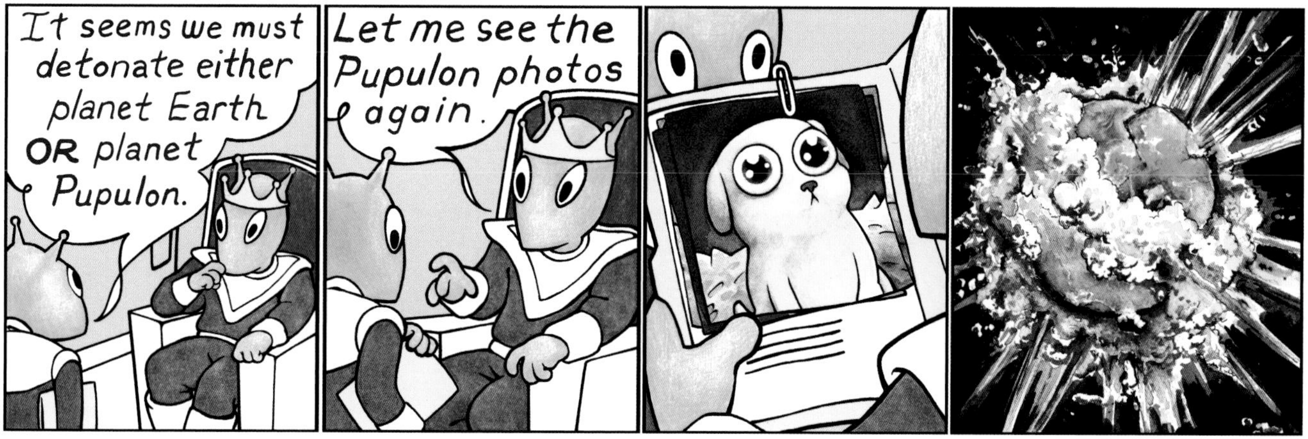
It seems we must detonate either planet Earth OR planet Pupulon.
Let me see the Pupulon photos again.

Durab, Inc.

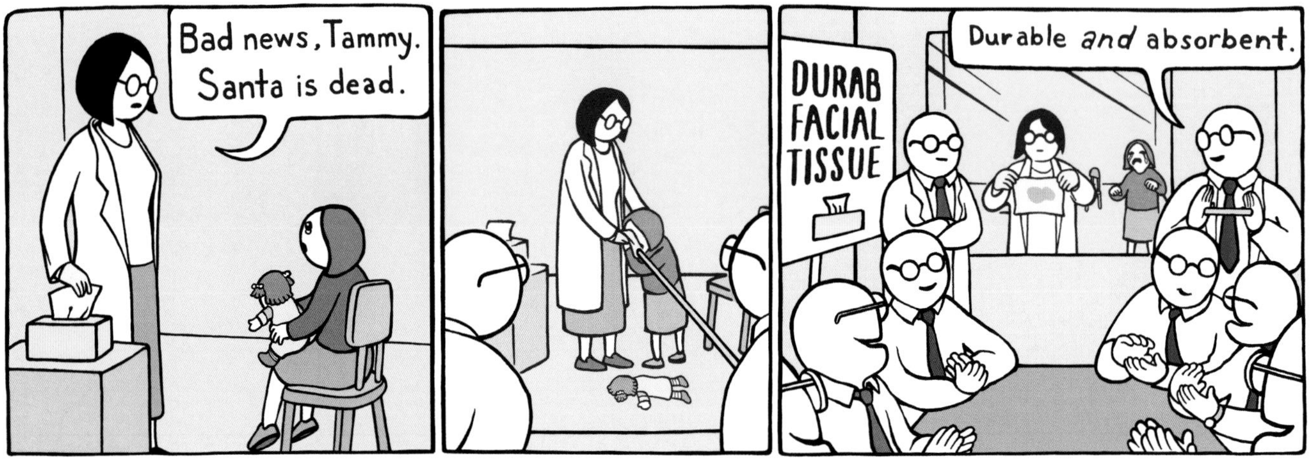
Bad news, Tammy. Santa is dead.
DURAB FACIAL TISSUE
Durable *and* absorbent.

Atlantis

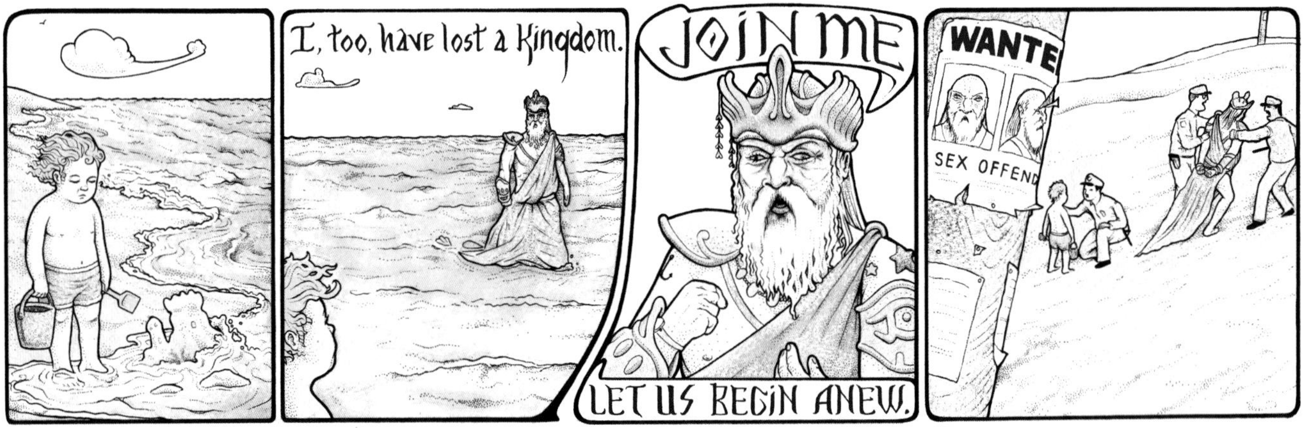
I, too, have lost a Kingdom.
JOIN ME
LET US BEGIN ANEW.
WANTE
SEX OFFEND

Doll Change

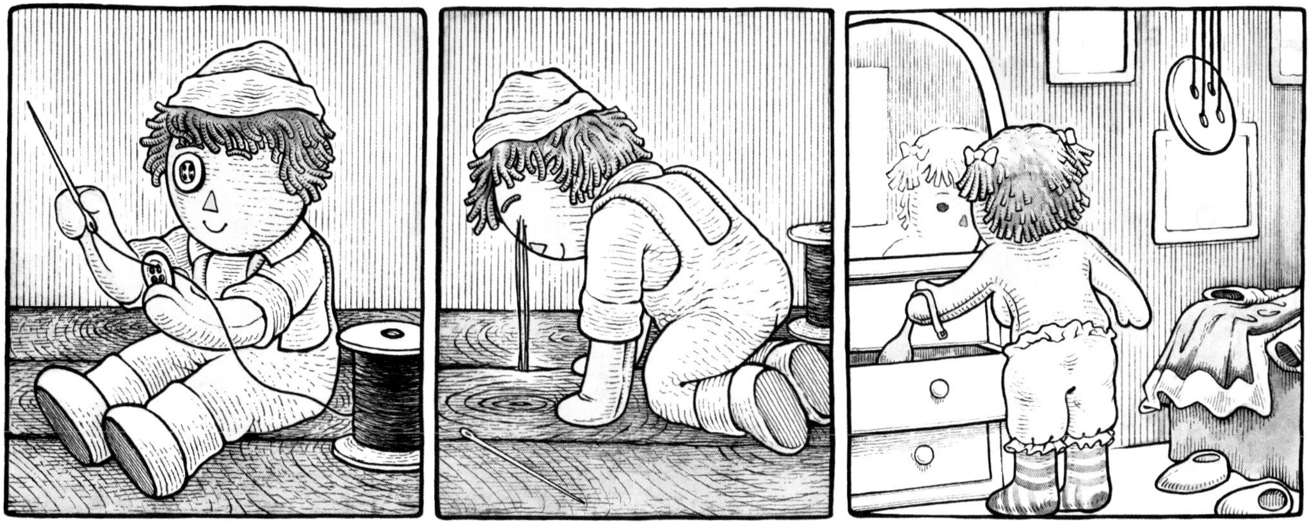

The Mercy of Admiral Shlork

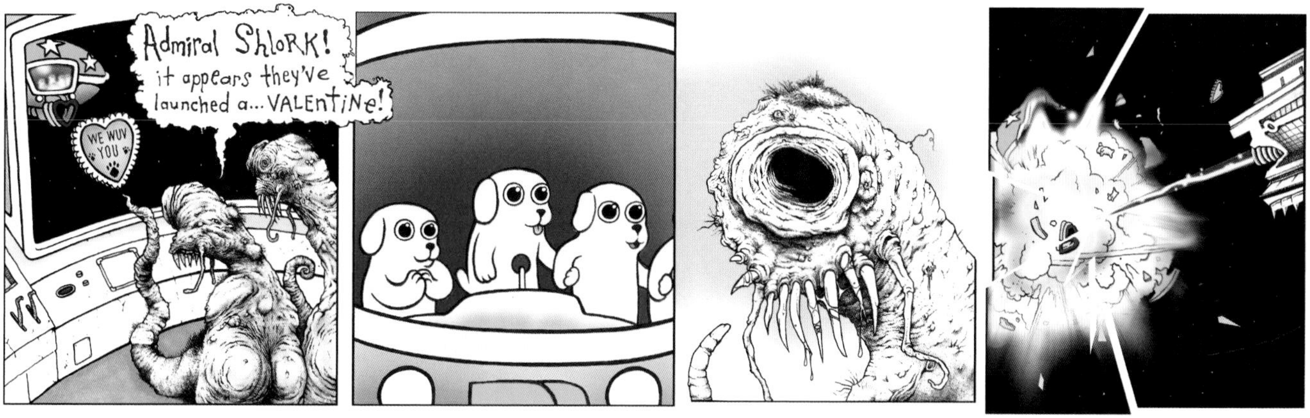
Admiral Shlork! it appears they've launched a... VALENTiNe!
WE WUV YOU

Left Brain / Right Brain

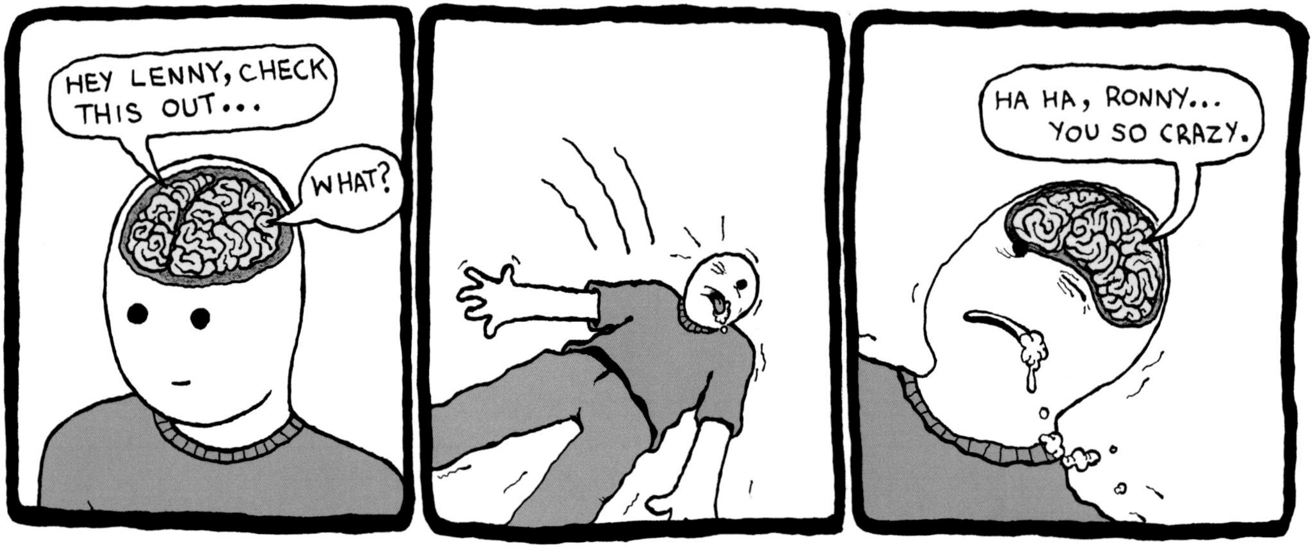
HEY LENNY, CHECK THIS OUT...
WHAT?
HA HA, RONNY... YOU SO CRAZY.

Mime City

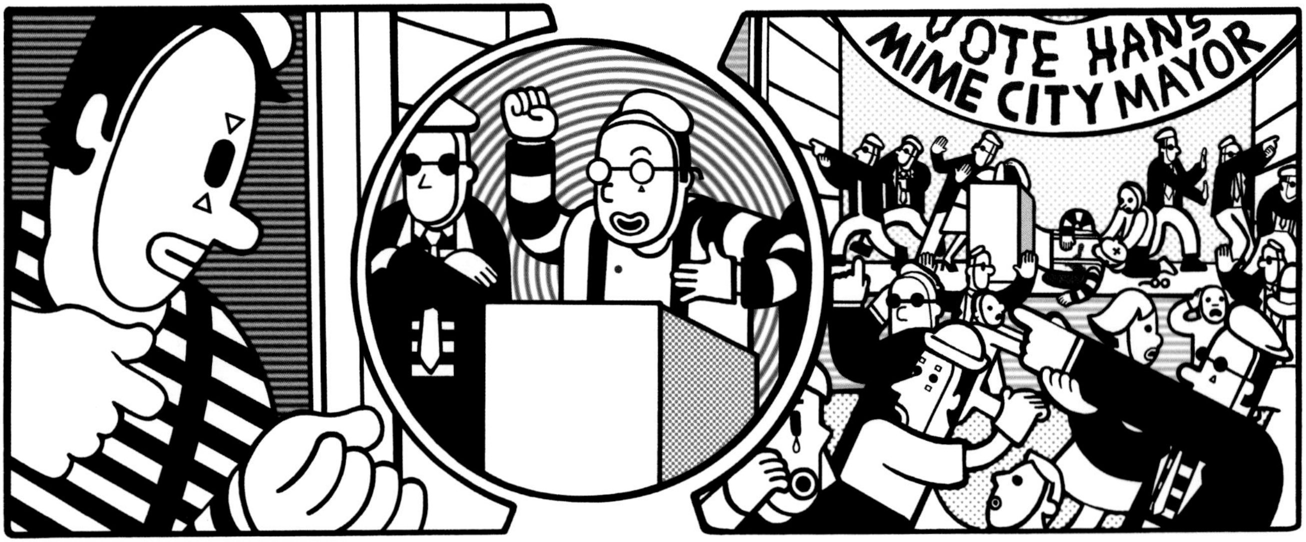
VOTE HANS
MIME CITY MAYOR

Kitty Stuck

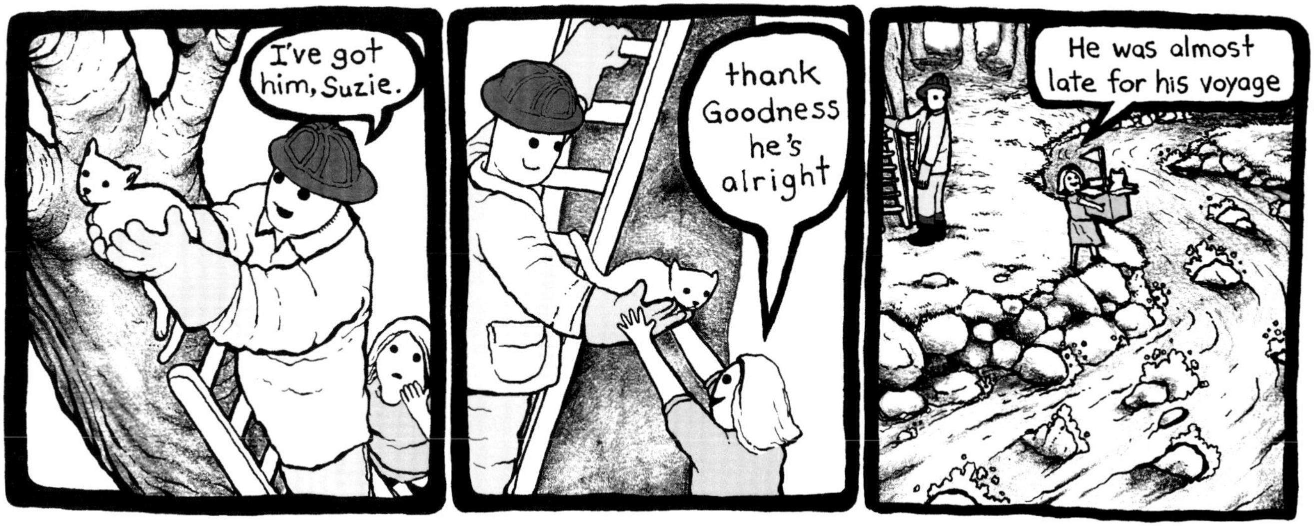
I've got him, Suzie.
thank Goodness he's alright
He was almost late for his voyage

Refridgeron and Magnimus

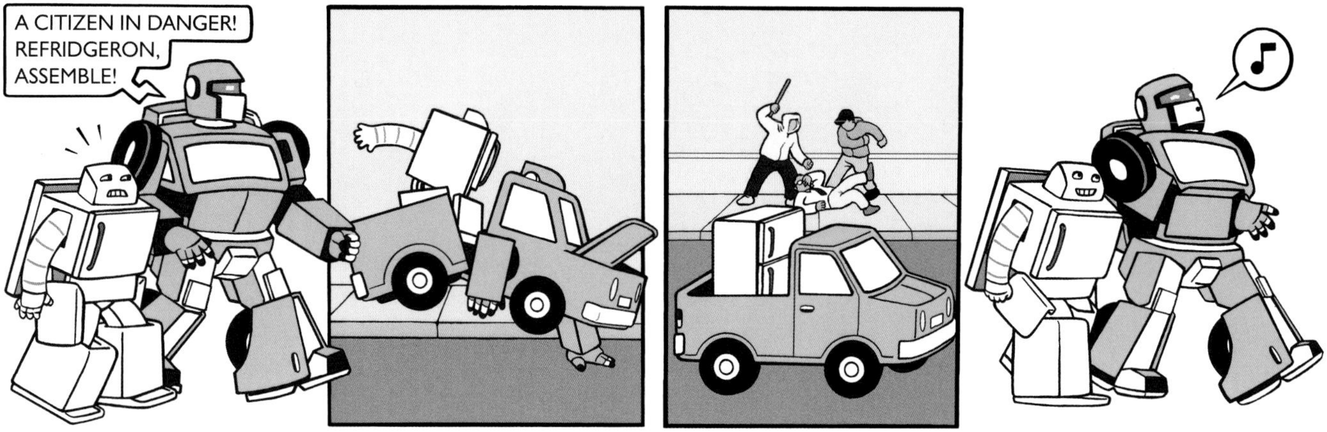
A CITIZEN IN DANGER! REFRIDGERON, ASSEMBLE!

The Other Girls

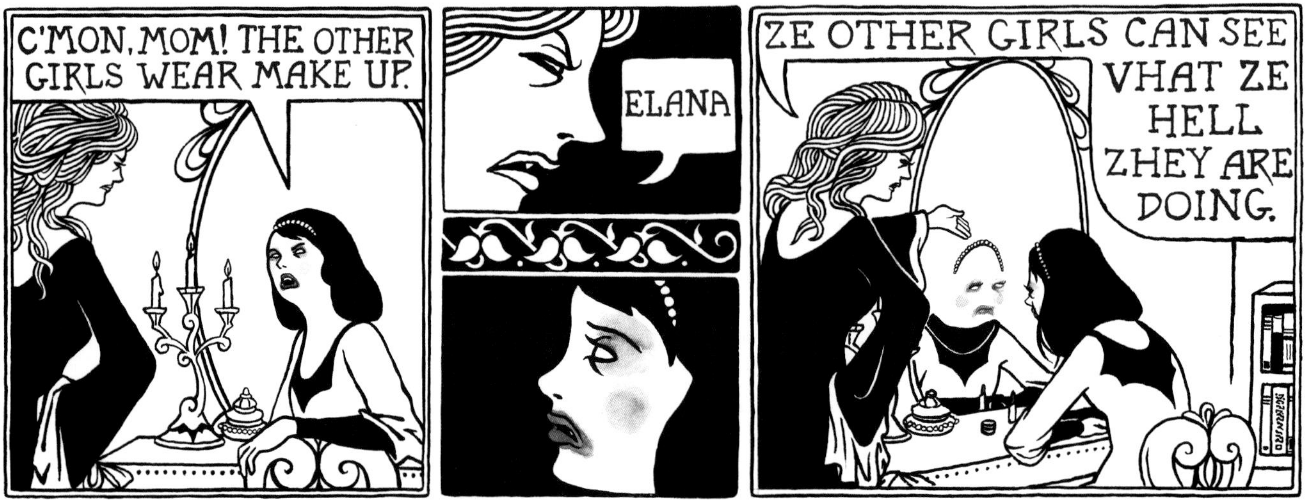
C'MON, MOM! THE OTHER GIRLS WEAR MAKE UP.
ELANA
ZE OTHER GIRLS CAN SEE VHAT ZE HELL ZHEY ARE DOING.

Book World

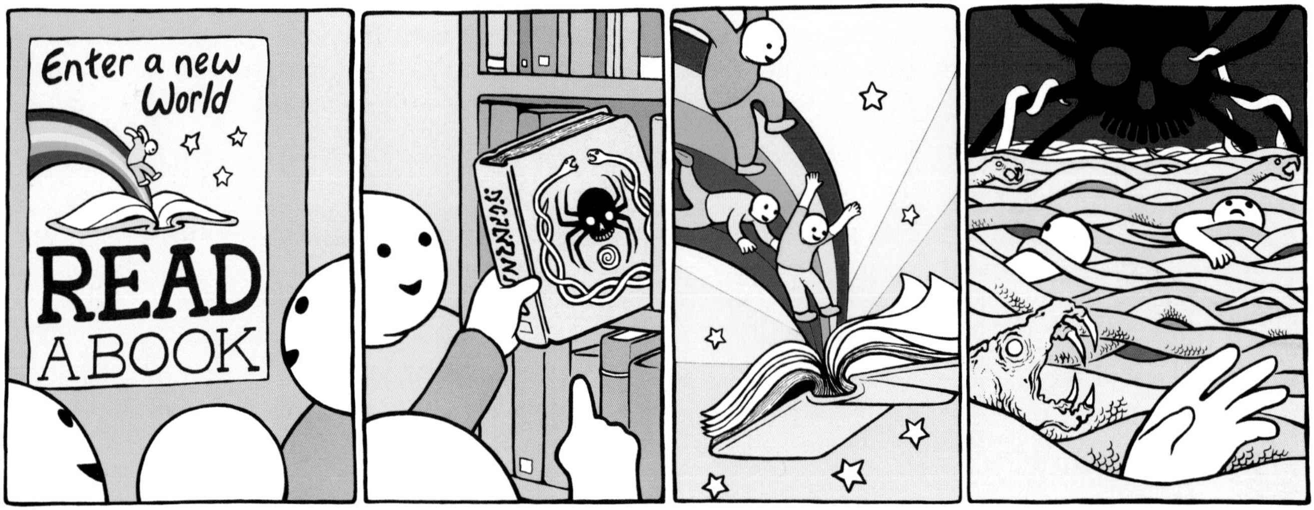
Enter a new World
READ A BOOK

A Hit for Bobby

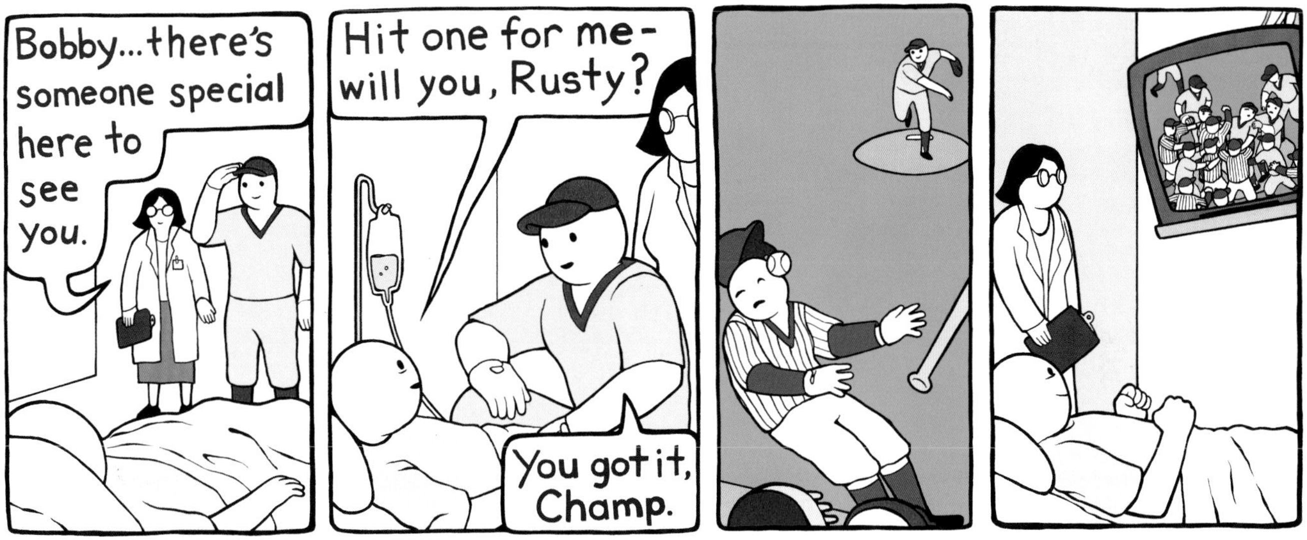
Bobby...there's someone special here to see you.
Hit one for me- will you, Rusty?
You got it, Champ.

Zuthulu's Resurrection

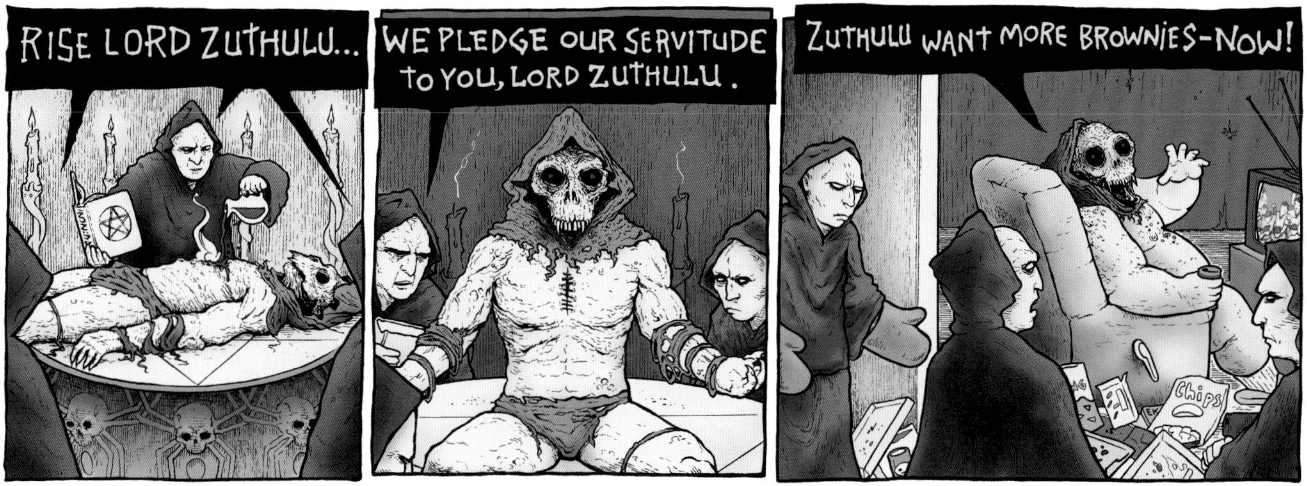
RISE LORD ZUTHULU...
WE PLEDGE OUR SERVITUDE TO YOU, LORD ZUTHULU.
ZUTHULU WANT MORE BROWNIES-NOW!
Chips

Hey Goat

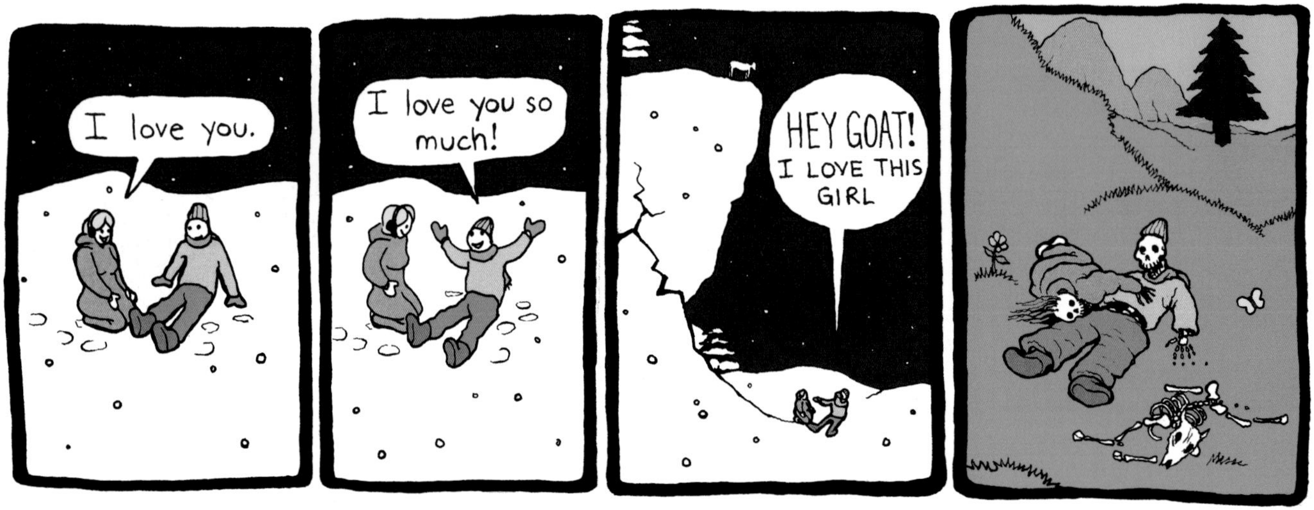
I love you.
I love you so much!
HEY GOAT! I LOVE THIS GIRL

X-mas Surgery

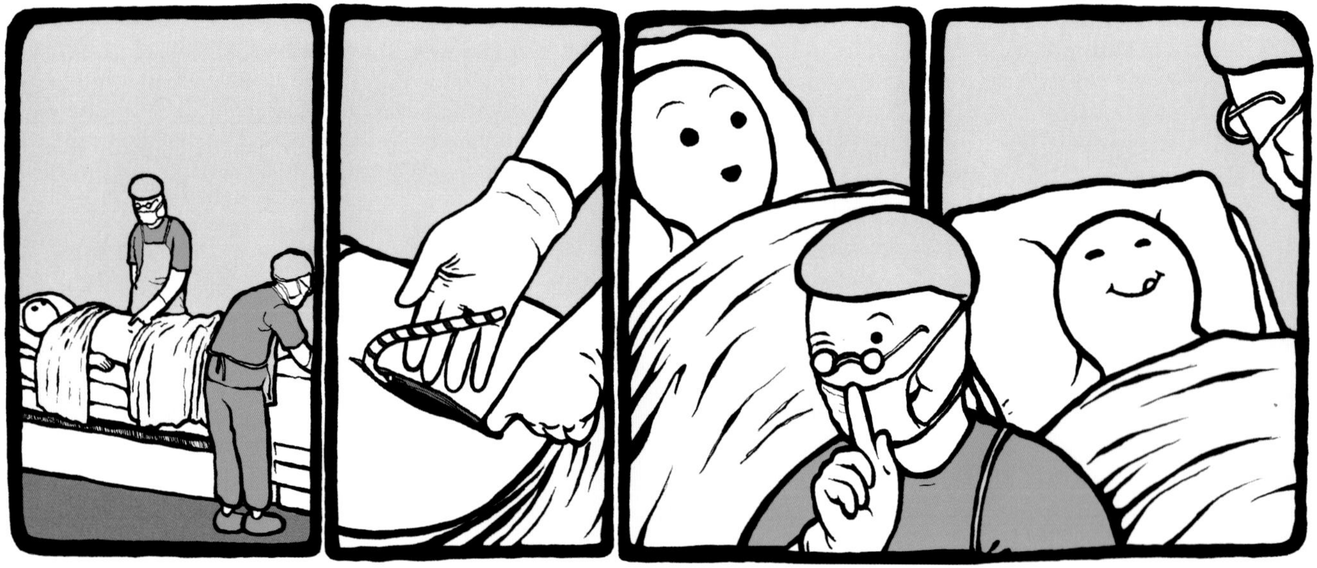

Eggnancy

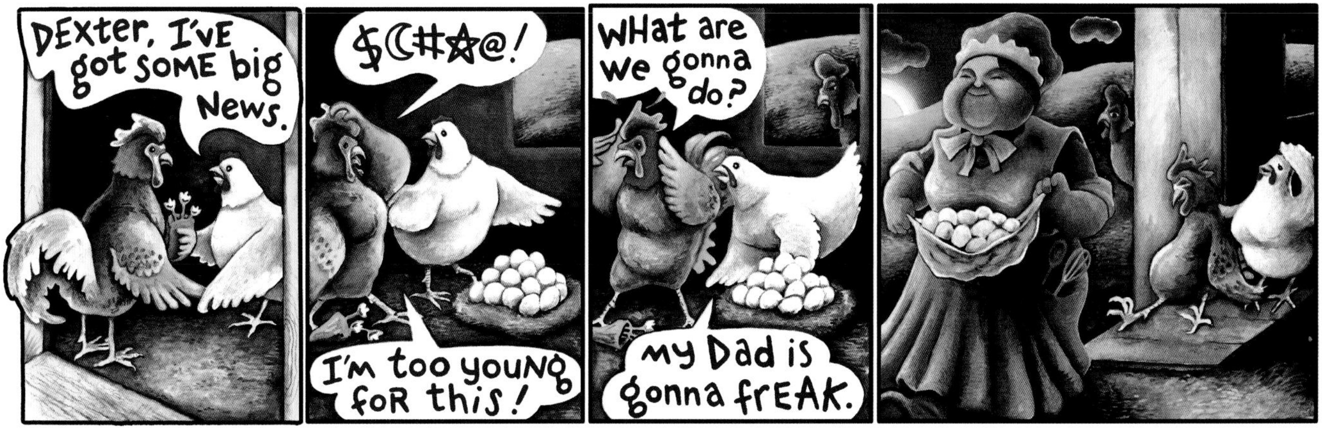
DExter, I'vE got SOME big News.
$☾#✪@!
I'm too youNg foR this!
WHat are we gonna do?
My Dad is gonna frEAK.

Stiff Breeze

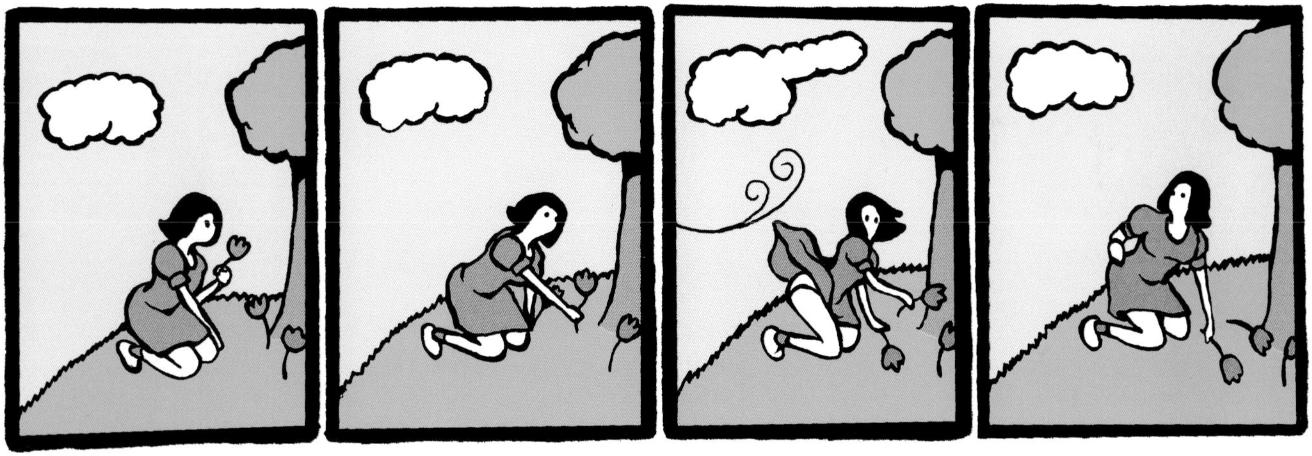

Captain Redbeard

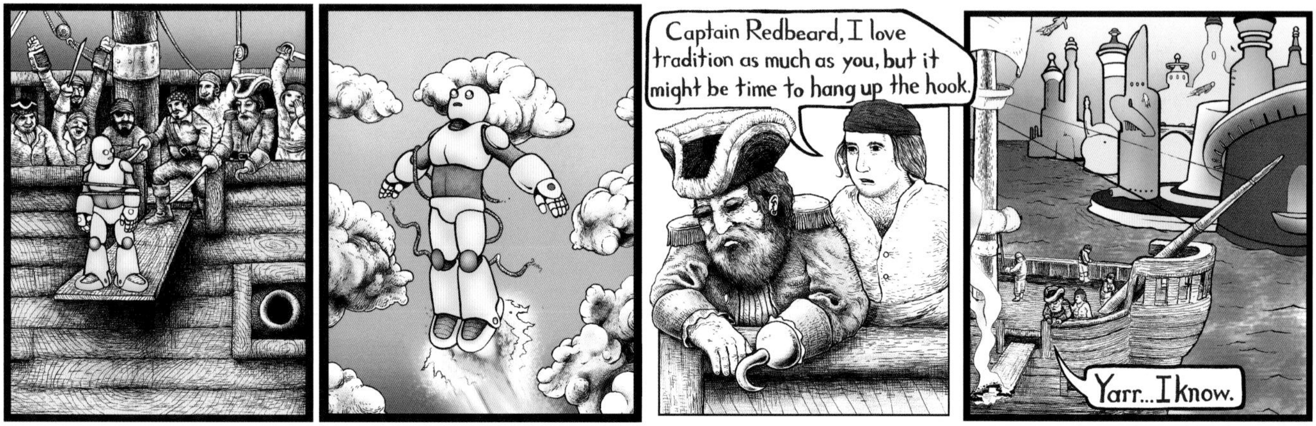
Captain Redbeard, I love tradition as much as you, but it might be time to hang up the hook.
Yarr...I know.

Reset

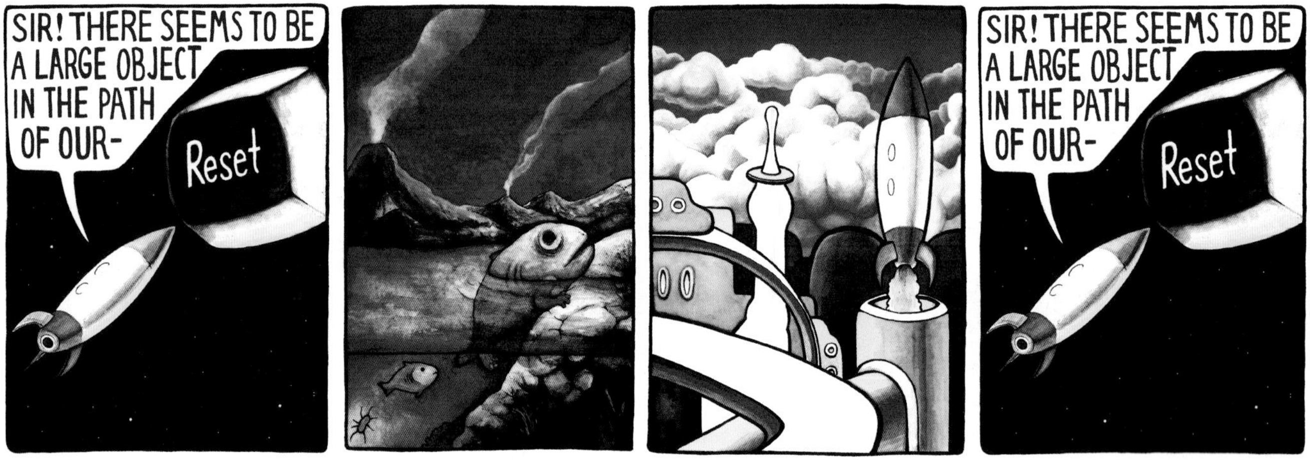
SIR! THERE SEEMS TO BE A LARGE OBJECT IN THE PATH OF OUR-
Reset
SIR! THERE SEEMS TO BE A LARGE OBJECT IN THE PATH OF OUR-
Reset

Kids are Thirsty

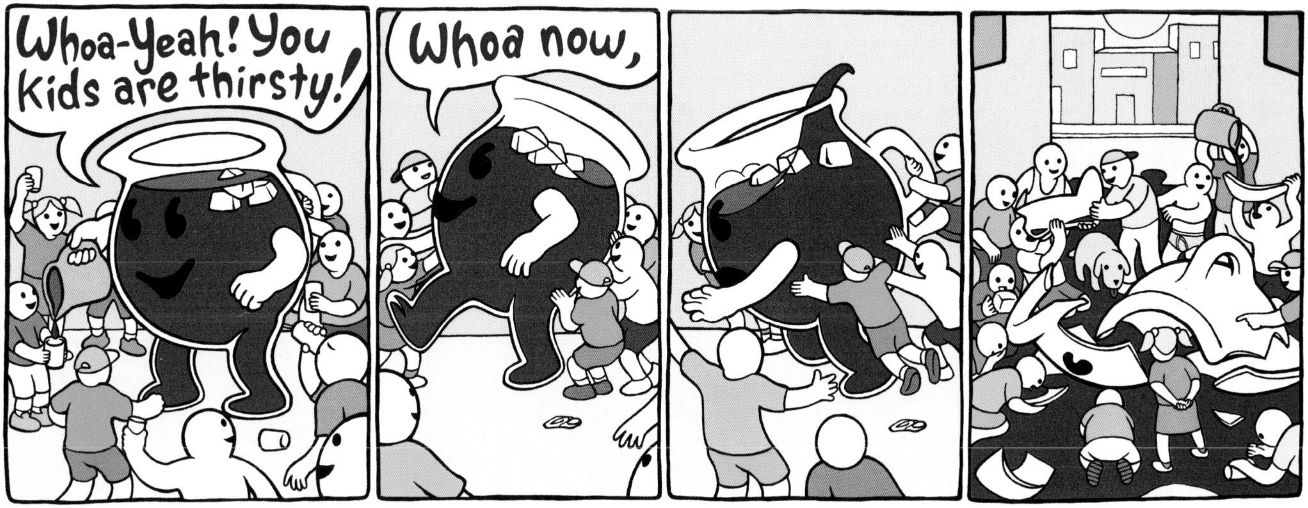
Whoa-Yeah! You kids are thirsty!
Whoa now,

Moon Bunny

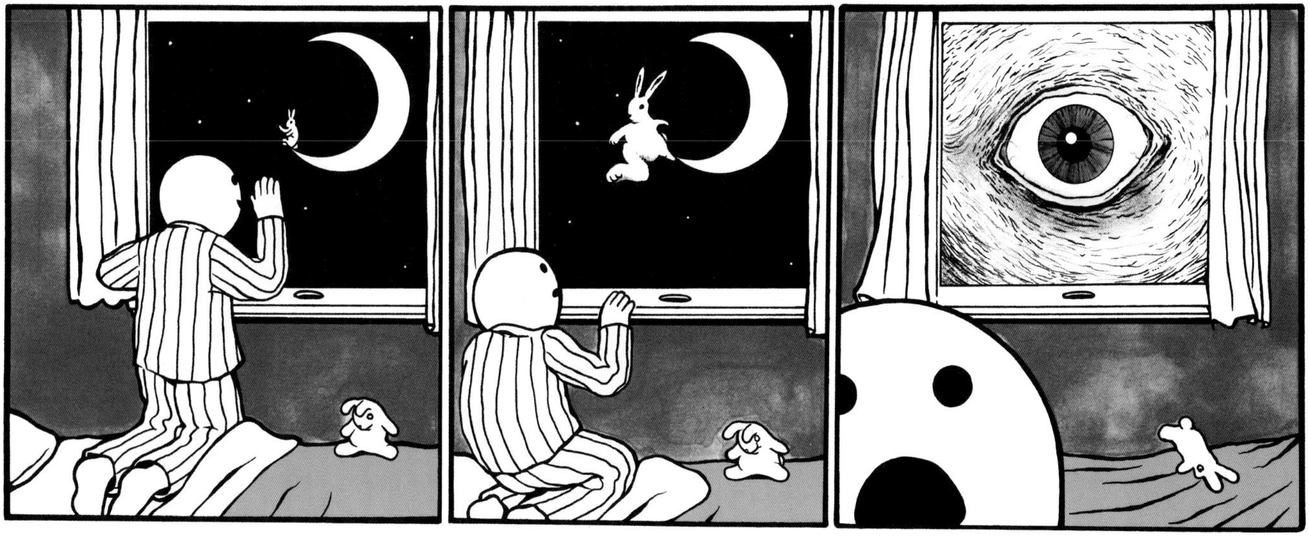

Q.P.I. Interview

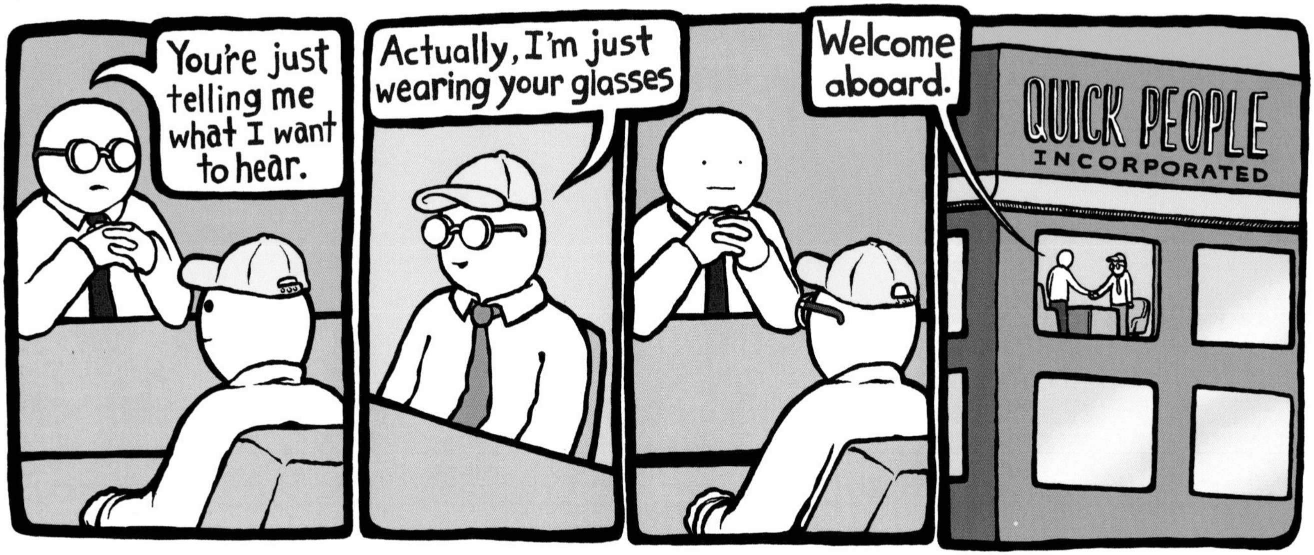
You're just telling me what I want to hear.
Actually, I'm just wearing your glasses
Welcome aboard.
QUICK PEOPLE
INCORPORATED

Earth Disorder

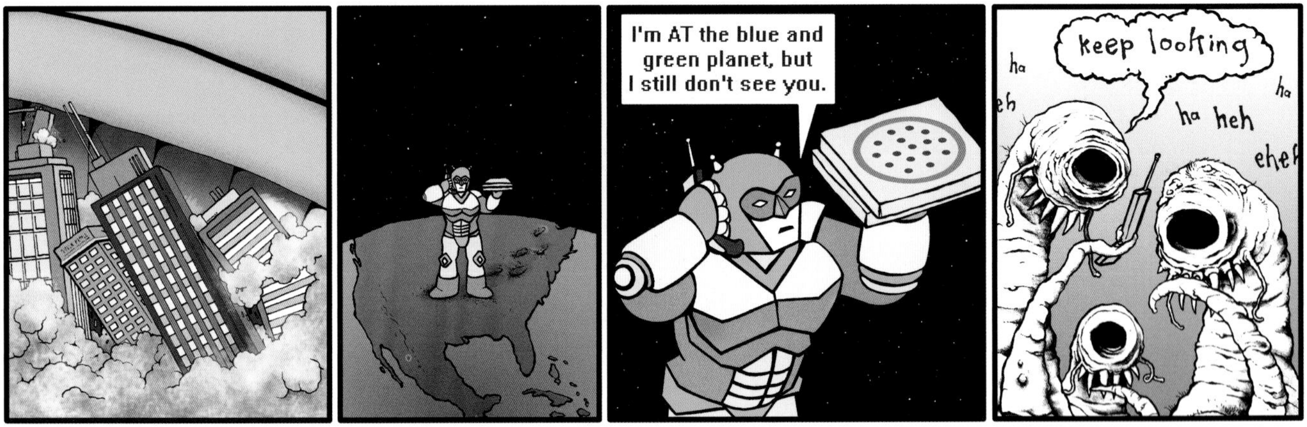
I'm AT the blue and green planet, but I still don't see you.
keep looking
ha
eh
ha
ha heh

No Survivors

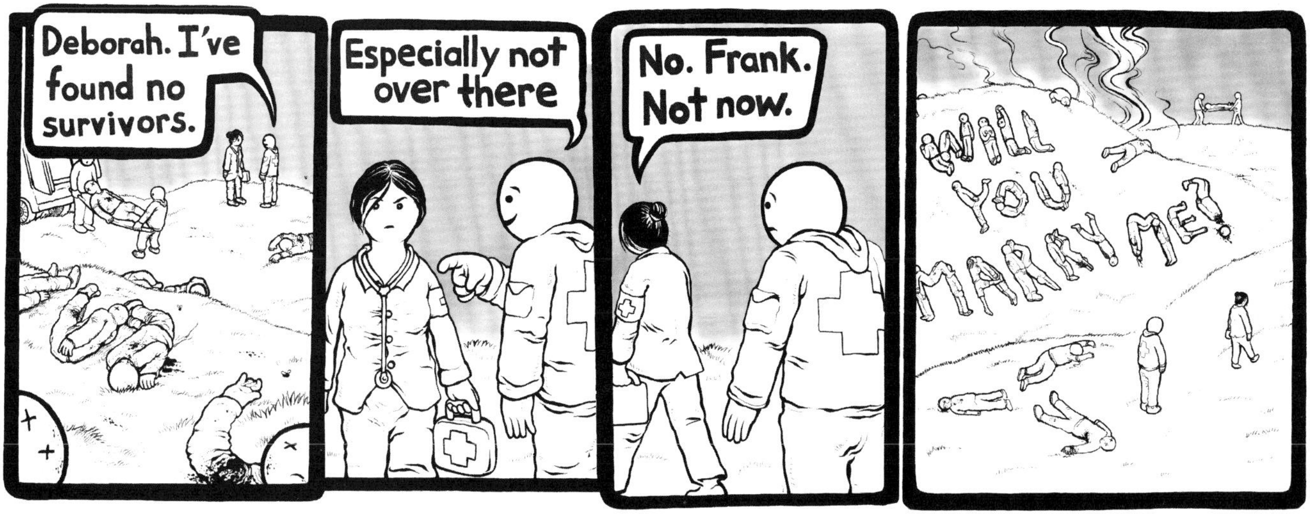
Deborah. I've found no survivors.
Especially not over there
No. Frank. Not now.
WILL YOU MARRY ME?

Martha's Orphanage

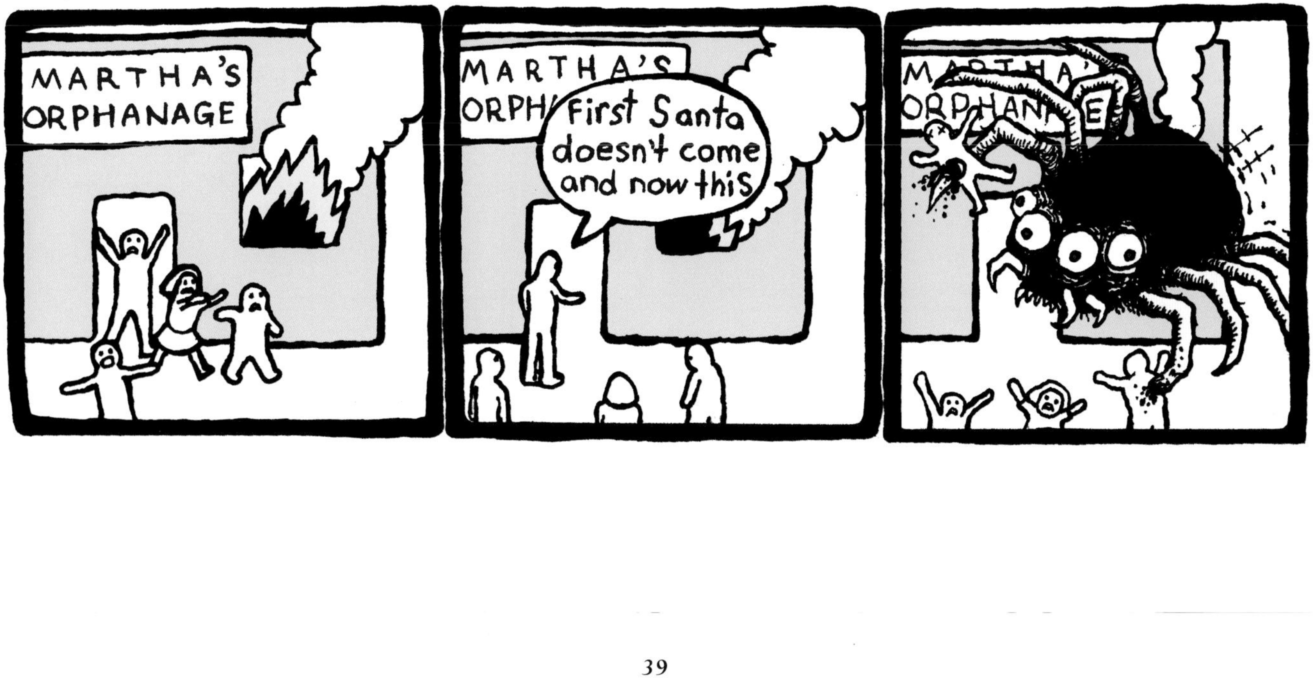
MARTHA'S ORPHANAGE
MARTHA'S ORPH
First Santa doesn't come and now this

Boss

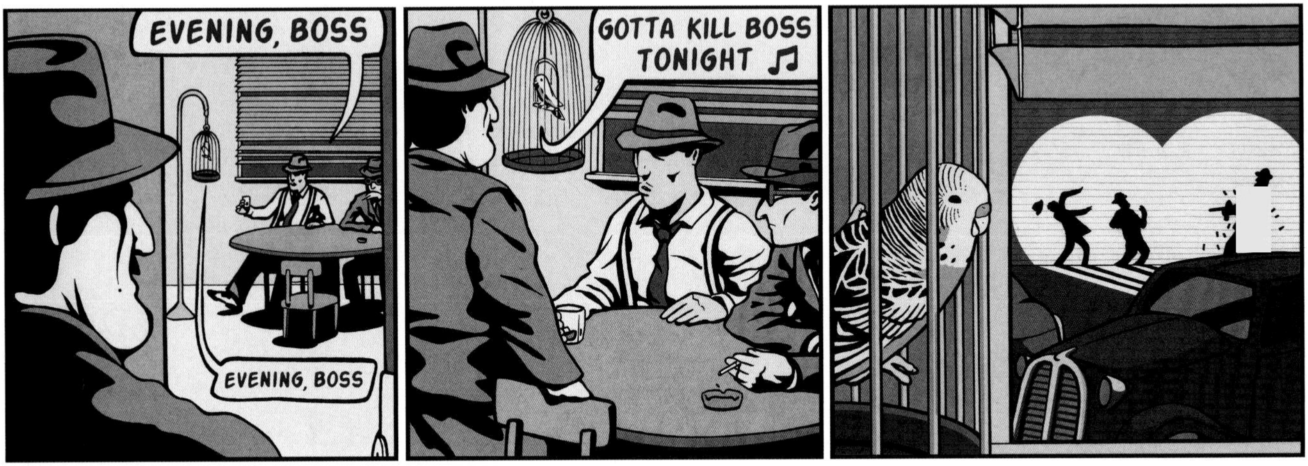
EVENING, BOSS
EVENING, BOSS
GOTTA KILL BOSS TONIGHT ♫

Automatic Business

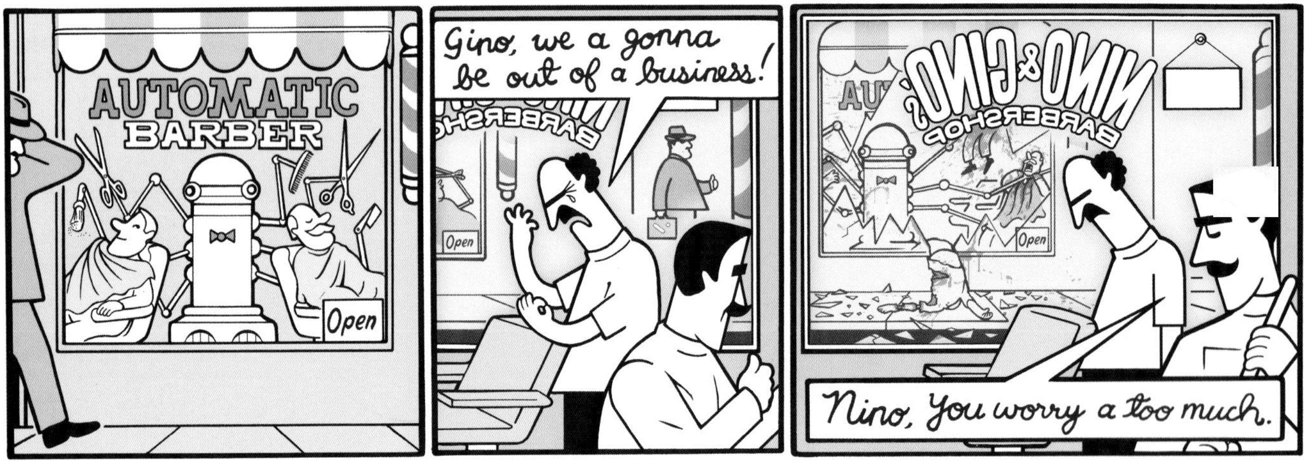
AUTOMATIC BARBER
Open
Gino, we a gonna be out of a business!
NINO & GINO'S BARBERSHOP
Nino, You worry a too much.

Goodbye Stanley

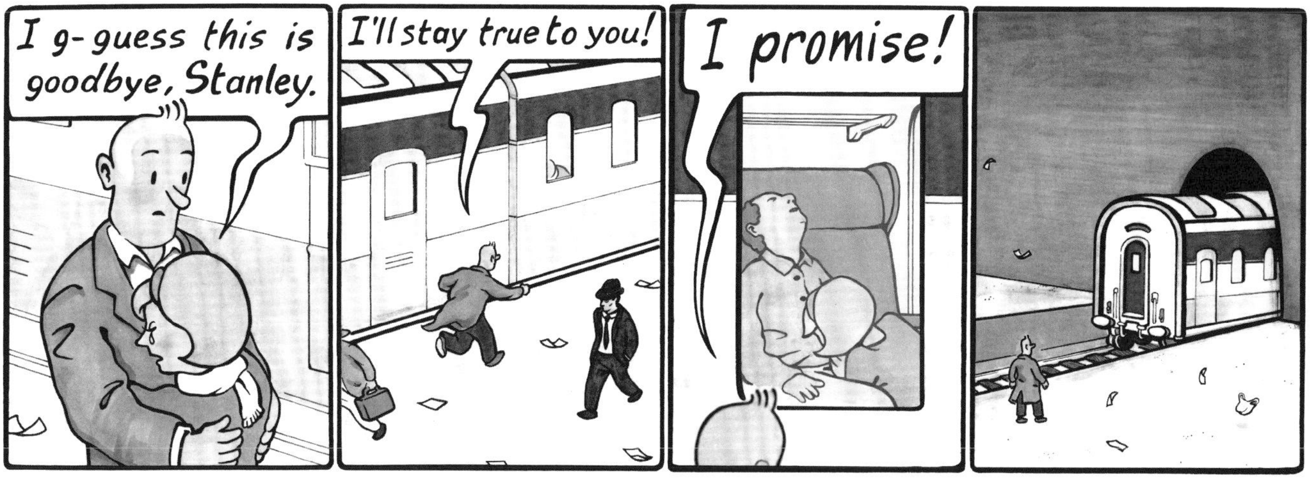
I g-guess this is goodbye, Stanley.
I'll stay true to you!
I promise!

Worm Squish

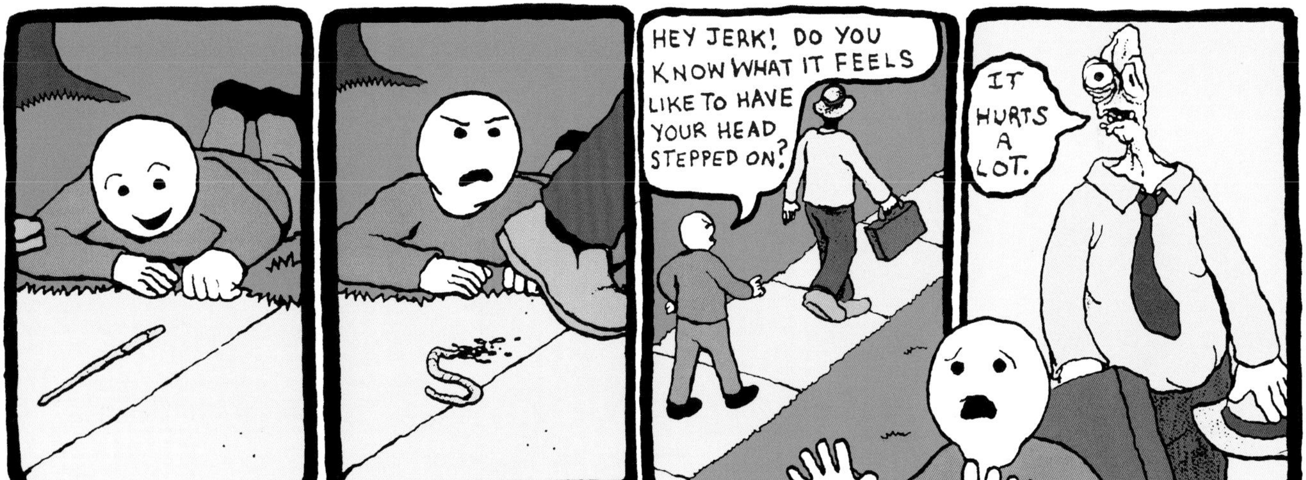
HEY JERK! DO YOU KNOW WHAT IT FEELS LIKE TO HAVE YOUR HEAD STEPPED ON?
IT HURTS A LOT.

Sven's Revenge

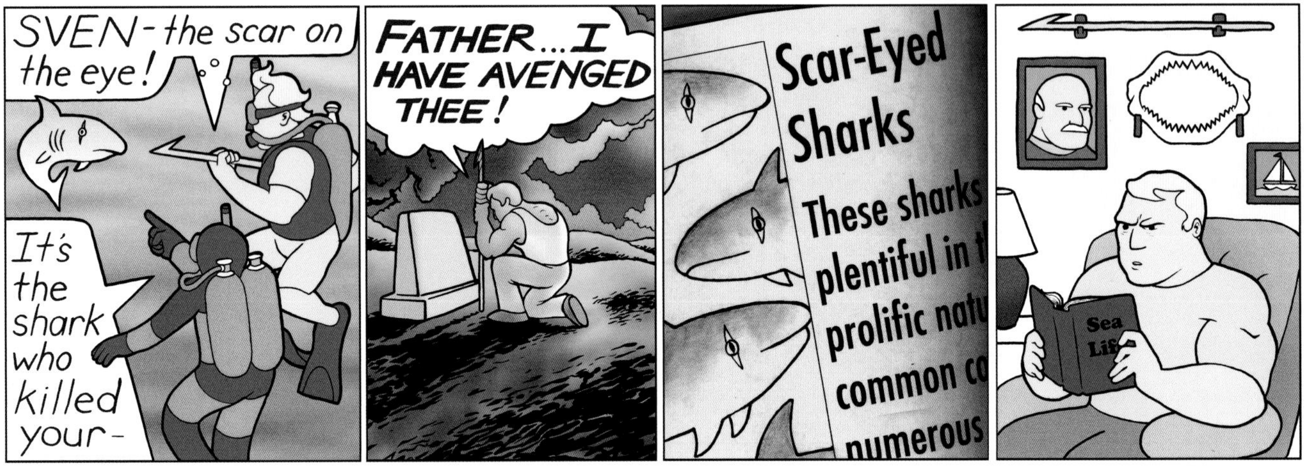
SVEN- the scar on the eye!
It's the shark who killed your-
FATHER... I HAVE AVENGED THEE!
Scar-Eyed Sharks
These sharks
plentiful in t
prolific natu
common co
numerous
Sea Lif

Peak Performance

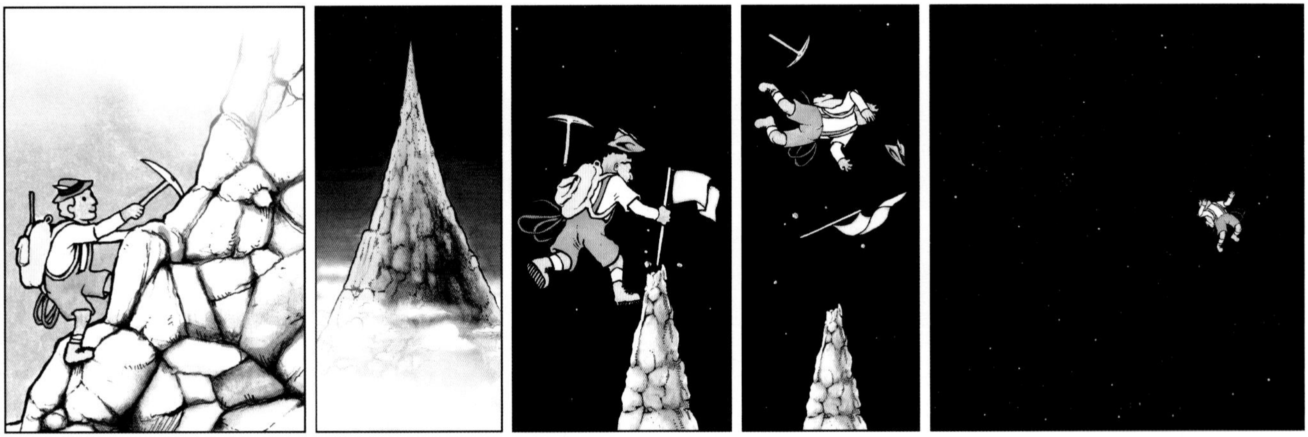

Lumberjack

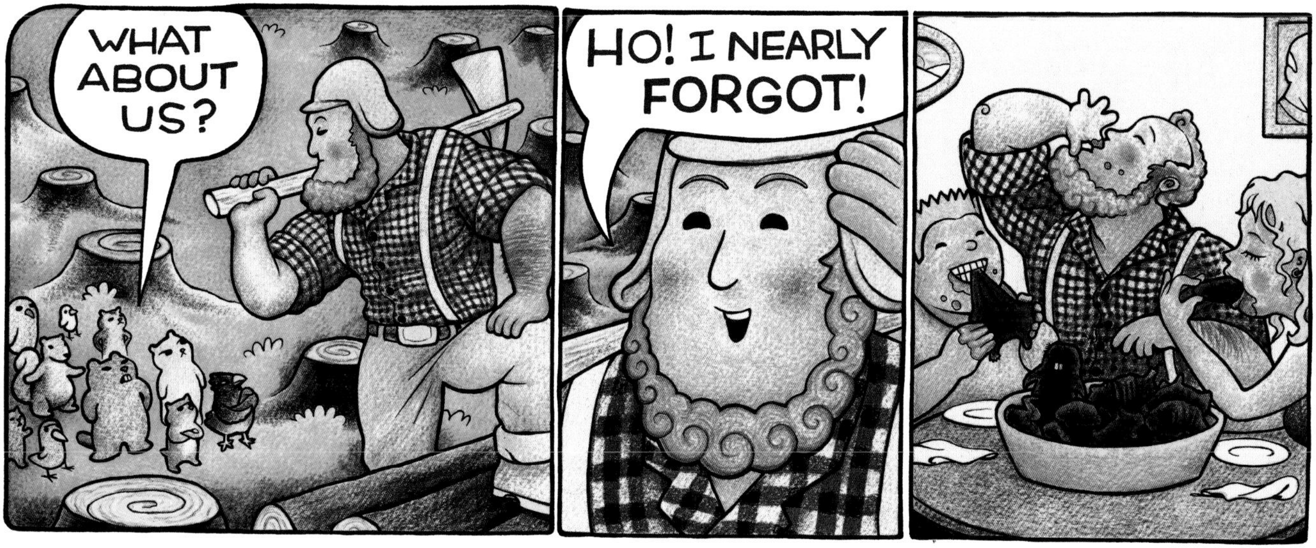
WHAT ABOUT US?
HO! I NEARLY FORGOT!

Tub Times

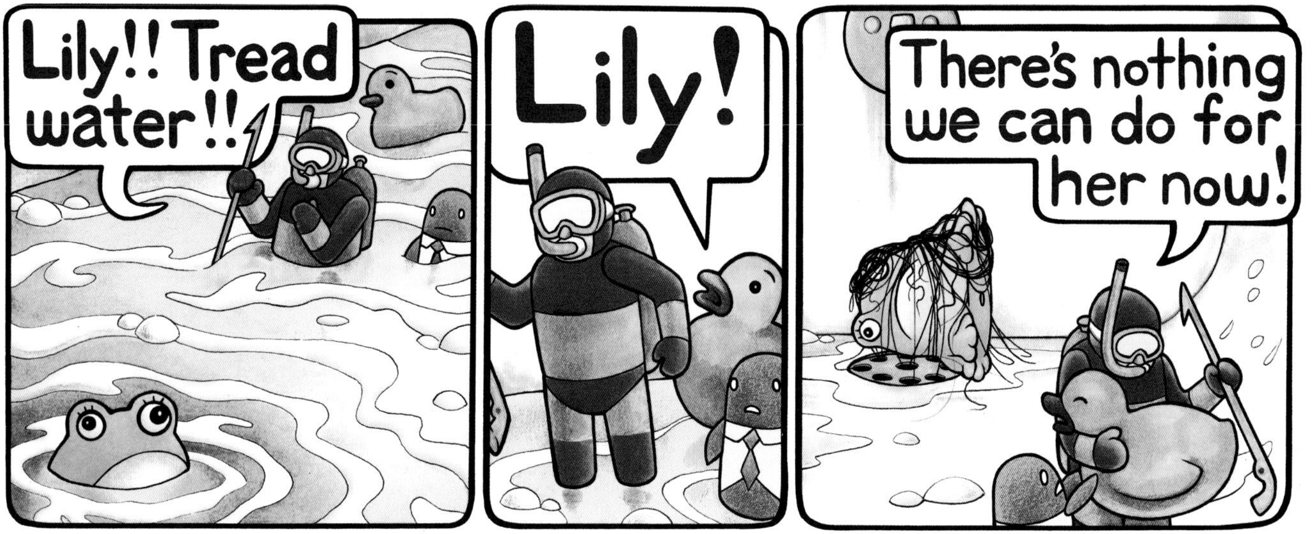
Lily!! Tread water!!
Lily!
There's nothing we can do for her now!

Special Delivery

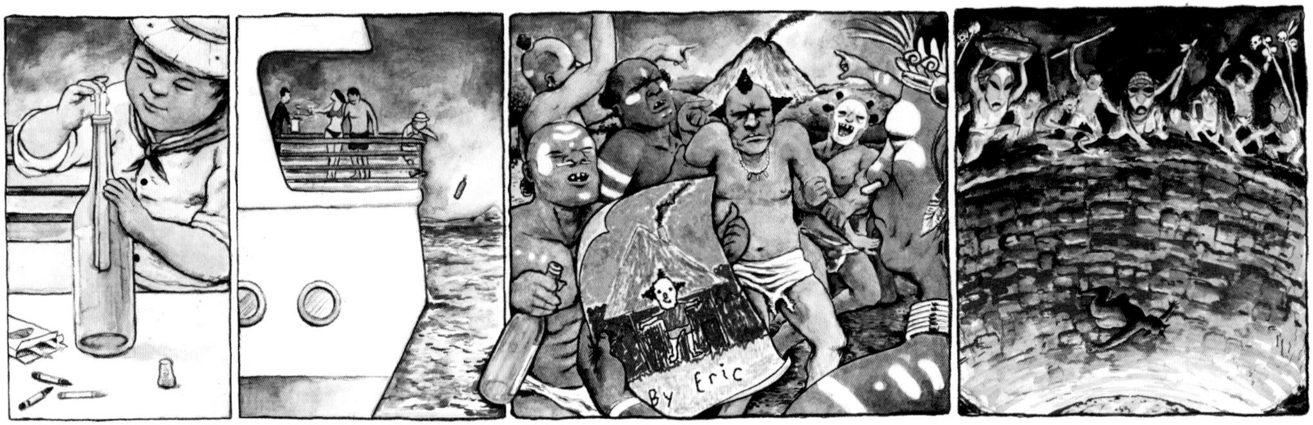

By Eric

The Pacific Council

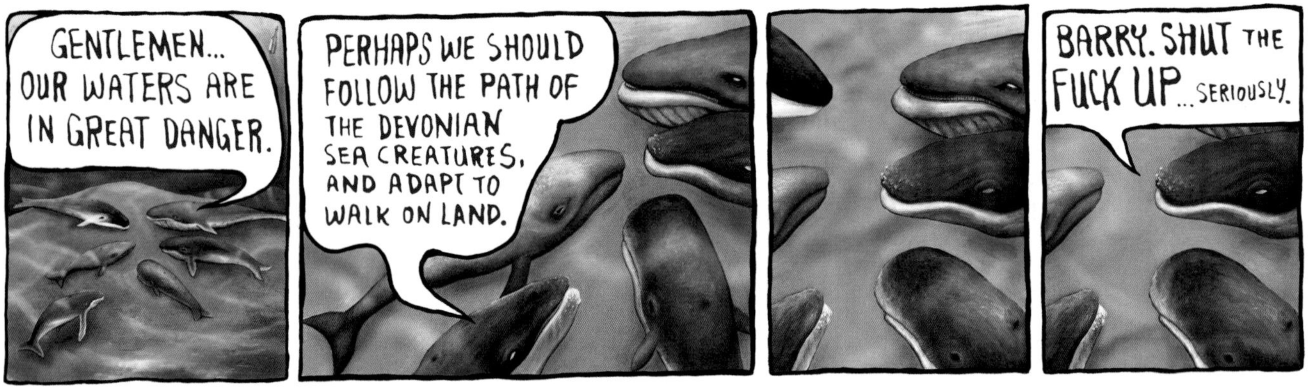

GENTLEMEN... OUR WATERS ARE IN GREAT DANGER.
PERHAPS WE SHOULD FOLLOW THE PATH OF THE DEVONIAN SEA CREATURES, AND ADAPT TO WALK ON LAND.
BARRY. SHUT THE FUCK UP... SERIOUSLY.

Chew Boy

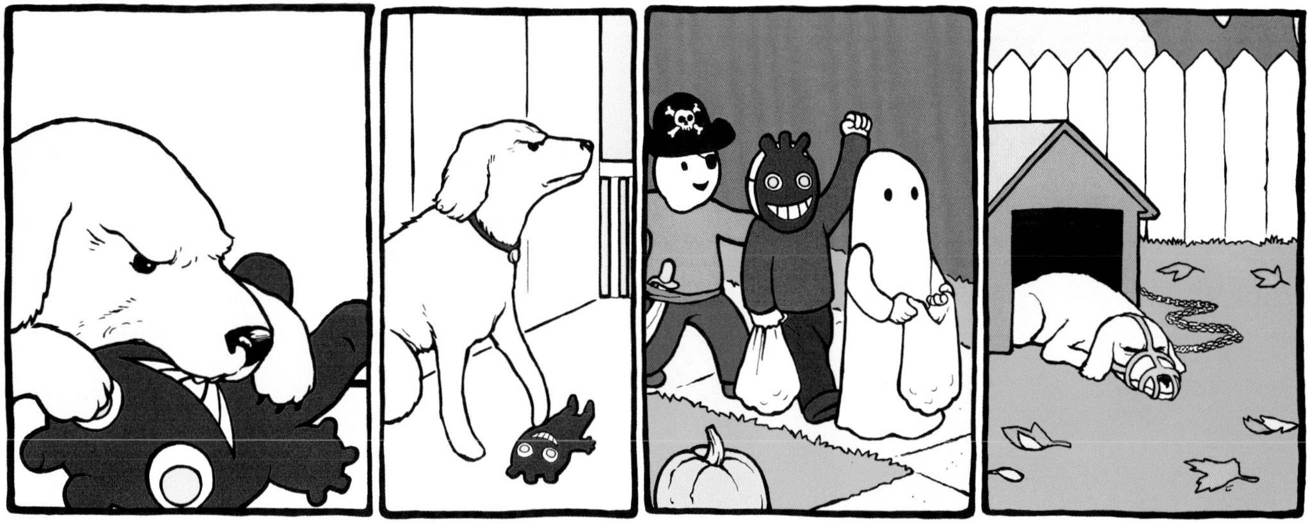

Allen the Hungry Alligator

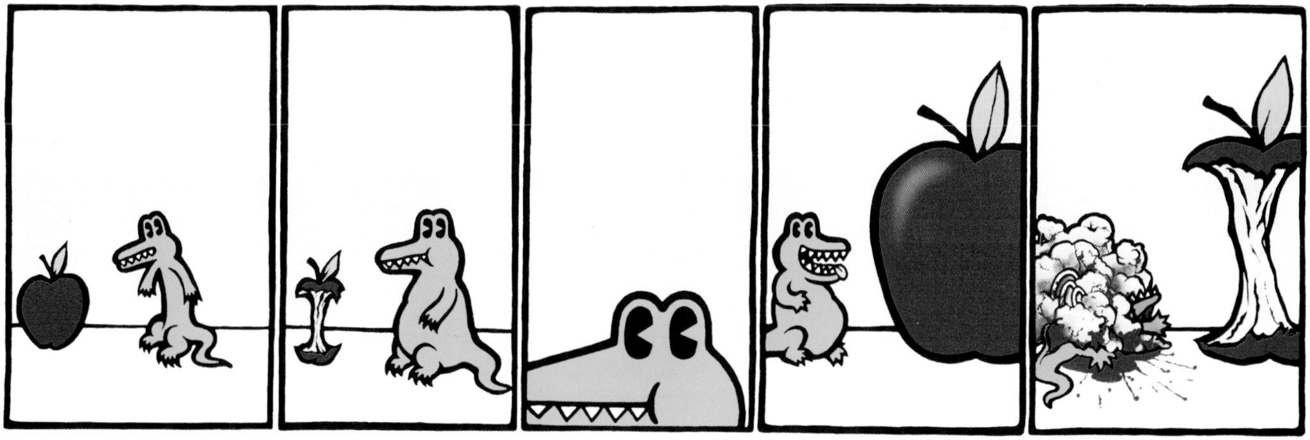

Wishing Well

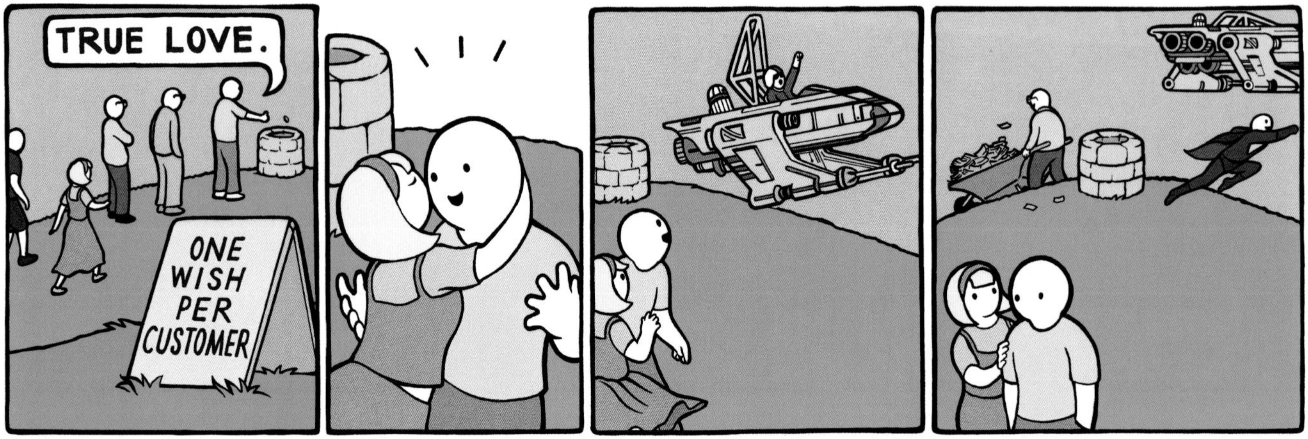

TRUE LOVE.
ONE WISH PER CUSTOMER

Super League

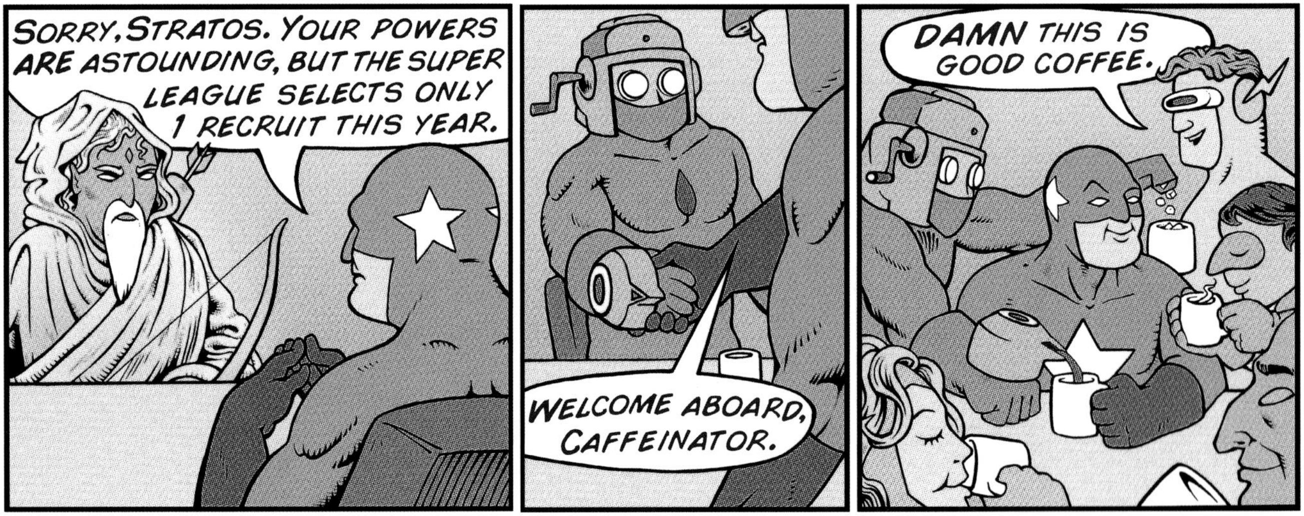

SORRY, STRATOS. YOUR POWERS ARE ASTOUNDING, BUT THE SUPER LEAGUE SELECTS ONLY 1 RECRUIT THIS YEAR.
WELCOME ABOARD, CAFFEINATOR.
DAMN THIS IS GOOD COFFEE.

Mrs. Hammer

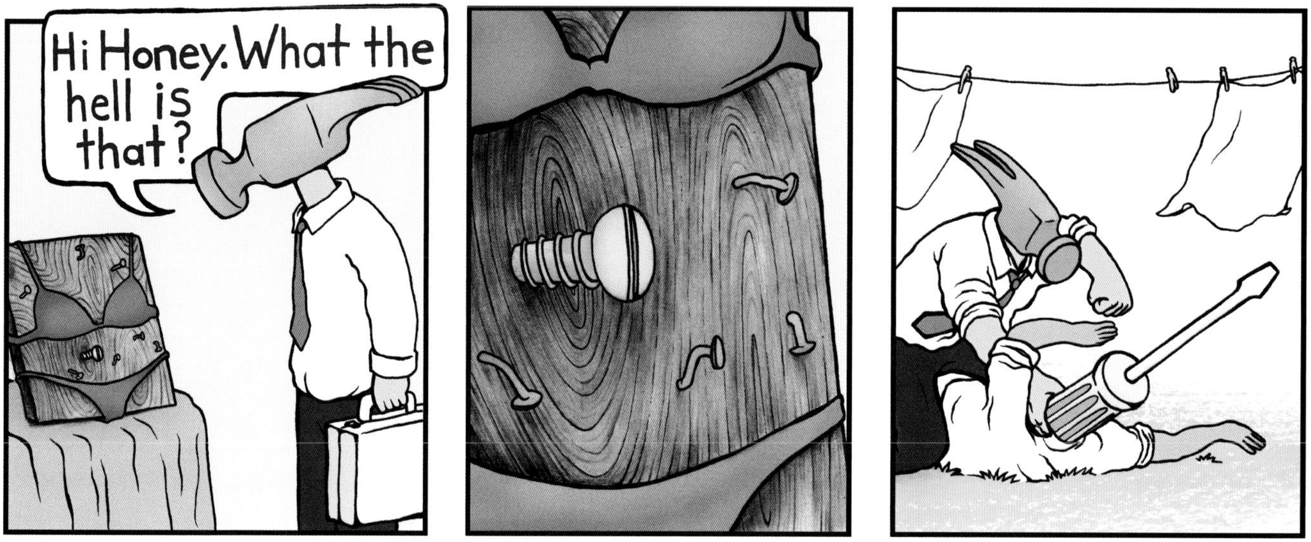
Hi Honey. What the hell is that?

Boy Scouts

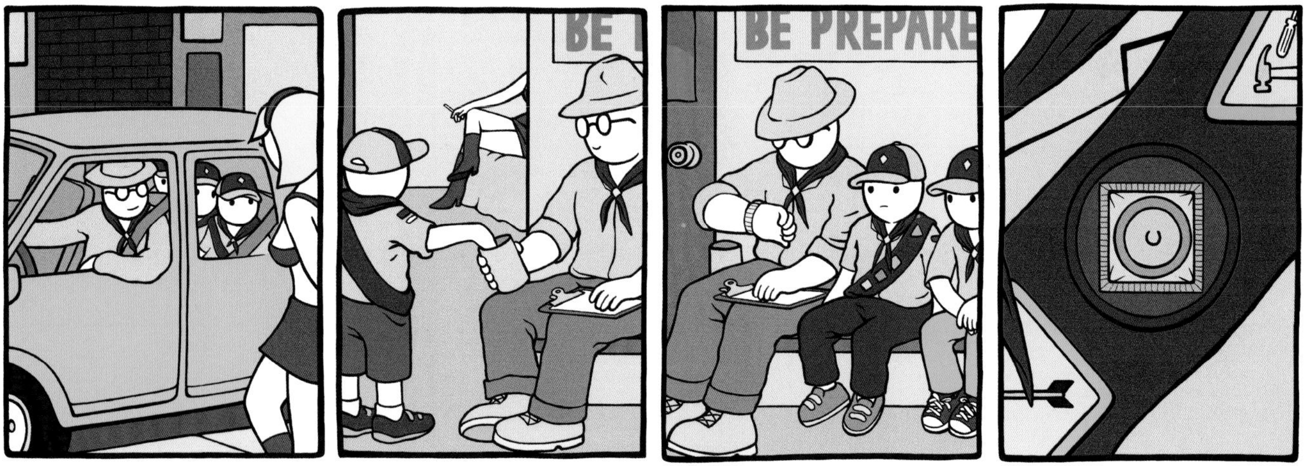
BE PREPARE

Today I am Going to Fly

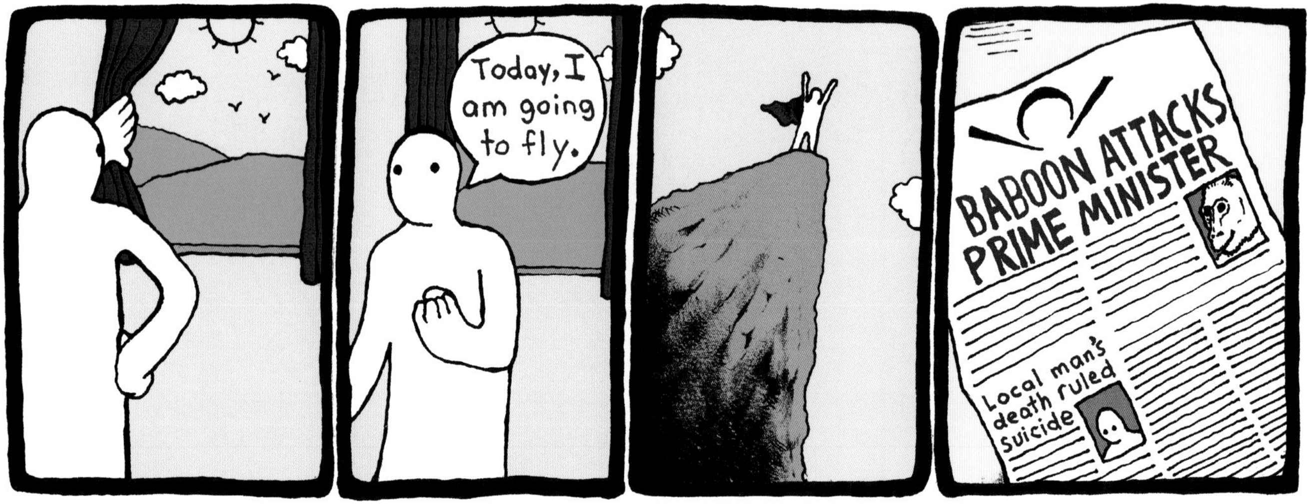

Today, I am going to fly.
BABOON ATTACKS PRIME MINISTER
Local man's death ruled suicide

Falling Dream

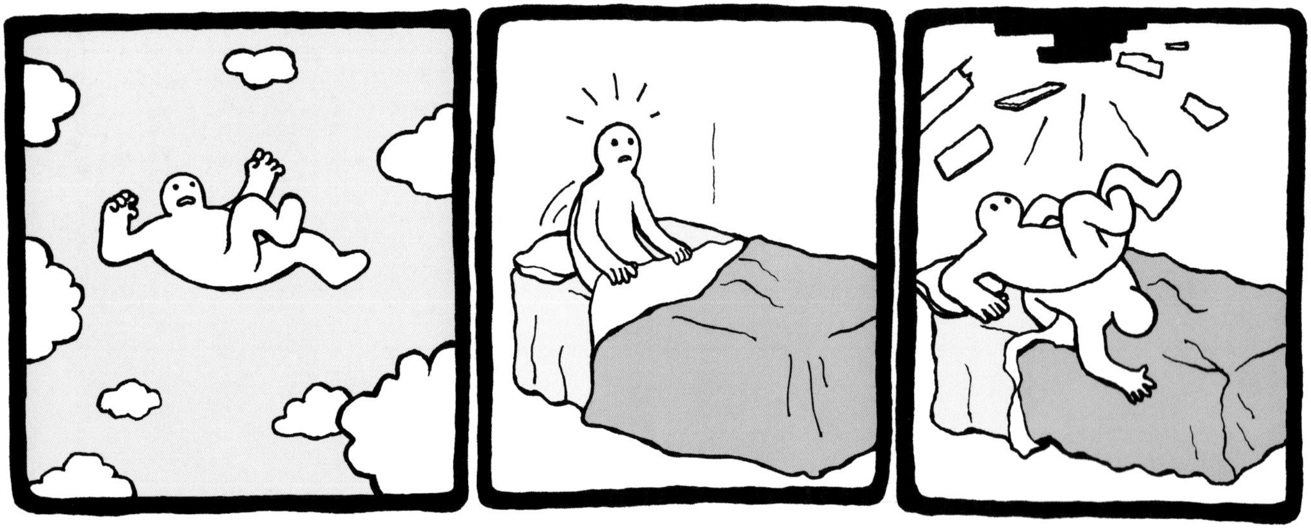

Way Too Much (Apologies to Bil Keane)

"David, that's way too much."

"The tooth fairy gave me 20 BUCKS!"

"We're gonna be RICH!!!"

Basebugs

OH COME ON, GONZALES.

GONZALES—WHAT THE *%$#* ARE YOU DOING!?!

Photo Album

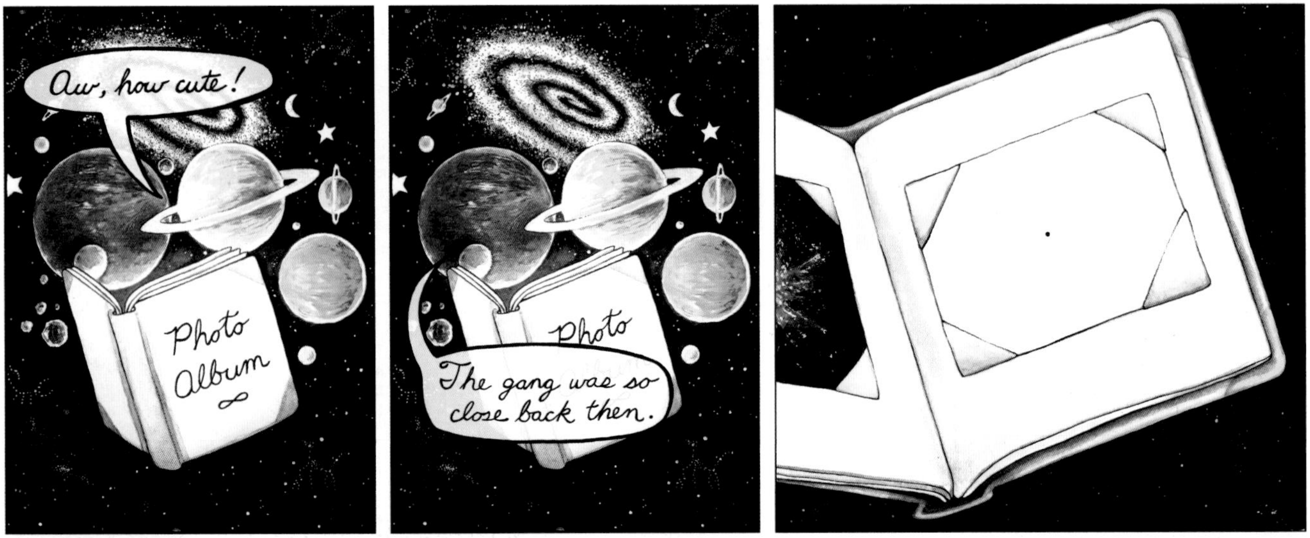
Aw, how cute!
Photo Album
Photo
The gang was so close back then.

Kitty Heaven

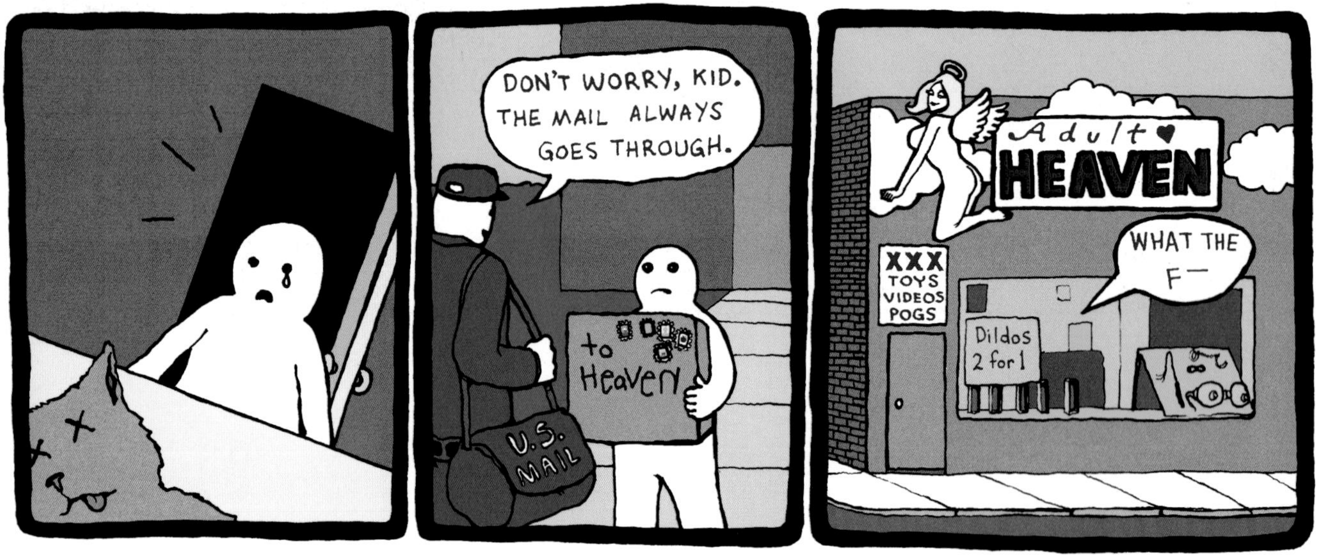
DON'T WORRY, KID. THE MAIL ALWAYS GOES THROUGH.
to Heaven
U.S. MAIL
Adult
HEAVEN
XXX TOYS VIDEOS POGS
Dildos 2 for 1
WHAT THE F—

The Agronox

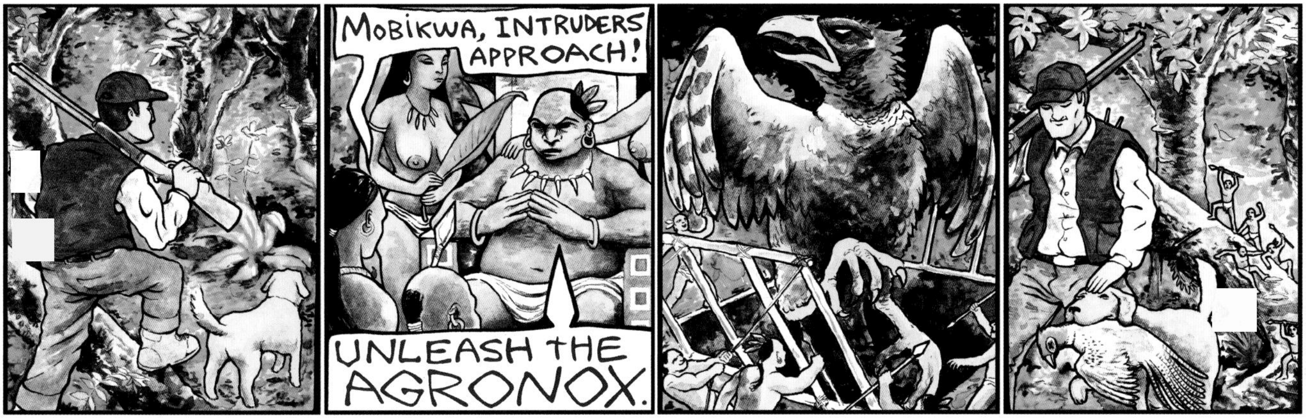
MOBIKWA, INTRUDERS APPROACH!
UNLEASH THE AGRONOX.

Space Helmet

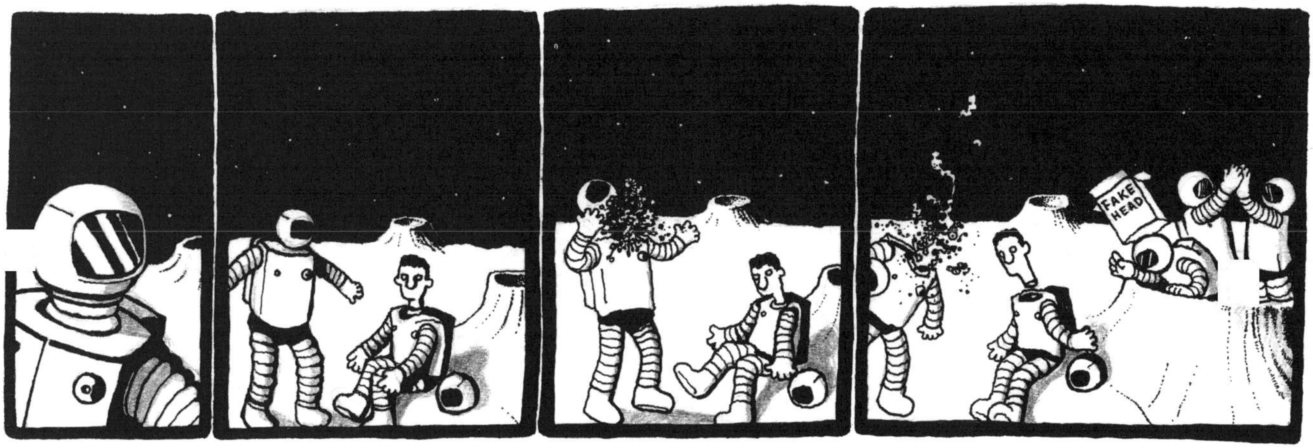
FAKE HEAD

Bumble Buzzin'

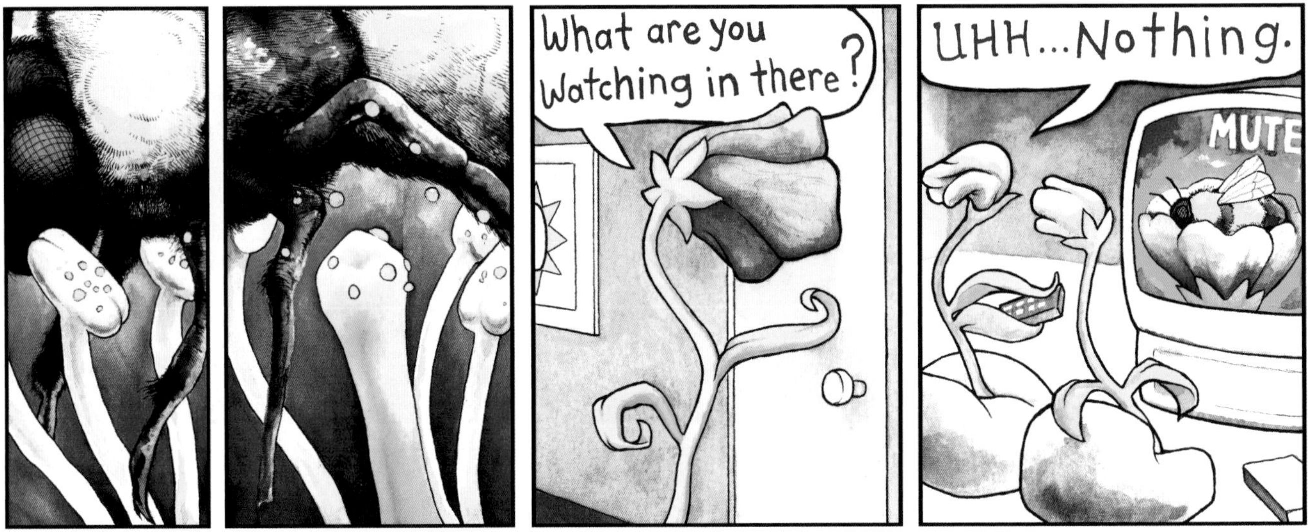

What are you Watching in there?
UHH...Nothing.
MUTE

Rhino and Boy

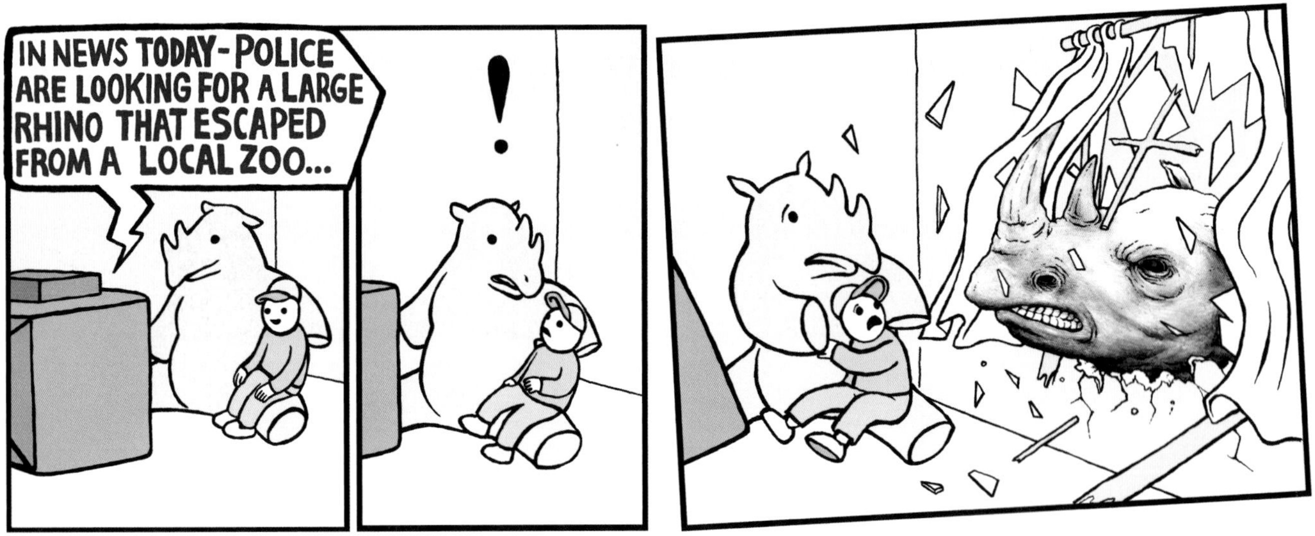

IN NEWS TODAY-POLICE ARE LOOKING FOR A LARGE RHINO THAT ESCAPED FROM A LOCAL ZOO...
!

Missing School

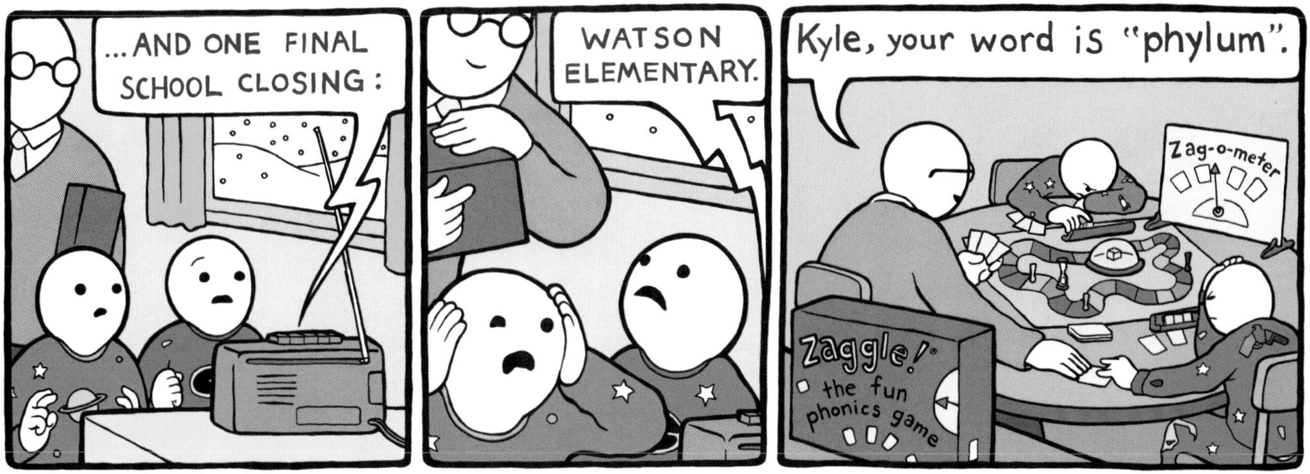
...AND ONE FINAL SCHOOL CLOSING:
WATSON ELEMENTARY.
Kyle, your word is "phylum".
Zag-o-meter
Zaggle!
the fun phonics game

Guntron Alliance Force

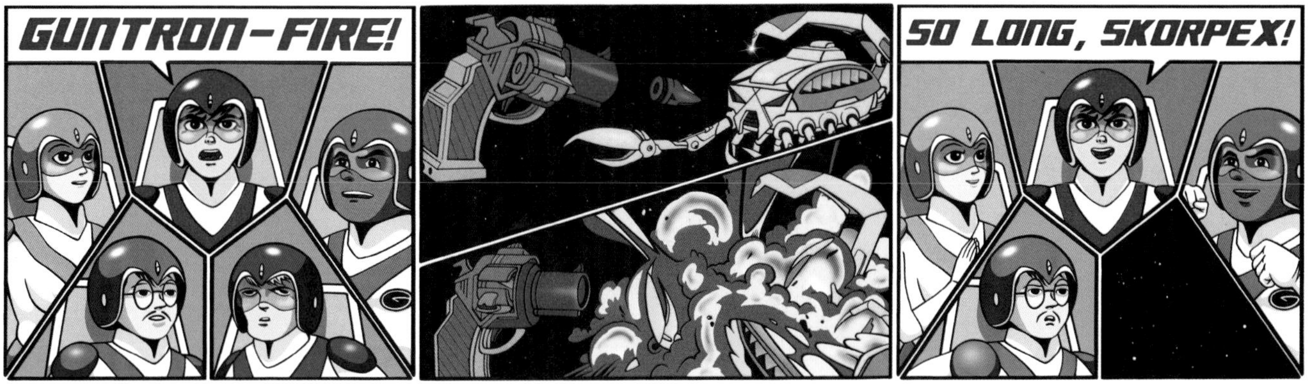
GUNTRON–FIRE!
SO LONG, SKORPEX!

Tunnel of Love

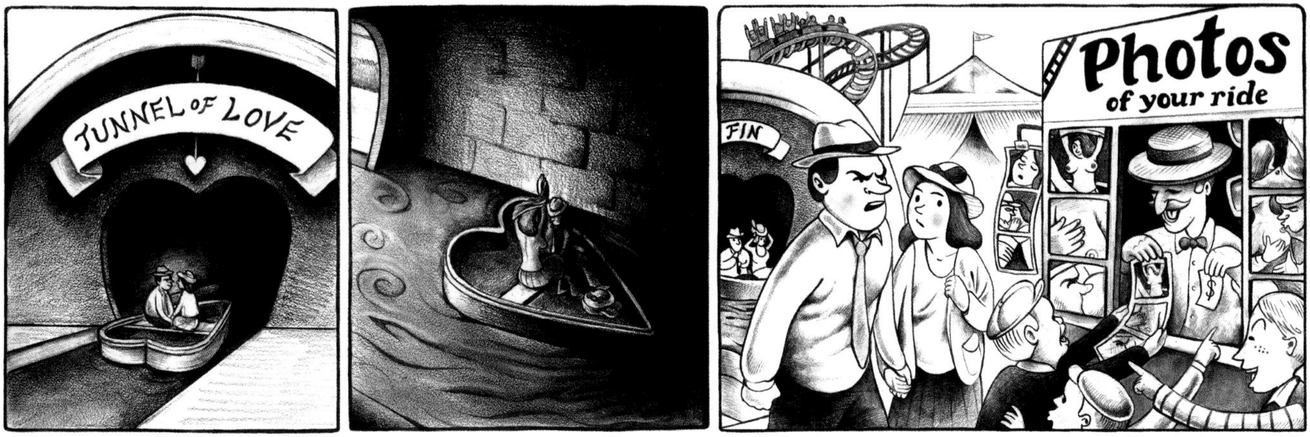
TUNNEL OF LOVE
FIN
Photos
of your ride

Happy Brothers

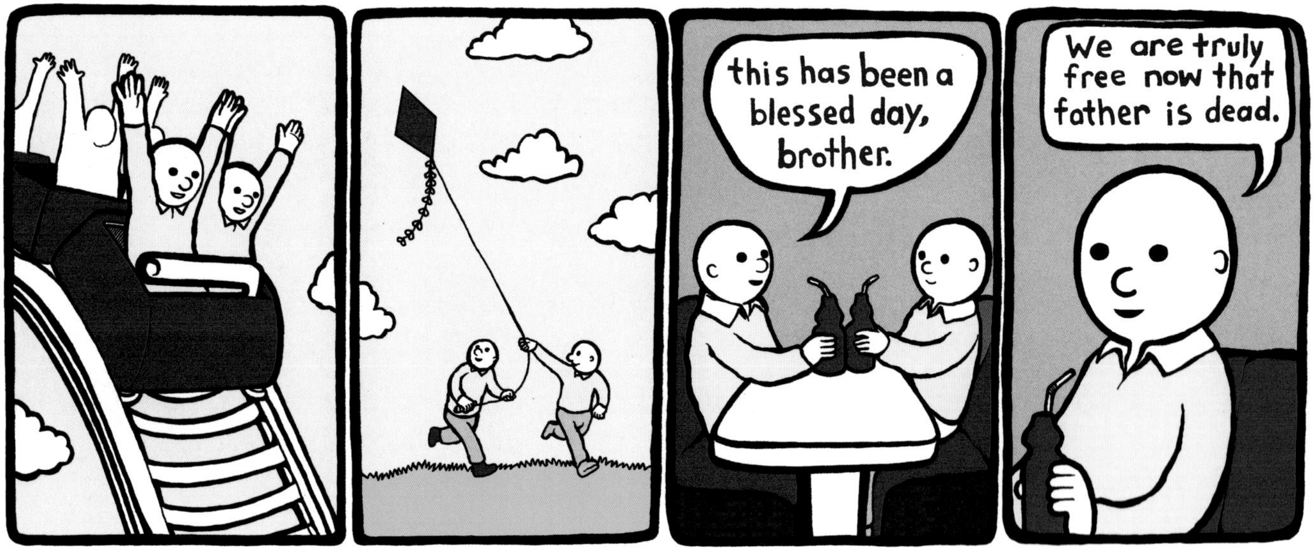
this has been a blessed day, brother.
We are truly free now that father is dead.

Nude Beach

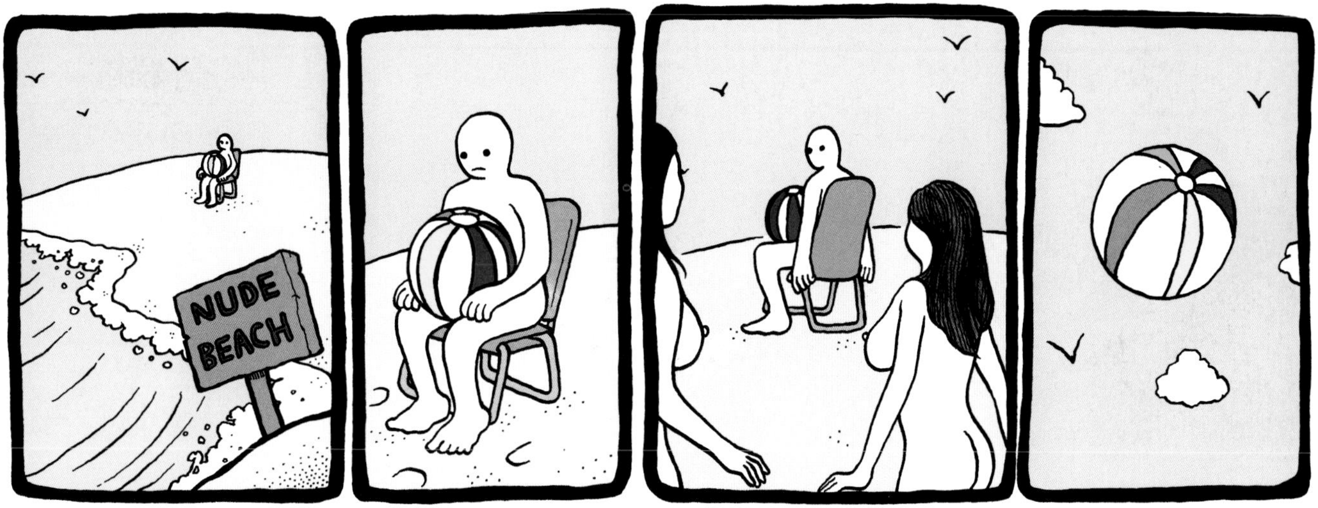
NUDE BEACH

Robin Hood

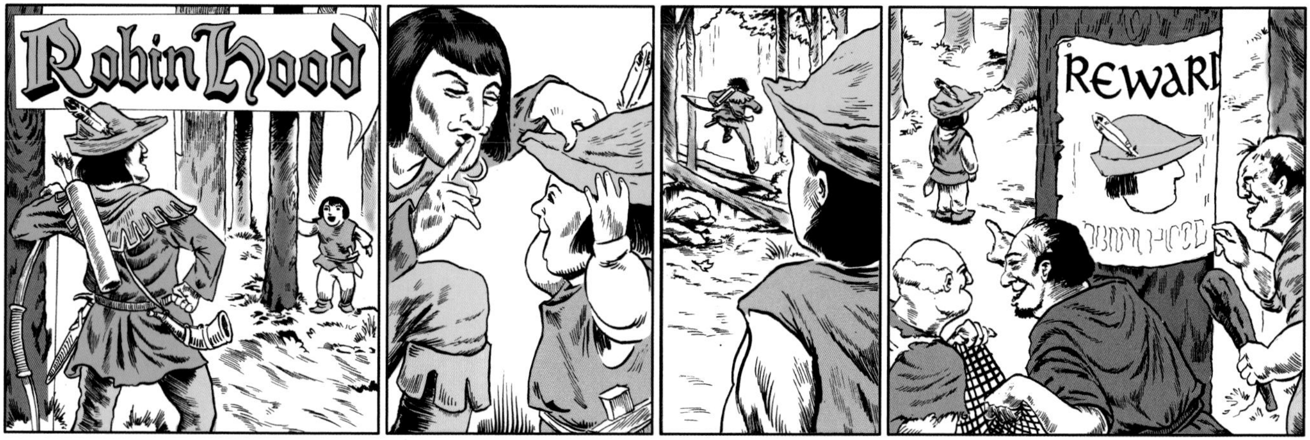
Robin Hood
REWARD

Rodeo

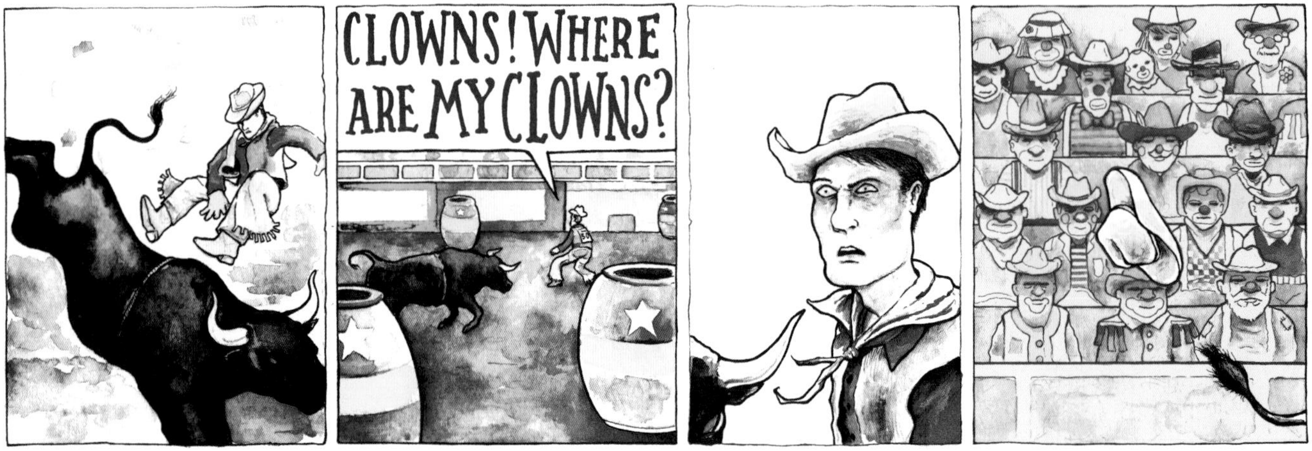
CLOWNS! WHERE ARE MY CLOWNS?

Disgusting Ted

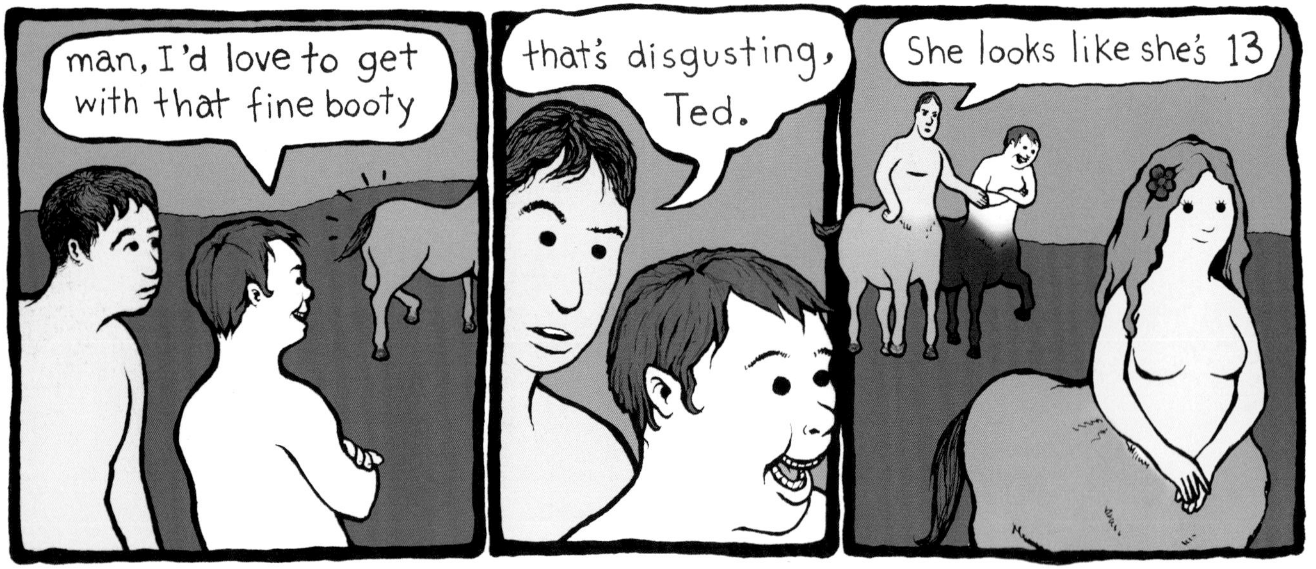
man, I'd love to get with that fine booty
that's disgusting, Ted.
She looks like she's 13

Game Boy

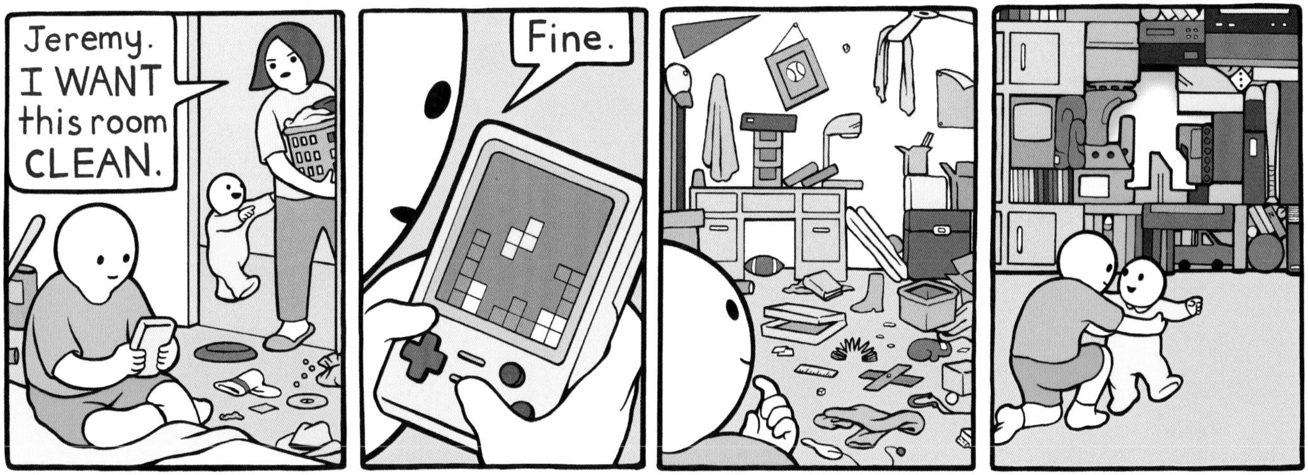
Jeremy.
I WANT
this room
CLEAN.
Fine.

Disassemble

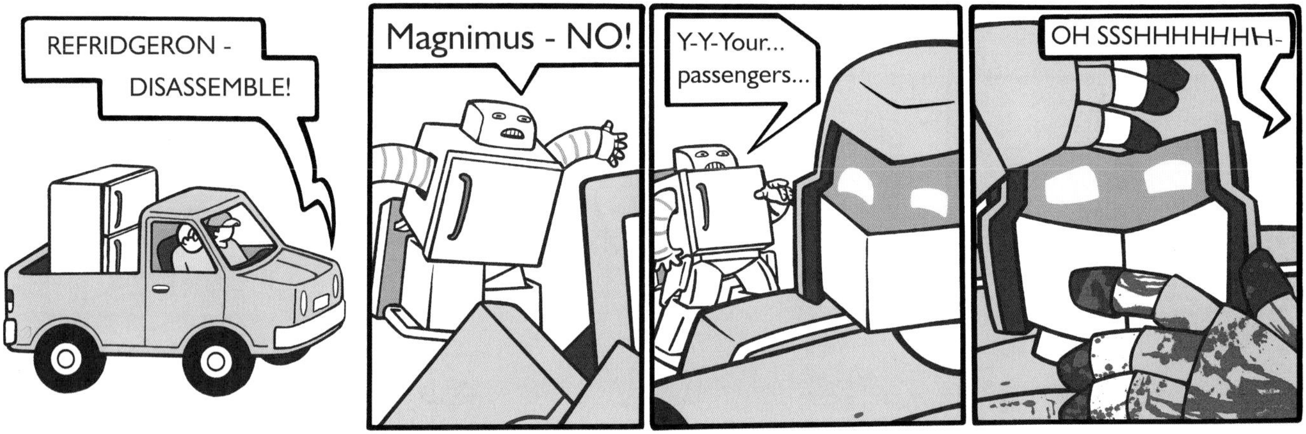
REFRIDGERON -
DISASSEMBLE!
Magnimus - NO!
Y-Y-Your...
passengers...
OH SSSHHHHHHHH-

Bacon Egg

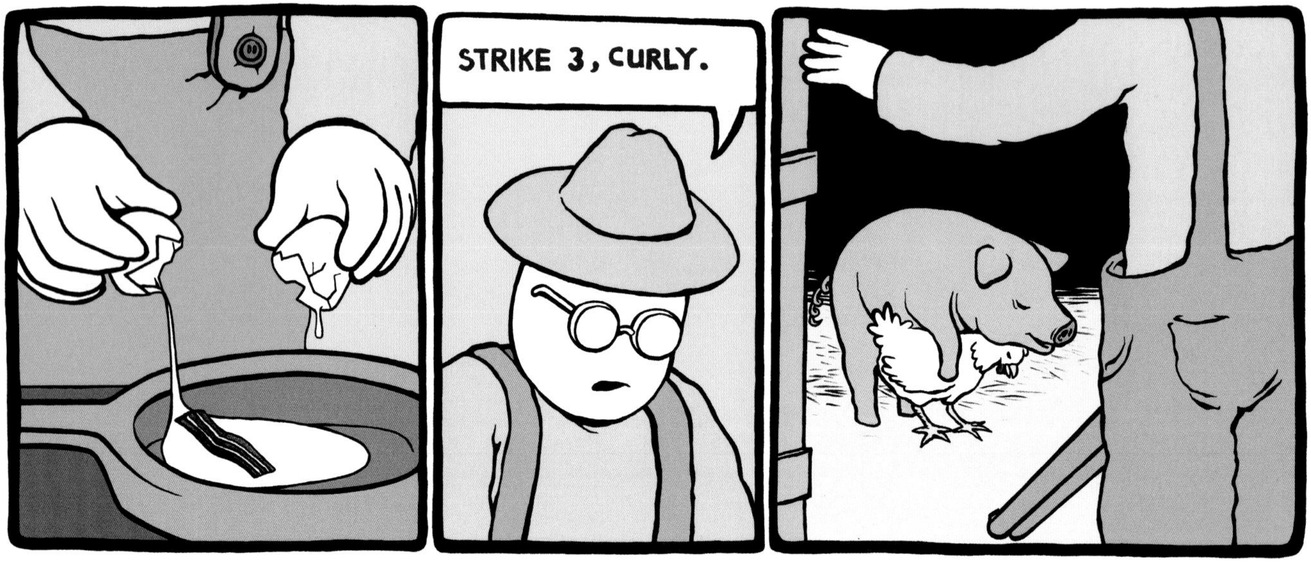
STRIKE 3, CURLY.

Mr. Rex

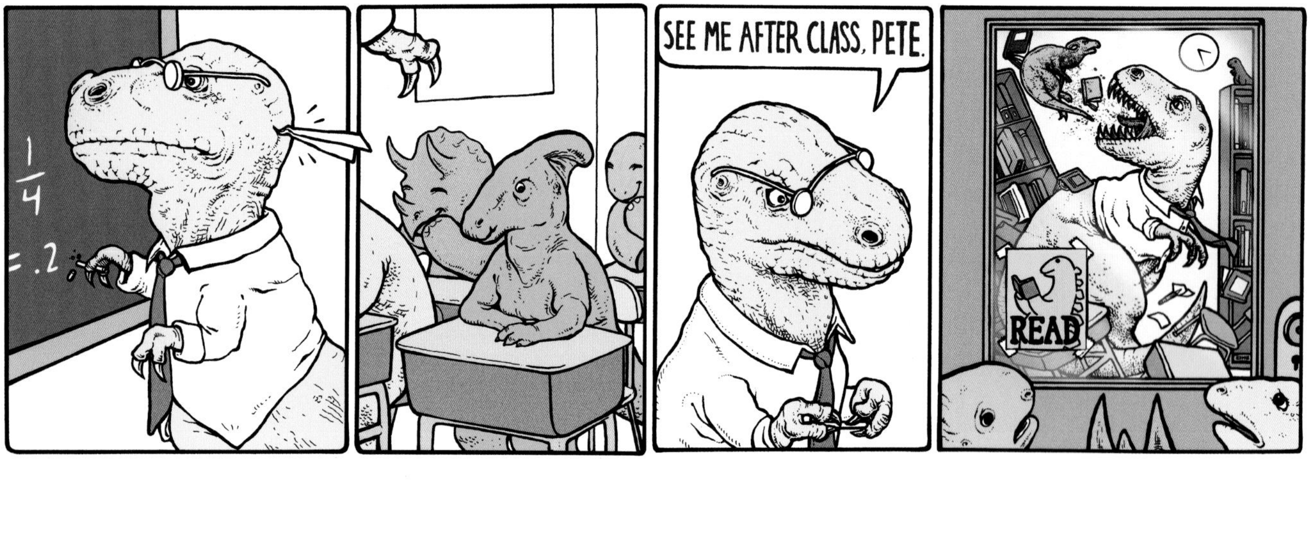
1/4
=.2
SEE ME AFTER CLASS, PETE.
READ

Mittens

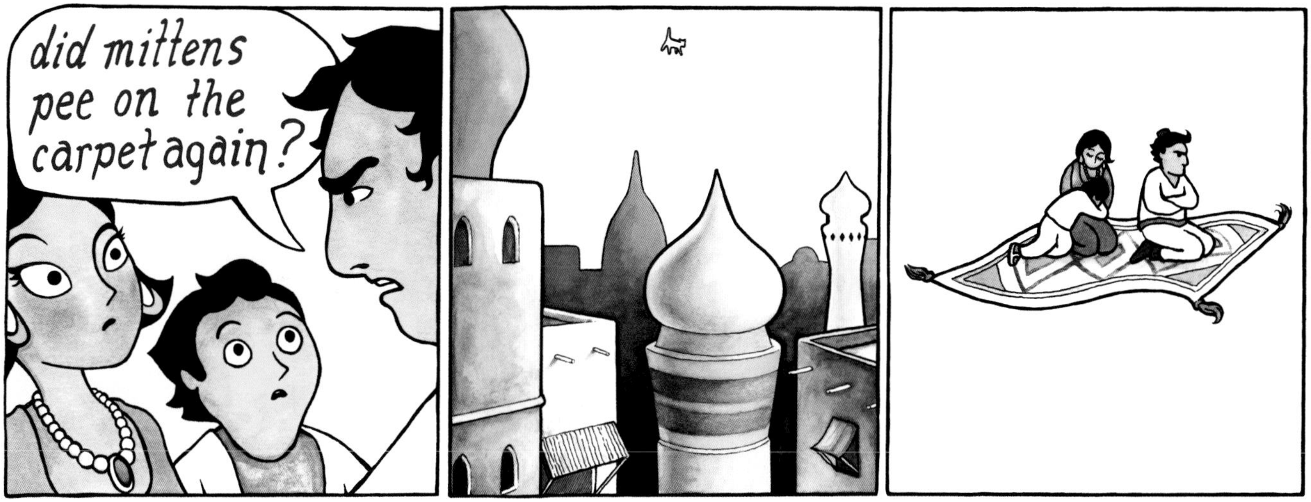
did mittens pee on the carpet again?

Check Shots

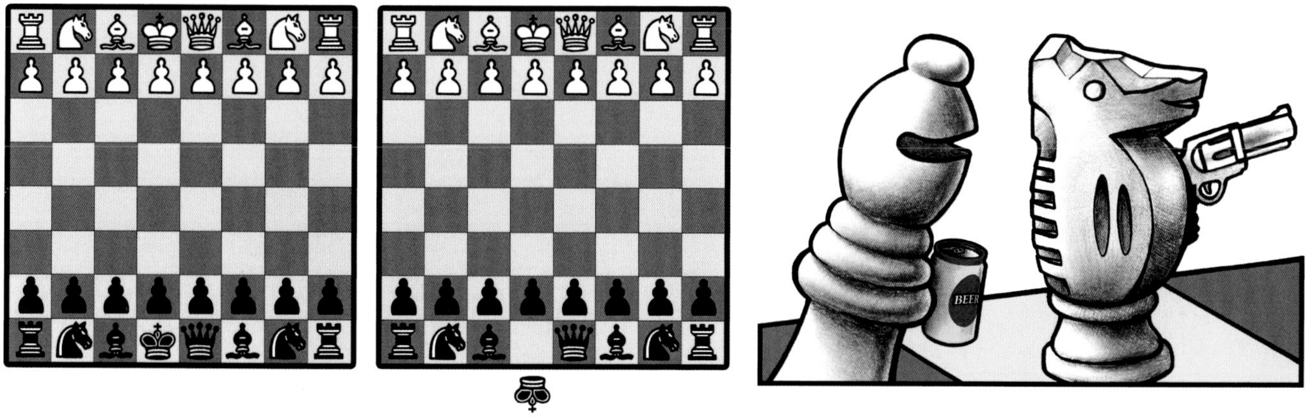
BEER

Scorpy the Forest Friend

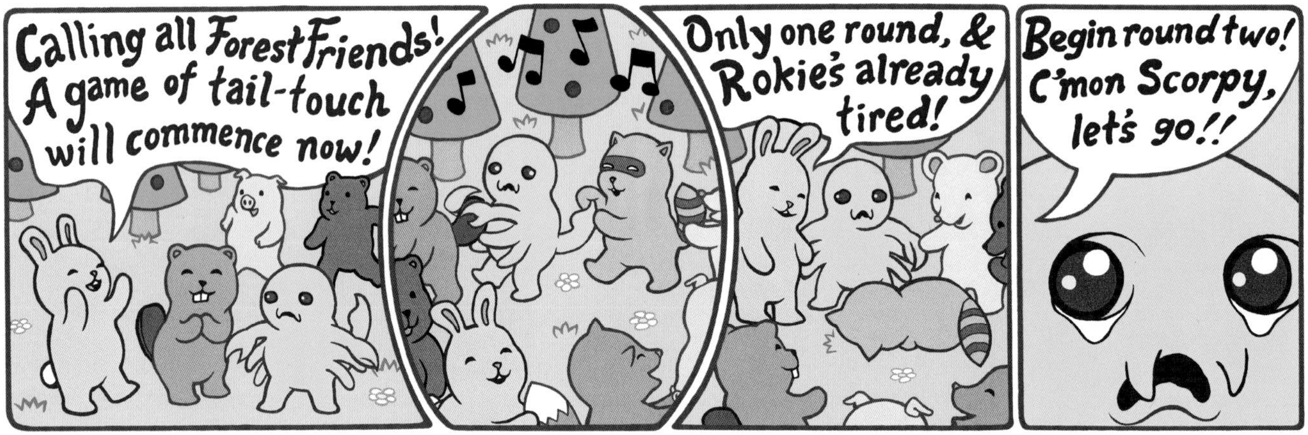
Calling all Forest Friends! A game of tail-touch will commence now!
Only one round, & Rokie's already tired!
Begin round two! C'mon Scorpy, let's go!!

Truancy Bot

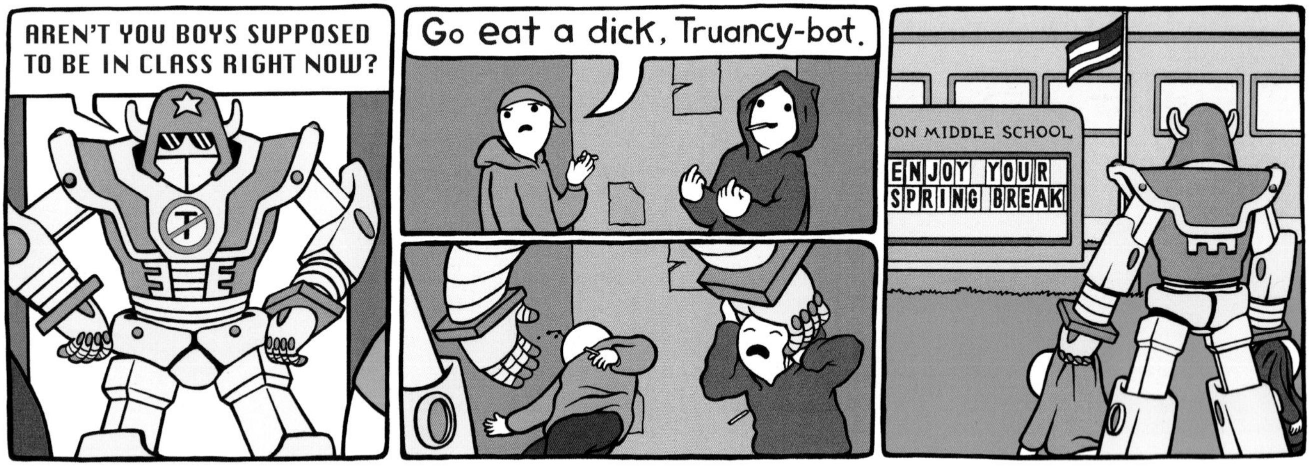
AREN'T YOU BOYS SUPPOSED TO BE IN CLASS RIGHT NOW?
Go eat a dick, Truancy-bot.
ON MIDDLE SCHOOL
ENJOY YOUR SPRING BREAK

Gigaknight™

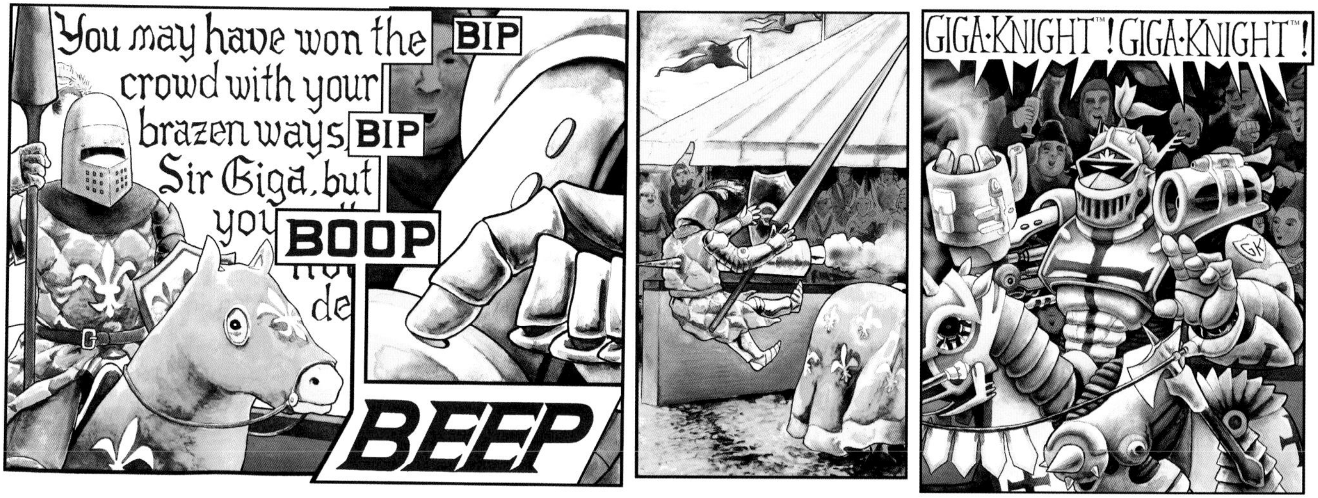
You may have won the crowd with your brazen ways,
BIP
BIP
Sir Giga, but you
BOOP
BEEP
GIGA·KNIGHT™! GIGA·KNIGHT™!

b

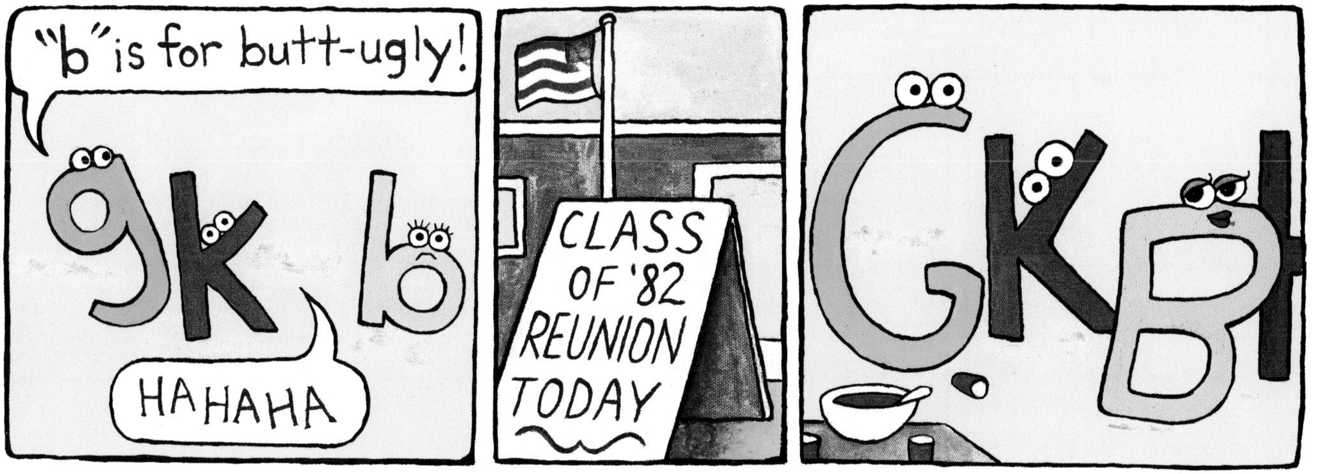
"b" is for butt-ugly!
HAHAHA
CLASS OF '82 REUNION TODAY

No One Is Thirsty

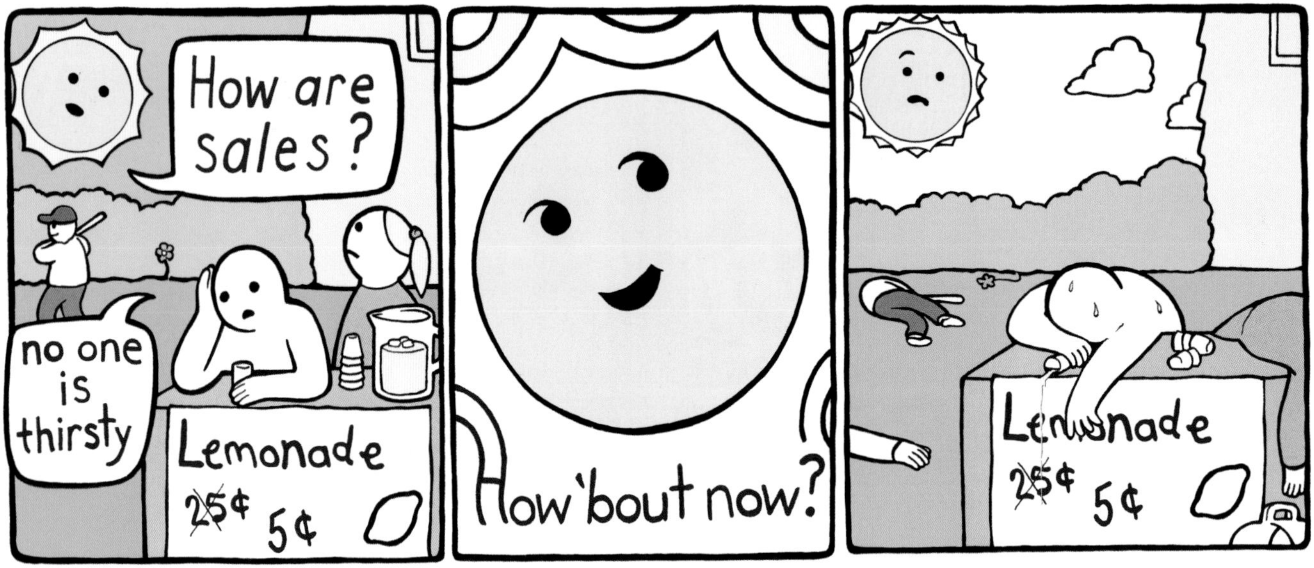
How are sales?
no one is thirsty
Lemonade
25¢ 5¢
How 'bout now?
25¢ 5¢

Bad Apple

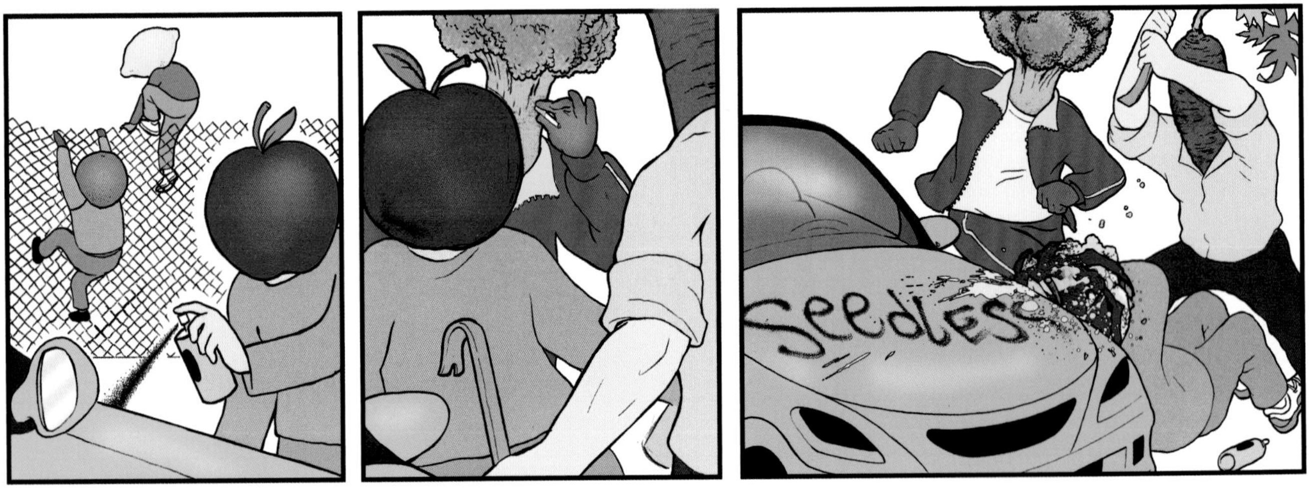
Seedles

Woolves

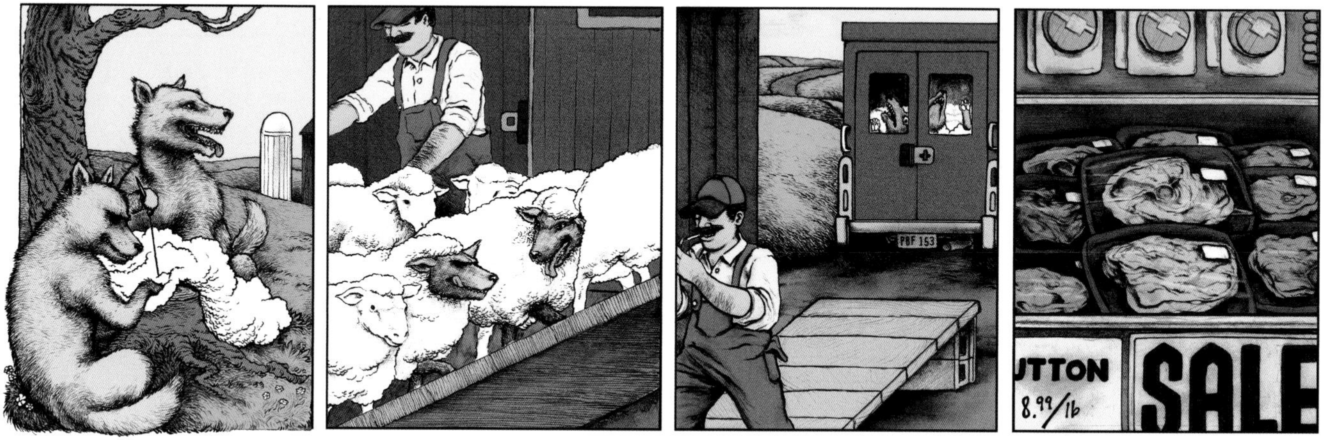
UTTON
8.99/lb
SALE

Cromax

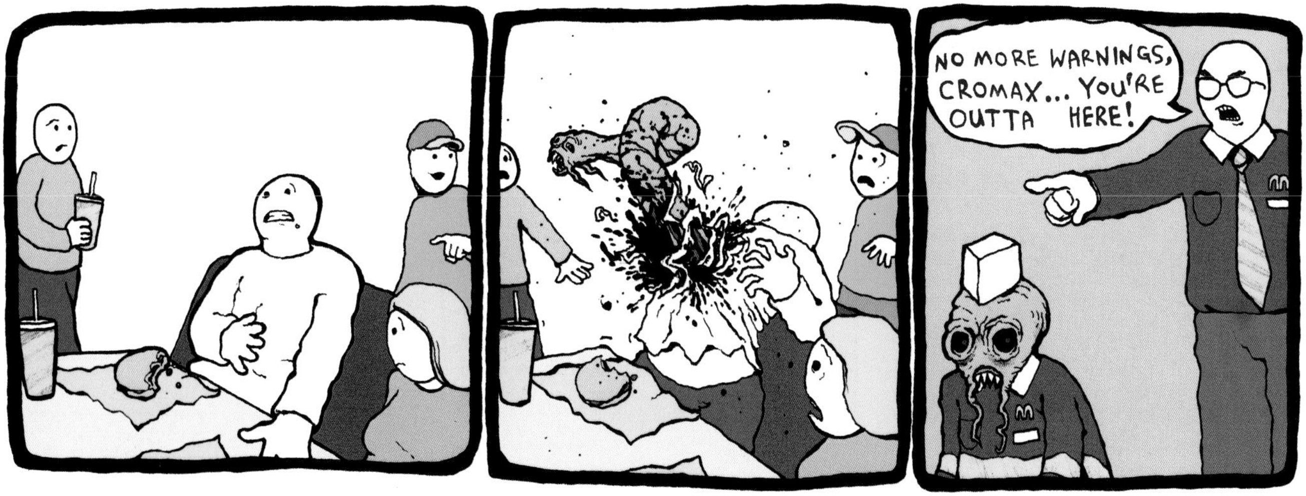
NO MORE WARNINGS, CROMAX... YOU'RE OUTTA HERE!

Better Luck

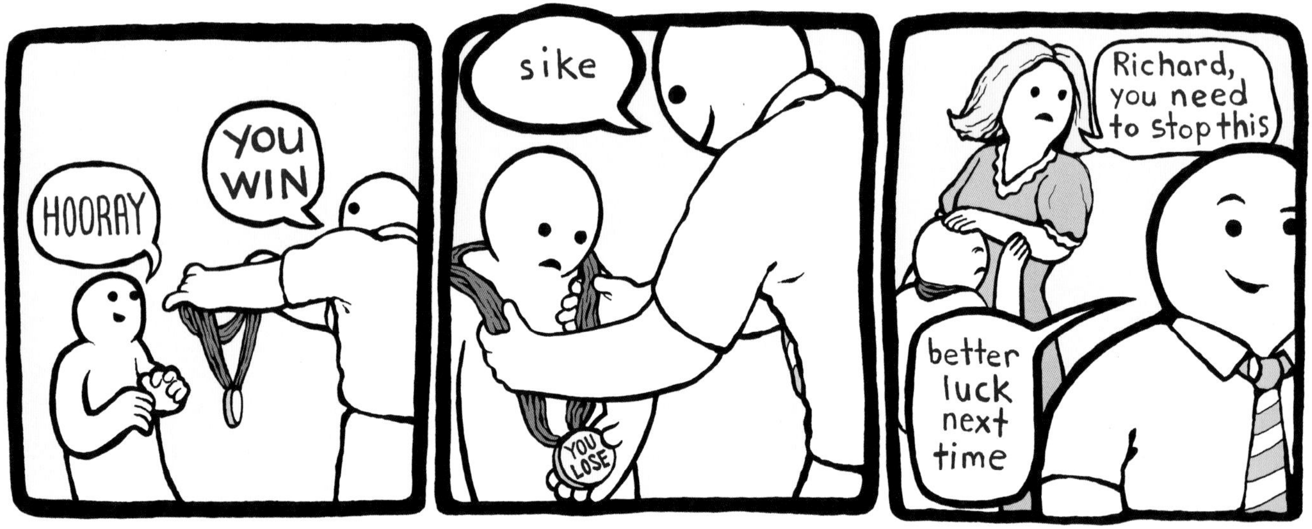
YOU WIN
HOORAY
sike
YOU LOSE
Richard, you need to stop this
better luck next time

Nuñez

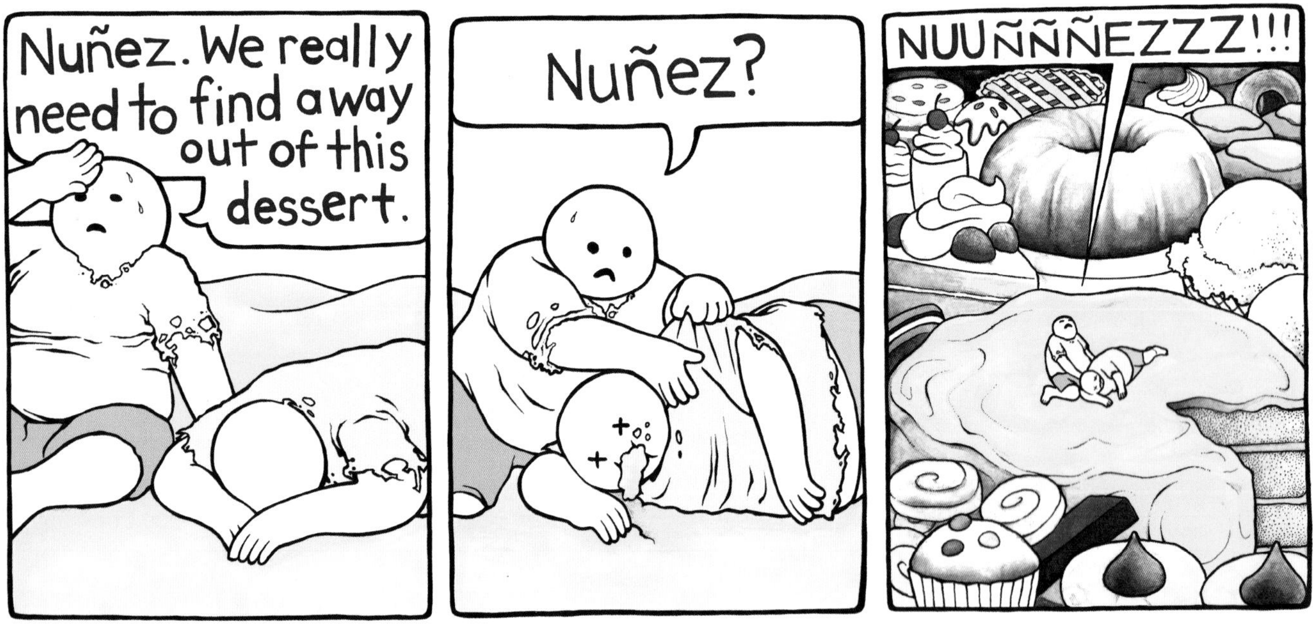
Nuñez. We really need to find a way out of this dessert.
Nuñez?
NUUÑÑÑEZZZZ!!!

The Golden Ticket (Apologies to Quentin Blake)

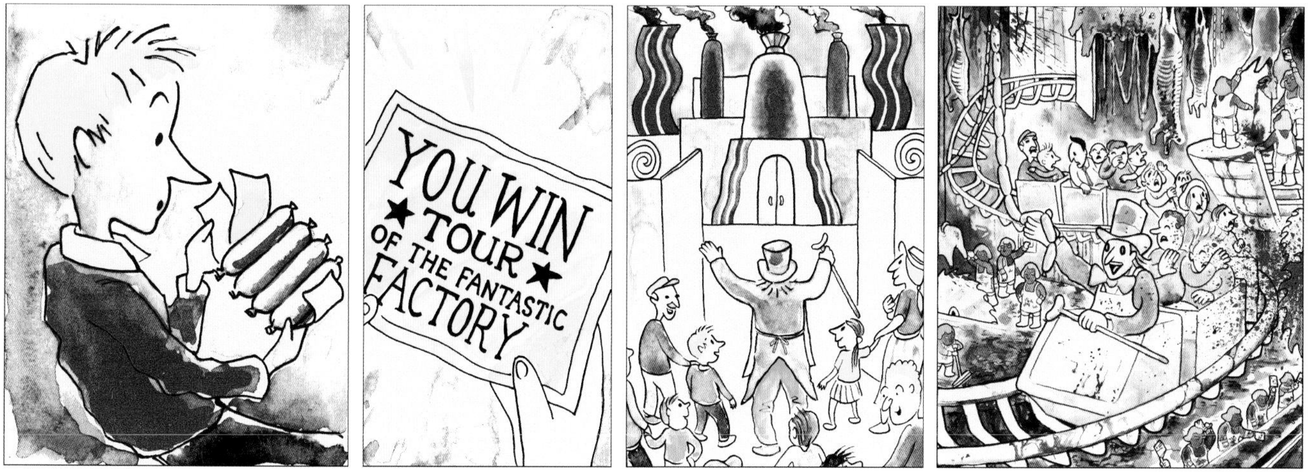
YOU WIN
★ TOUR ★
OF THE FANTASTIC
FACTORY

Weeaboo

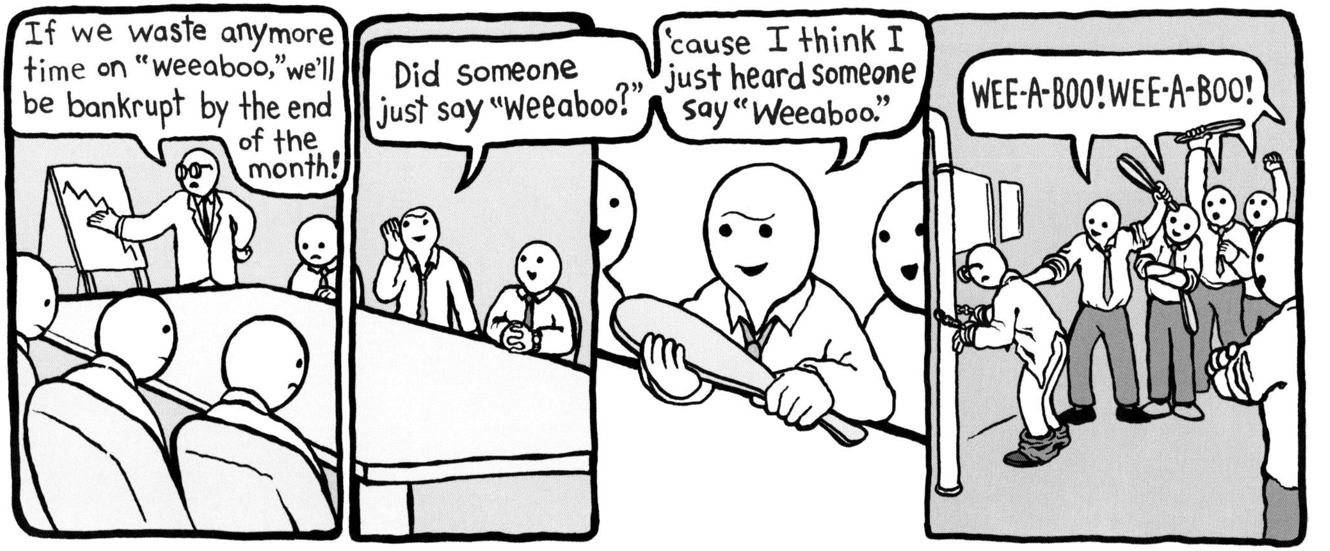
If we waste anymore time on "weeaboo," we'll be bankrupt by the end of the month!
Did someone just say "Weeaboo?"
'cause I think I just heard someone say "Weeaboo."
WEE-A-BOO! WEE-A-BOO!

The Tree of Irony

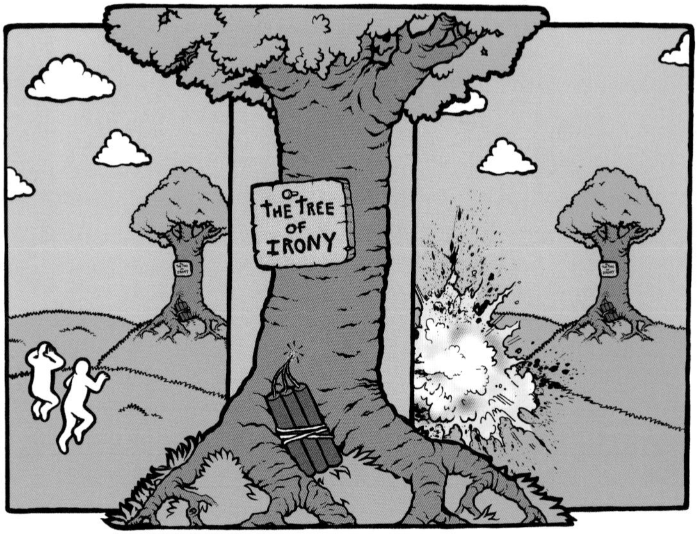
THE TREE OF IRONY

Little One

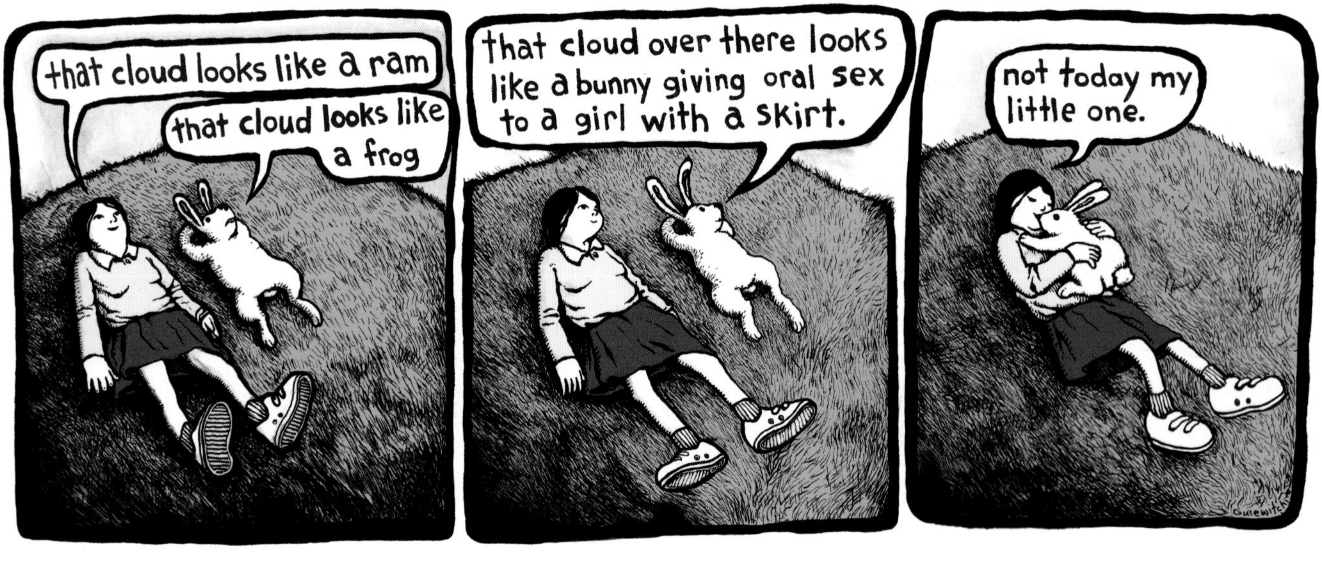
that cloud looks like a ram
that cloud looks like a frog
that cloud over there looks like a bunny giving oral sex to a girl with a skirt.
not today my little one.
Gurewitch

The Dreamcatcher 3000

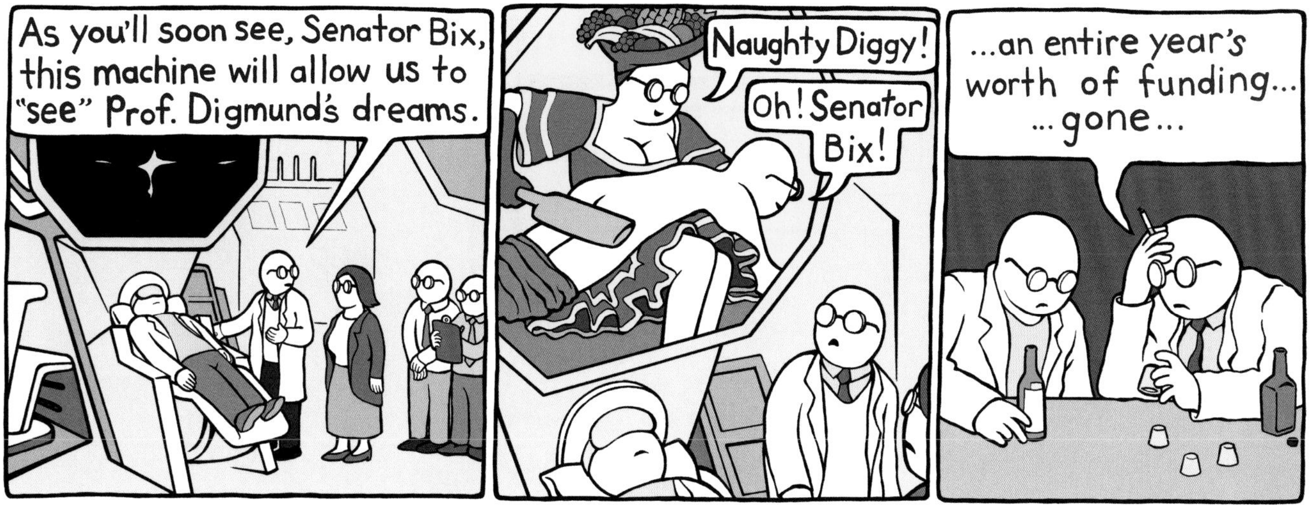
As you'll soon see, Senator Bix, this machine will allow us to "see" Prof. Digmund's dreams.
Naughty Diggy!
Oh! Senator Bix!
...an entire year's worth of funding... ...gone...

Lord Gloom

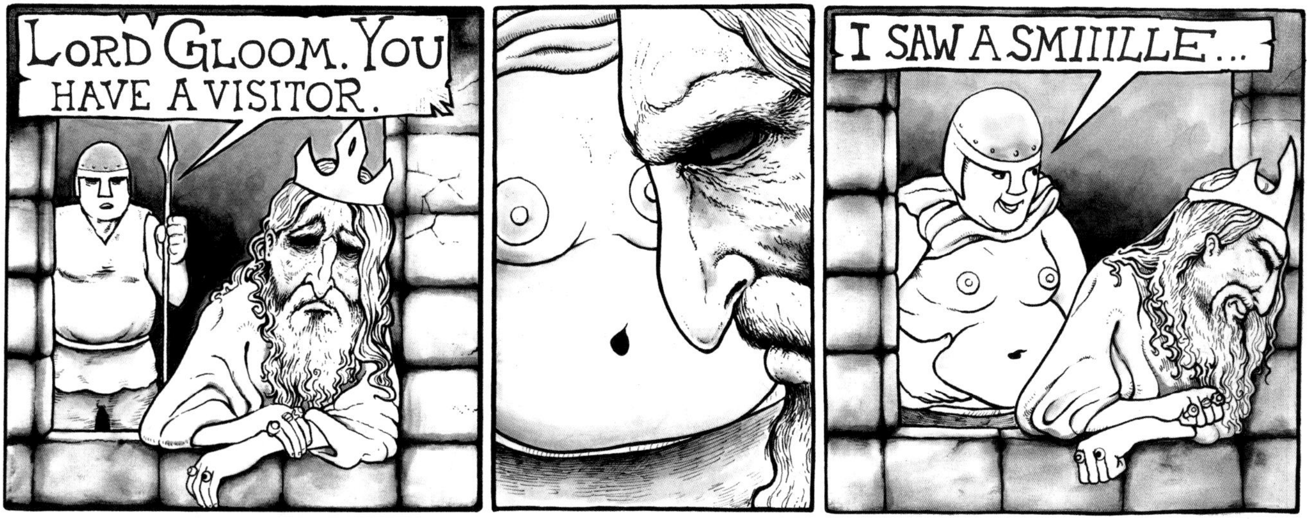
LORD GLOOM. YOU HAVE A VISITOR.
I SAW A SMIIILLE...

Freaking Vortex

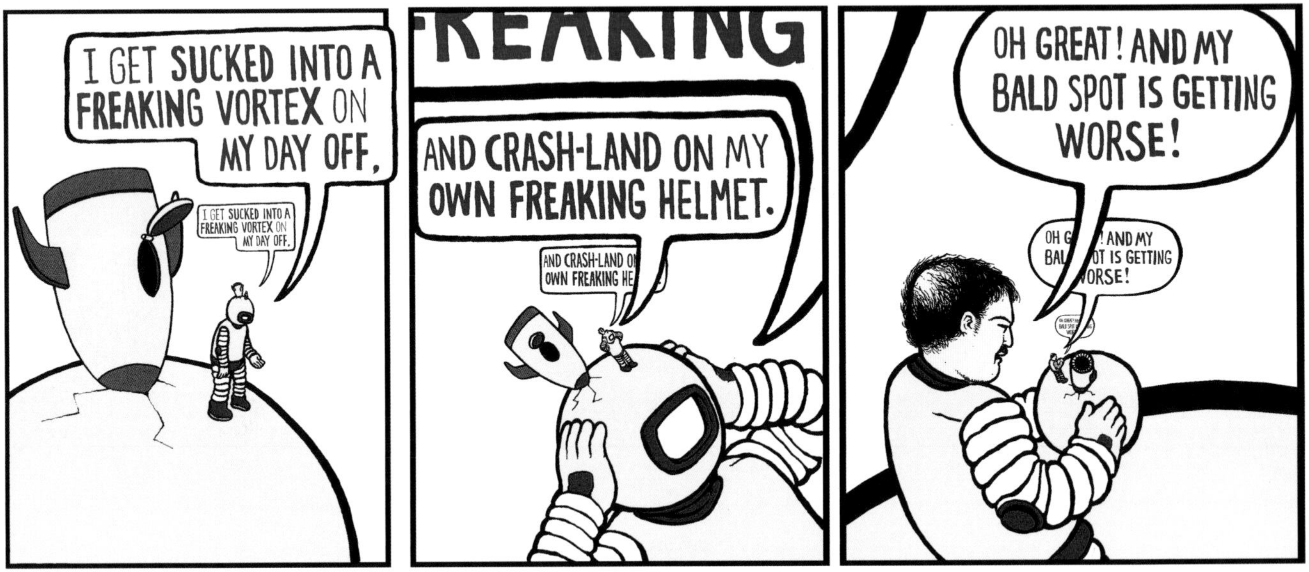
I GET SUCKED INTO A FREAKING VORTEX ON MY DAY OFF,
I GET SUCKED INTO A FREAKING VORTEX ON MY DAY OFF.
FREAKING
AND CRASH-LAND ON MY OWN FREAKING HELMET.
OH GREAT! AND MY BALD SPOT IS GETTING WORSE!

Butterfly Catchers

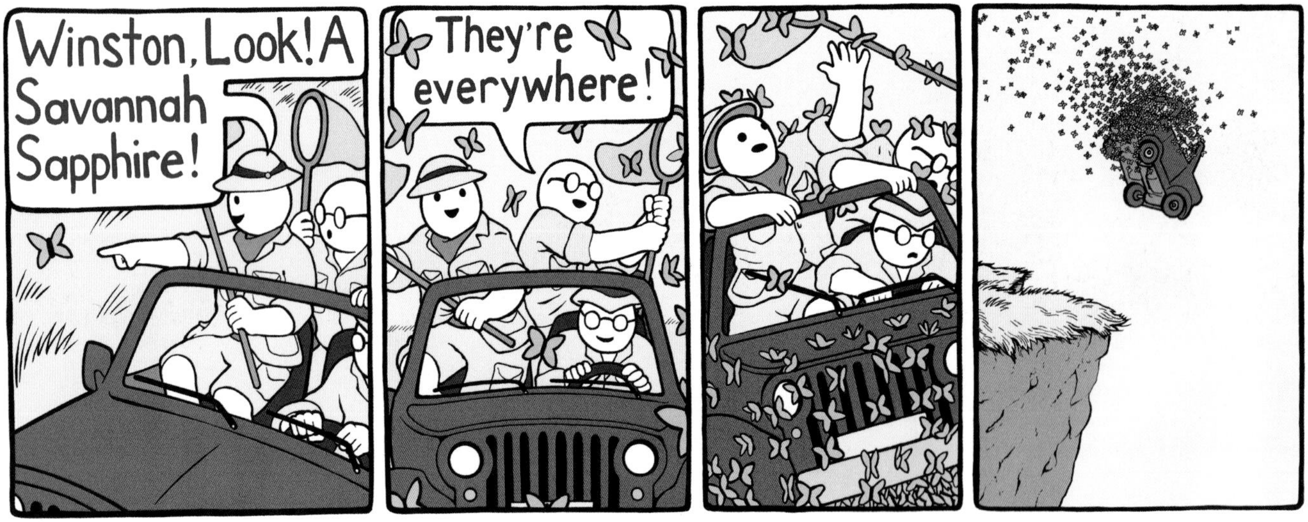
Winston, Look! A Savannah Sapphire!
They're everywhere!

Fun Bot

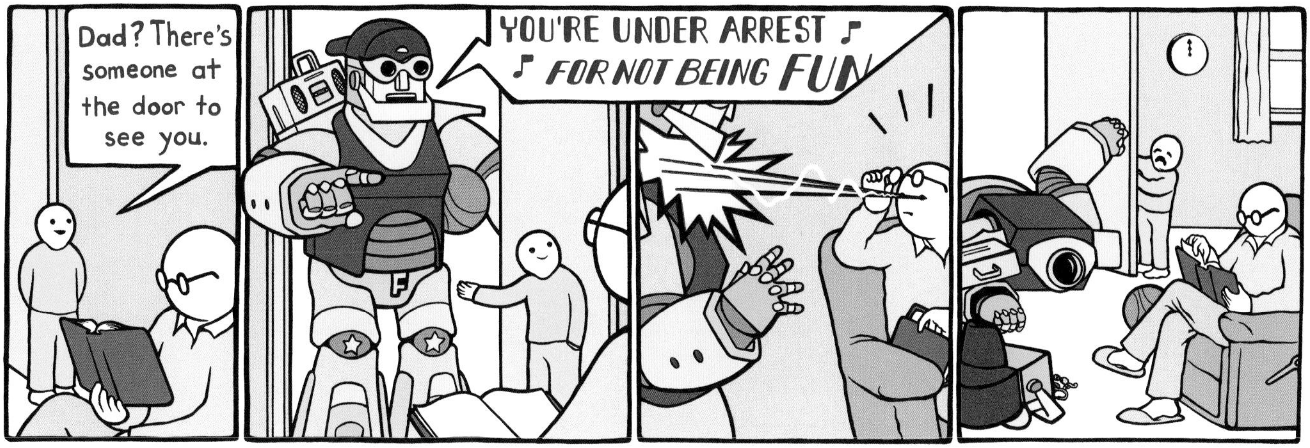
Dad? There's someone at the door to see you.
YOU'RE UNDER ARREST ♪
♪ FOR NOT BEING FUN

The Throbblefoot Aquarium,
OR: Notes from a Velvet Dulcimer (Apologies to Edward Gorey)

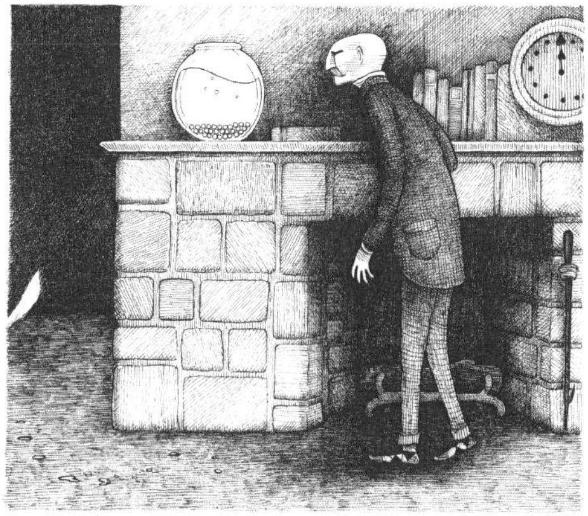

Lochlan's dear goldfish went missing that noon.

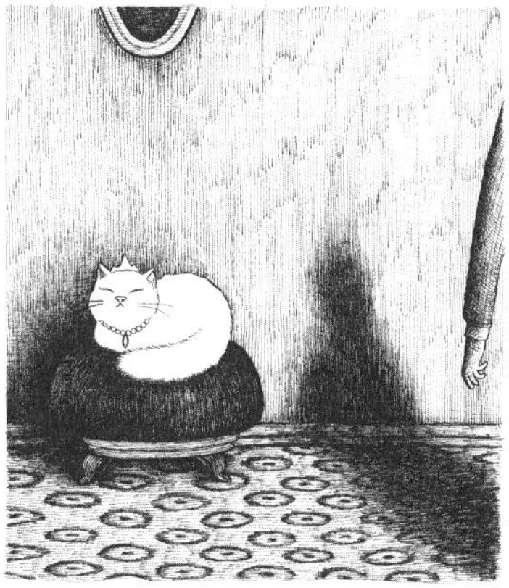

The Duchess was summoned

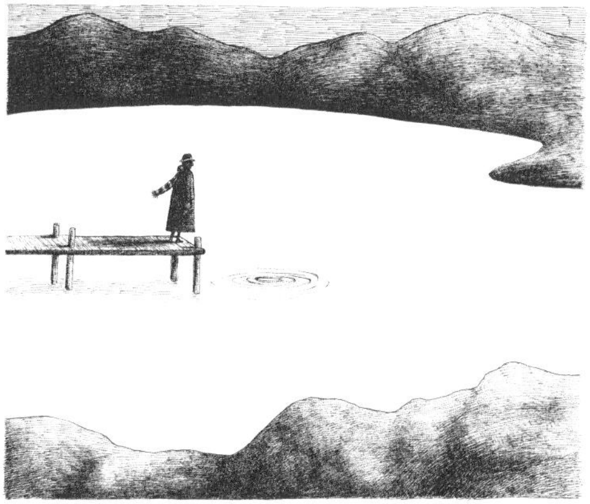

to search the lagoon.

Billy the Bunny

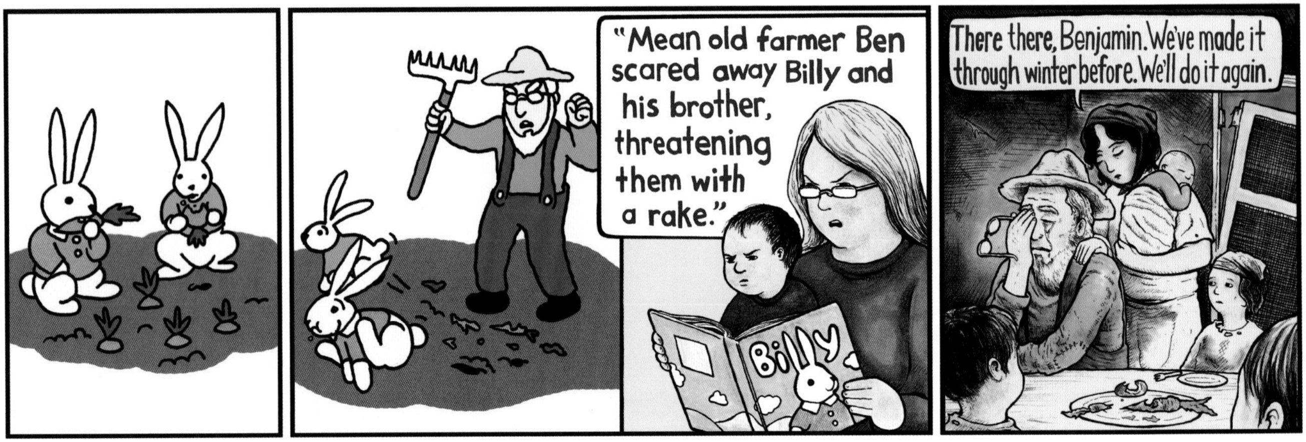
"Mean old farmer Ben scared away Billy and his brother, threatening them with a rake."
Billy
There there, Benjamin. We've made it through winter before. We'll do it again.

An End to Gopher Trouble

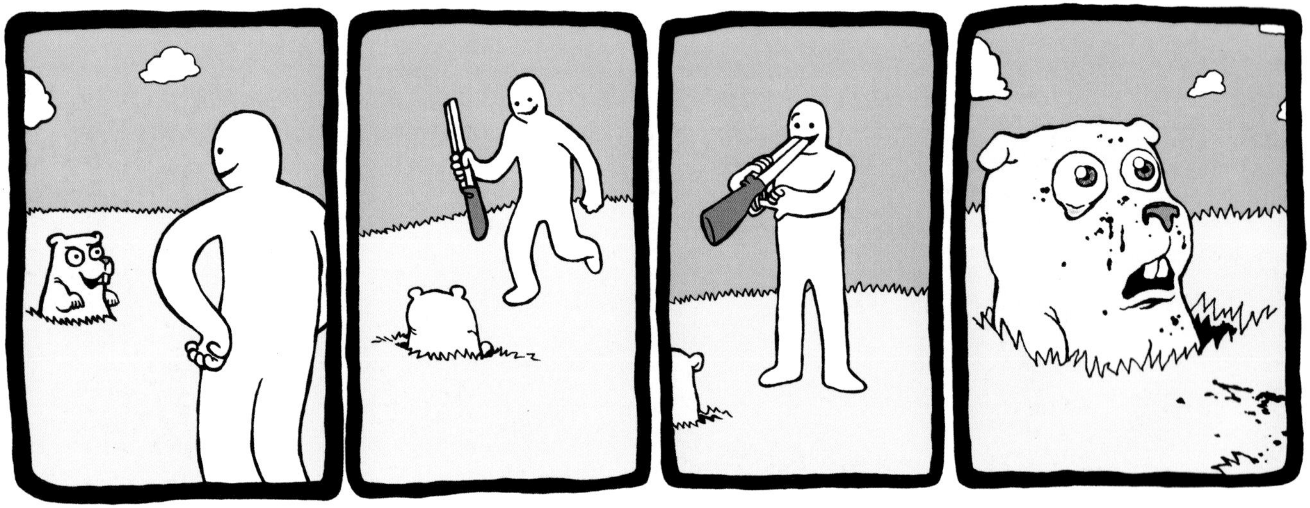

Birch Street

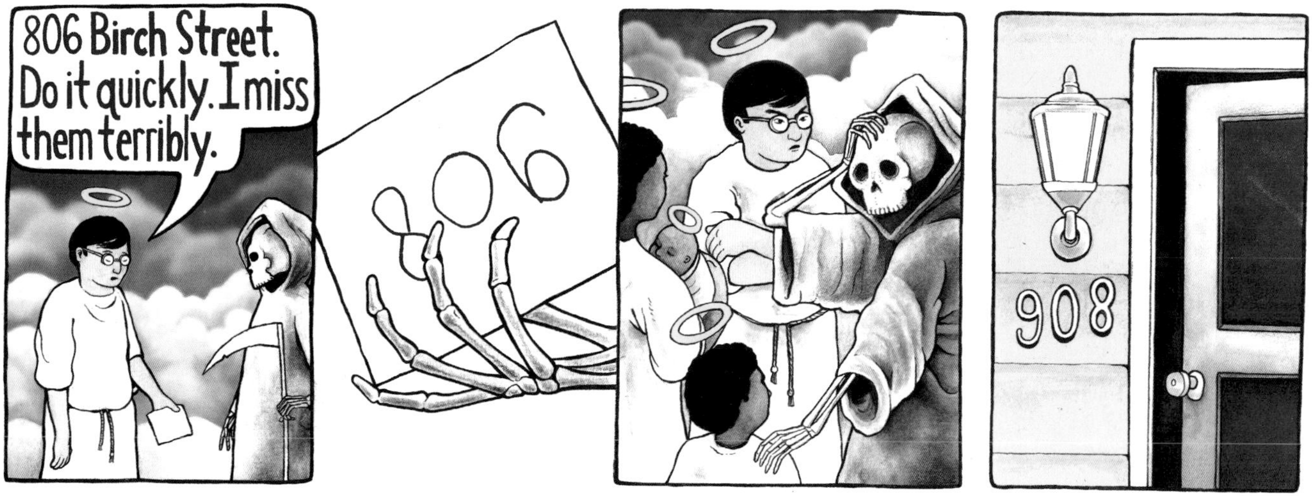
806 Birch Street. Do it quickly. I miss them terribly.
806
908

Hug Bot

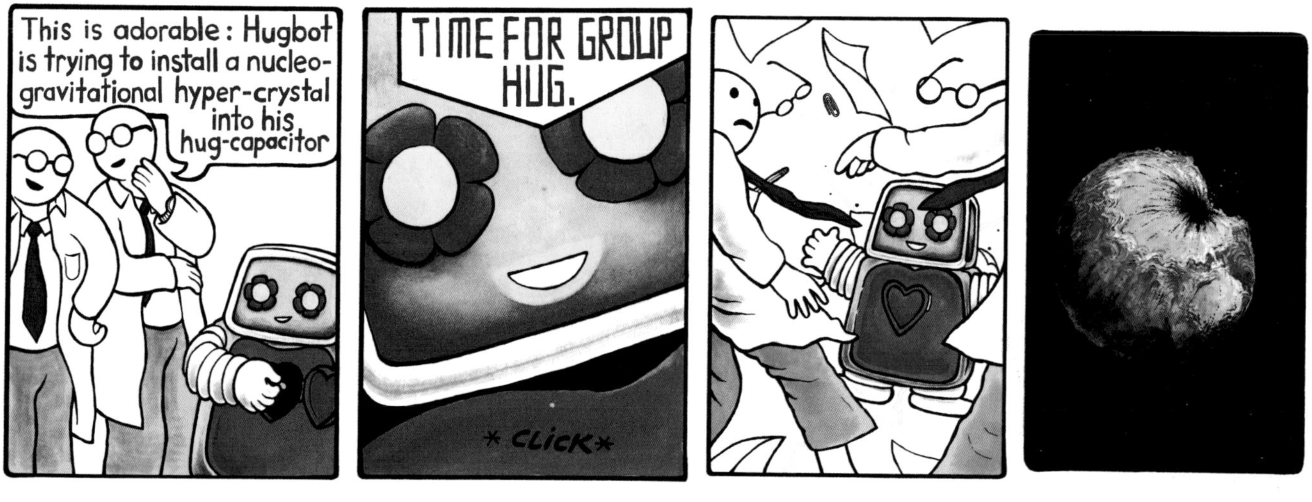
This is adorable: Hugbot is trying to install a nucleo-gravitational hyper-crystal into his hug-capacitor
TIME FOR GROUP HUG.
CLICK

Pyro Billy

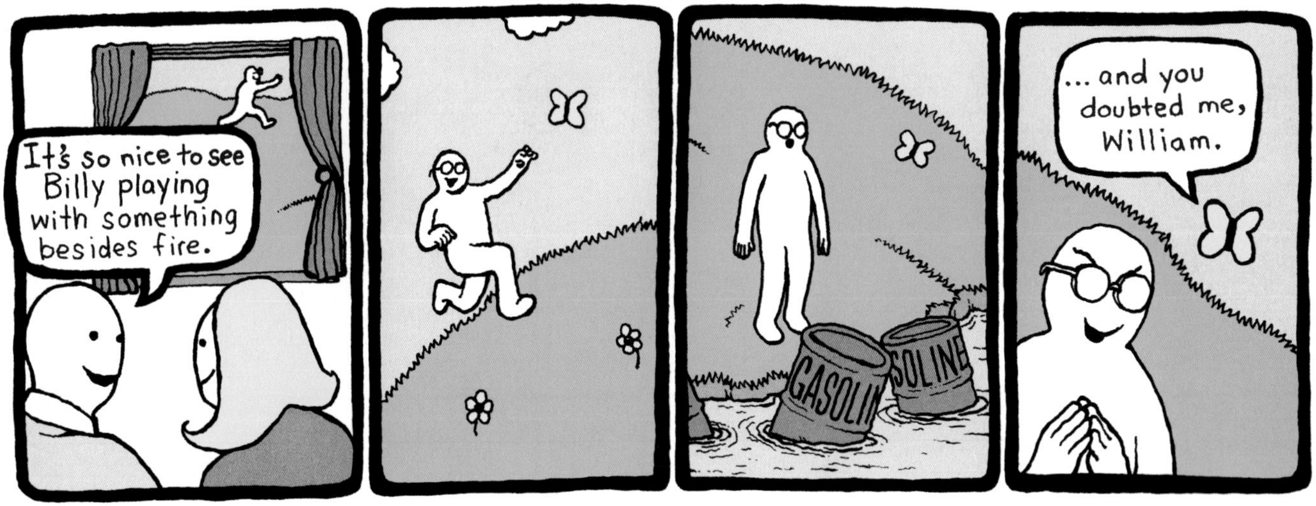
It's so nice to see Billy playing with something besides fire.
GASOLI
SOLINE
... and you doubted me, William.

Mountain Dad

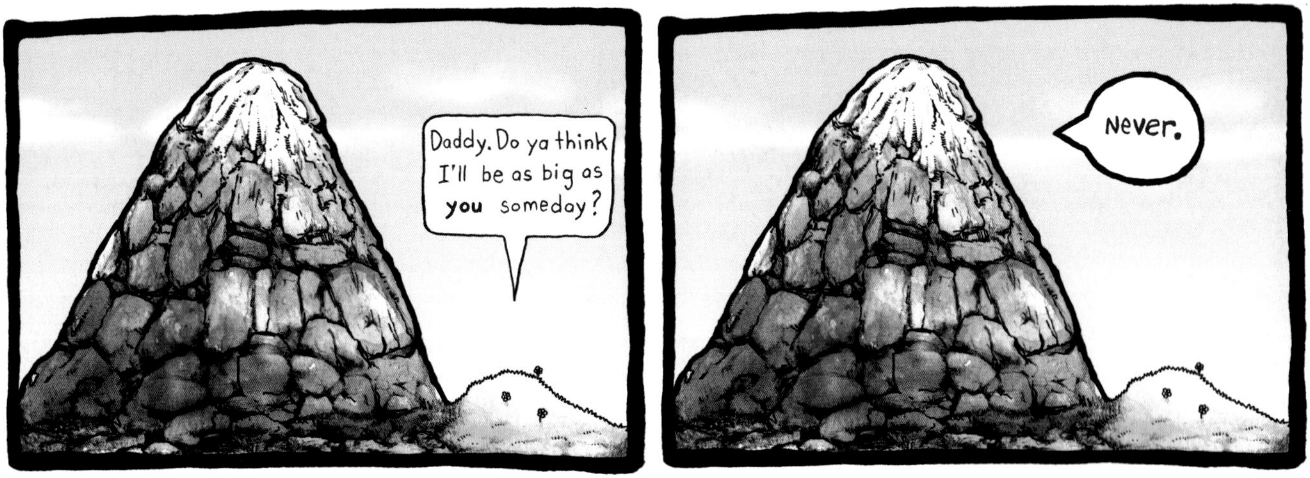
Daddy. Do ya think I'll be as big as **you** someday?
Never.

Gingerbread Man

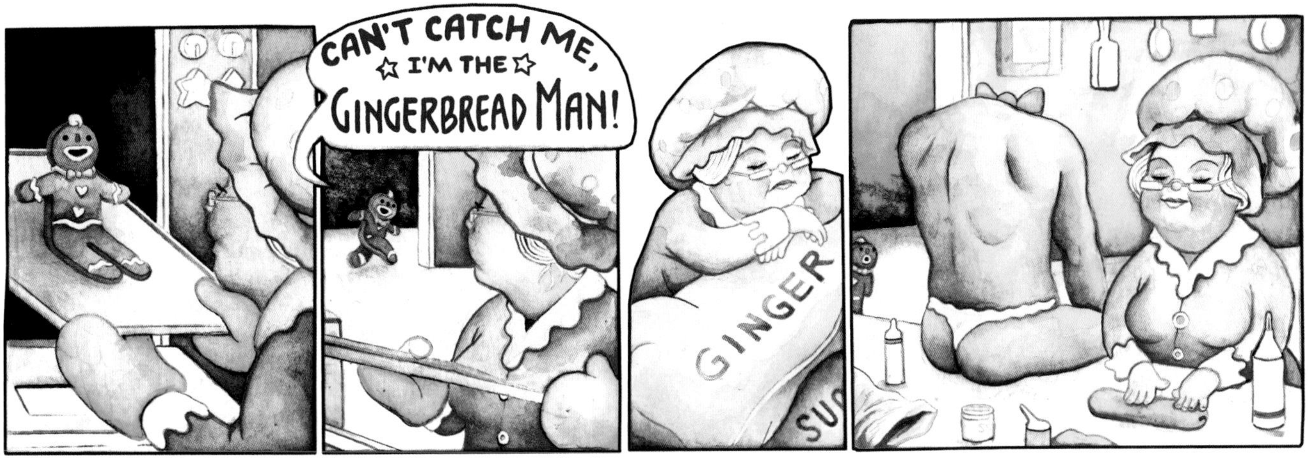
CAN'T CATCH ME, I'M THE GINGERBREAD MAN!
GINGER
SU

Skub

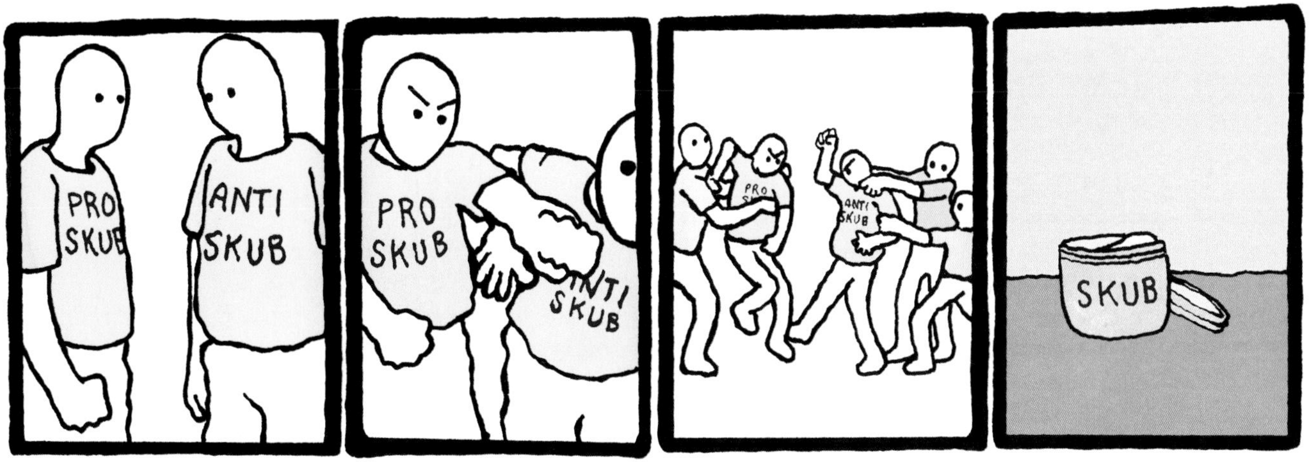
PRO SKUB
ANTI SKUB
PRO SKUB
ANTI SKUB
SKUB

Skeleton Clown

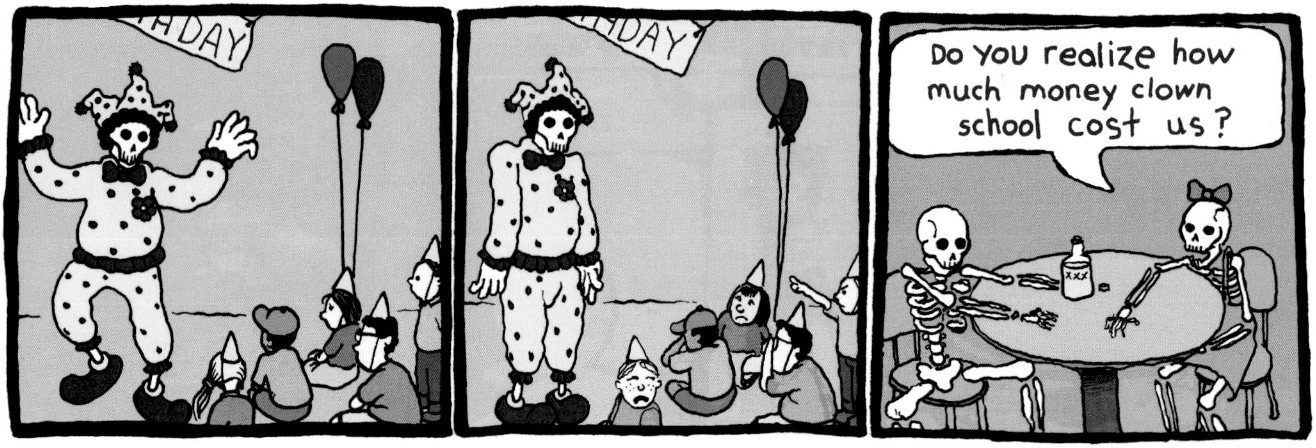
Do you realize how much money clown school cost us?

Dinosaur Meteors

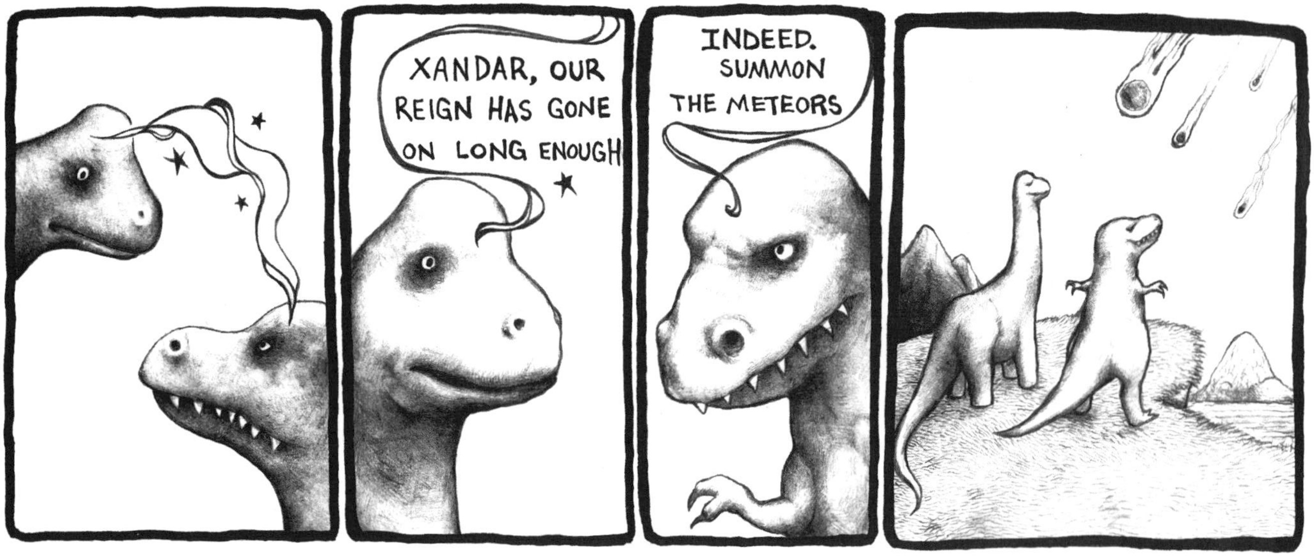
XANDAR, OUR REIGN HAS GONE ON LONG ENOUGH
INDEED. SUMMON THE METEORS

Wise Shitashi

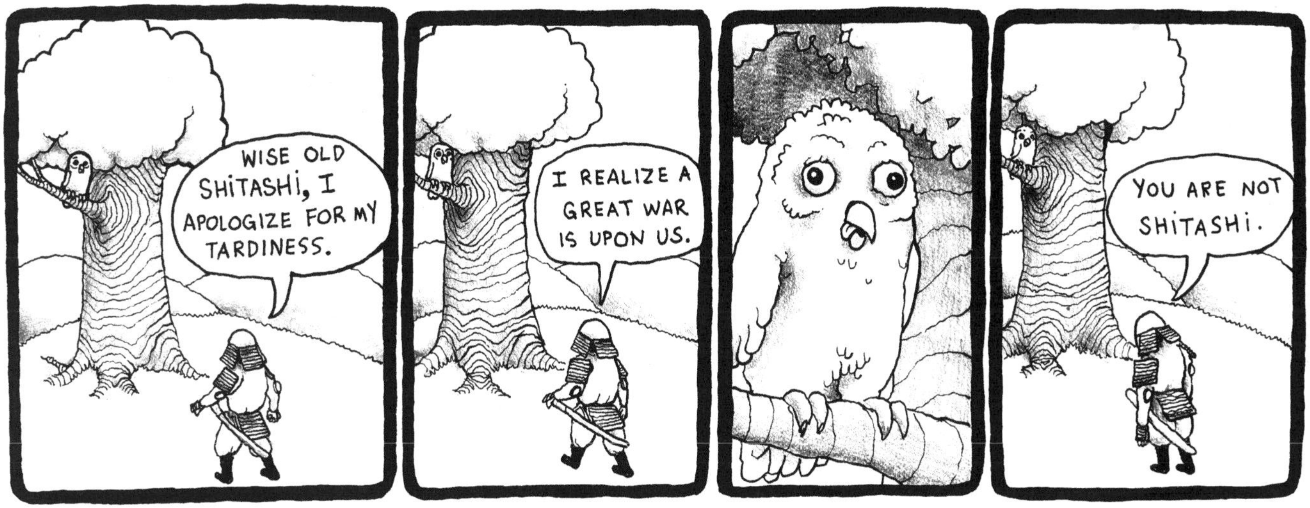
WISE OLD SHITASHI, I APOLOGIZE FOR MY TARDINESS.
I REALIZE A GREAT WAR IS UPON US.
YOU ARE NOT SHITASHI.

April 2

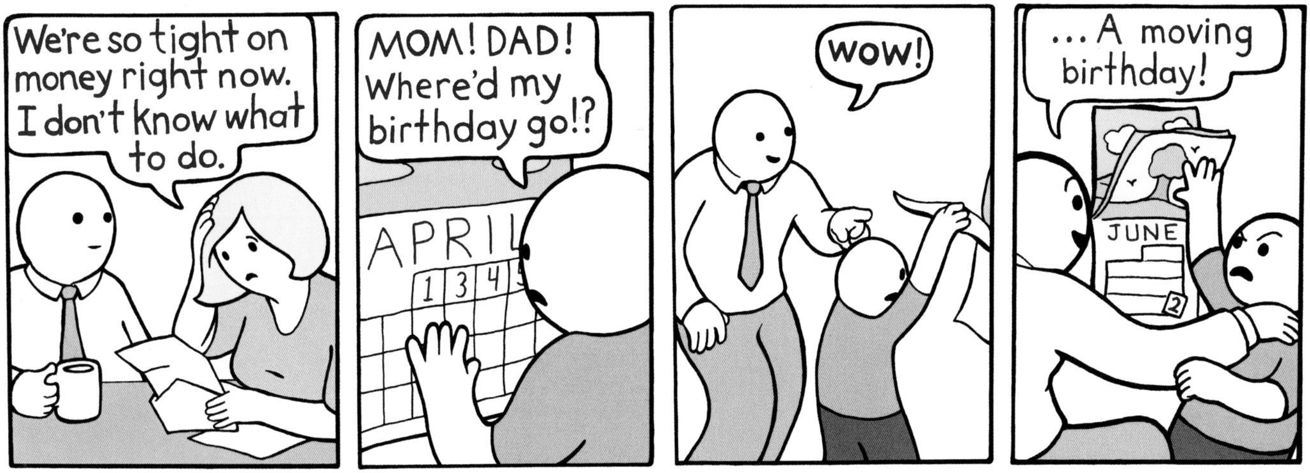
We're so tight on money right now. I don't know what to do.
MOM! DAD! Where'd my birthday go!?
APRIL
1 3 4
WOW!
...A moving birthday!
JUNE
2

Small Man

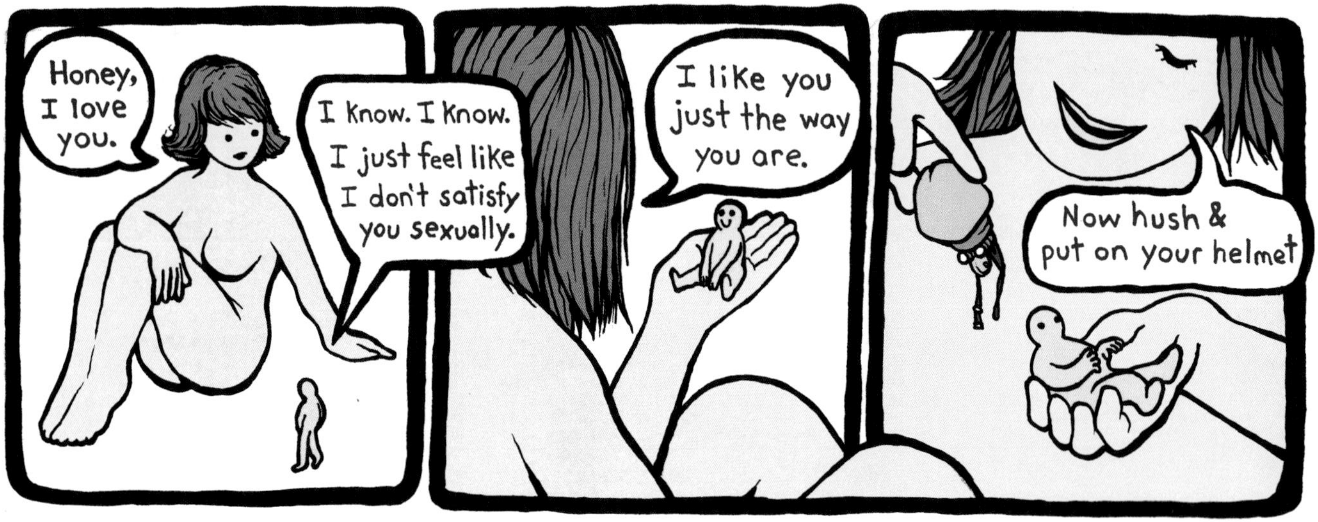
Honey, I love you.
I know. I know. I just feel like I don't satisfy you sexually.
I like you just the way you are.
Now hush & put on your helmet

Toad Race

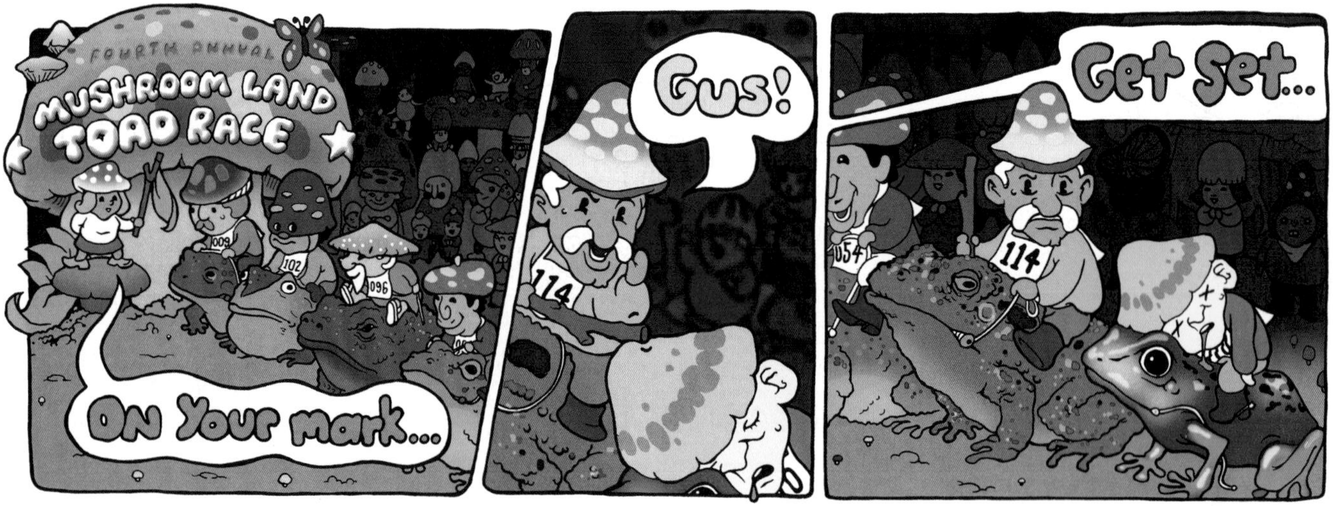
FOURTH ANNUAL
MUSHROOM LAND TOAD RACE
On Your mark...
Gus!
Get Set...

Keep on Truckin' (Apologies to Robert Crumb)

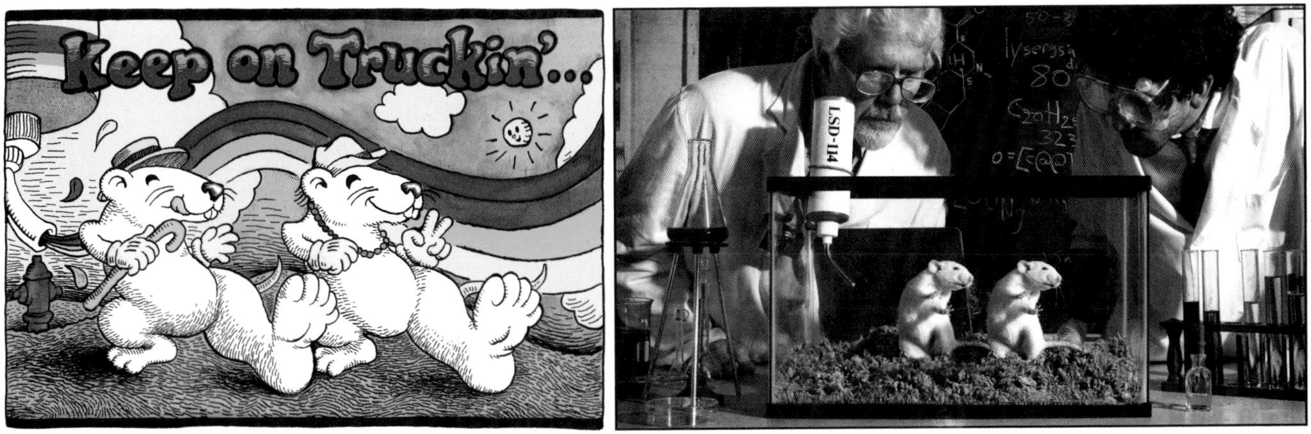
Keep on Truckin'...
LSD-114

Sun Love

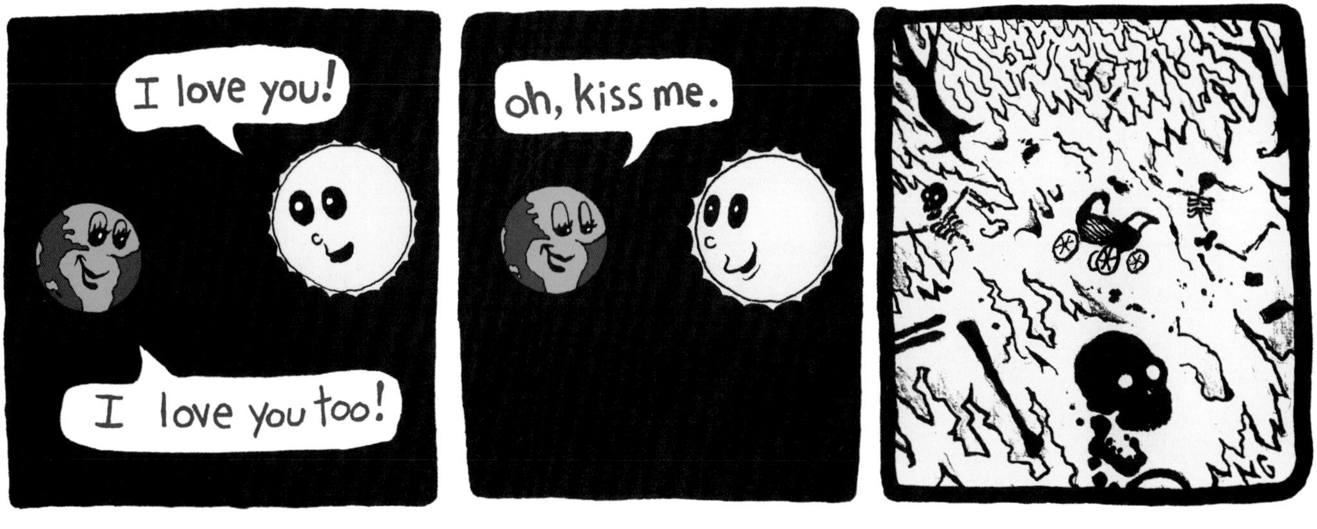
I love you!
I love you too!
oh, kiss me.

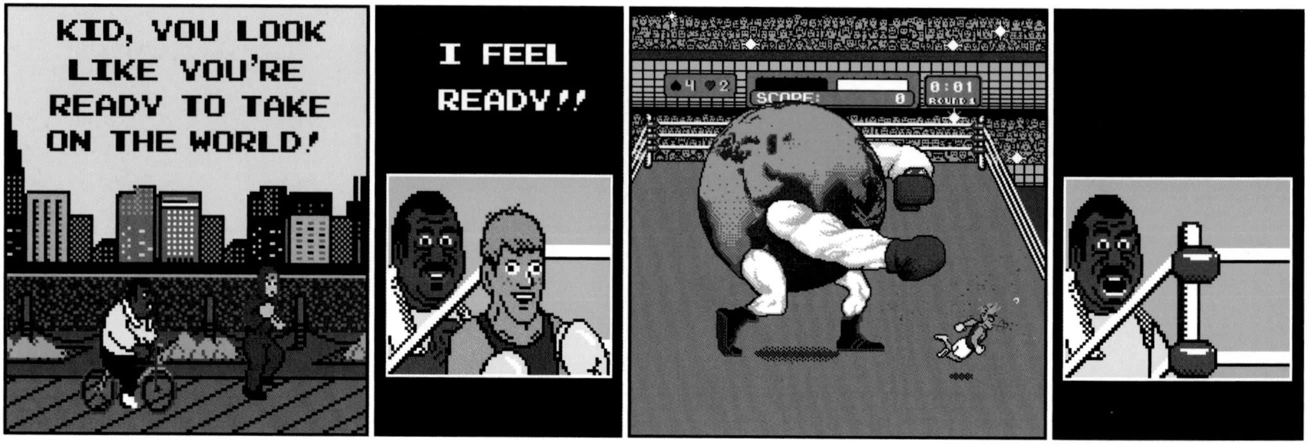
KID, YOU LOOK LIKE YOU'RE READY TO TAKE ON THE WORLD!
I FEEL READY!!

One More Day

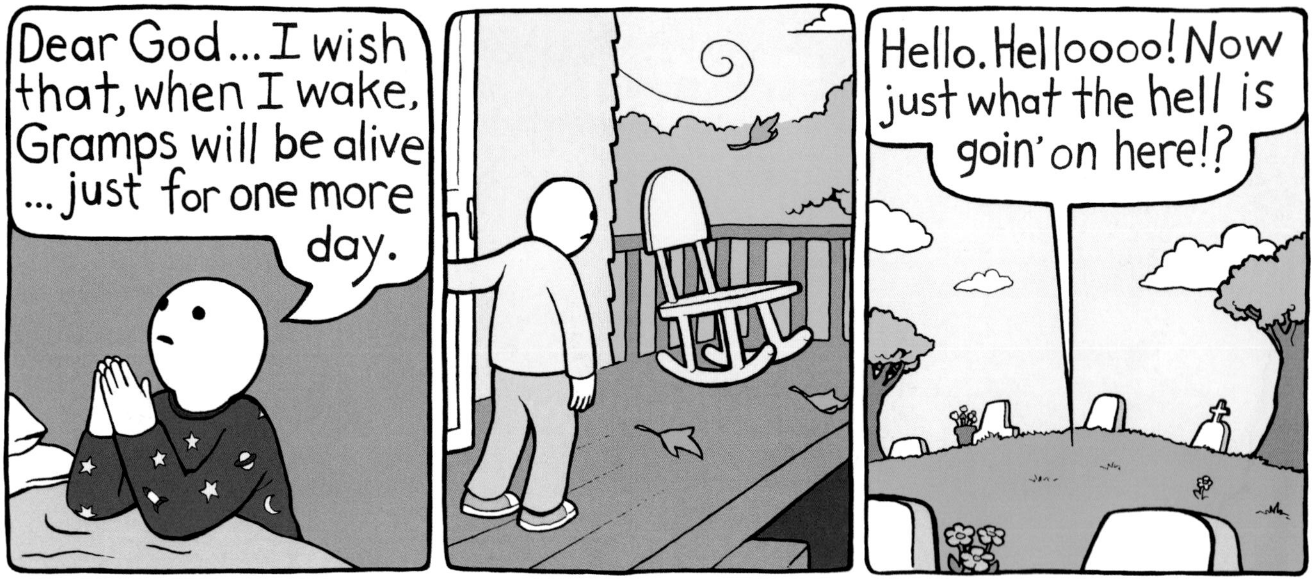
Dear God... I wish that, when I wake, Gramps will be alive ...just for one more day.
Hello. Helloooo! Now just what the hell is goin' on here!?

Cave Explorer

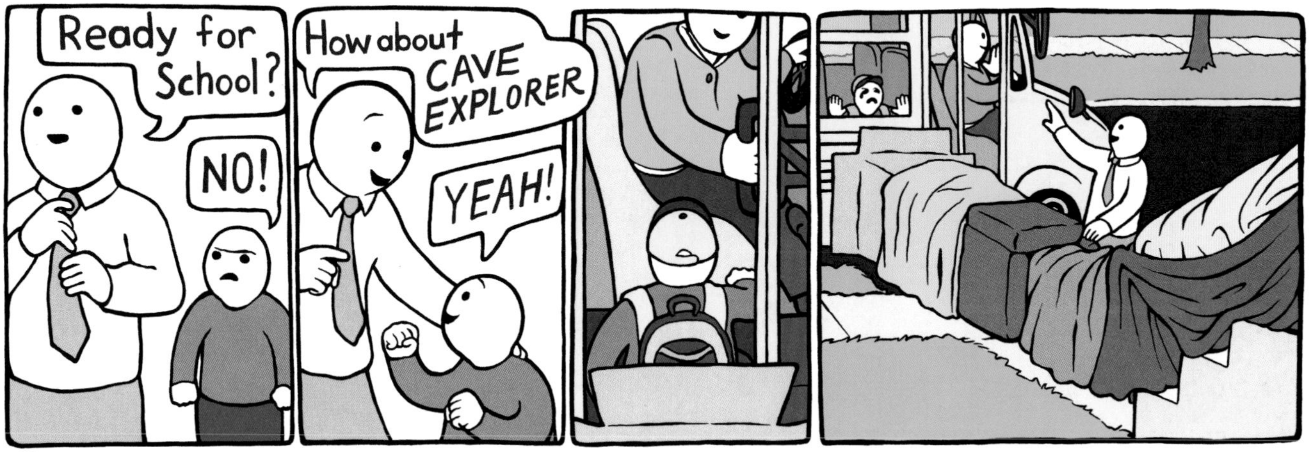
Ready for School?
NO!
How about CAVE EXPLORER
YEAH!

Christmas Cards

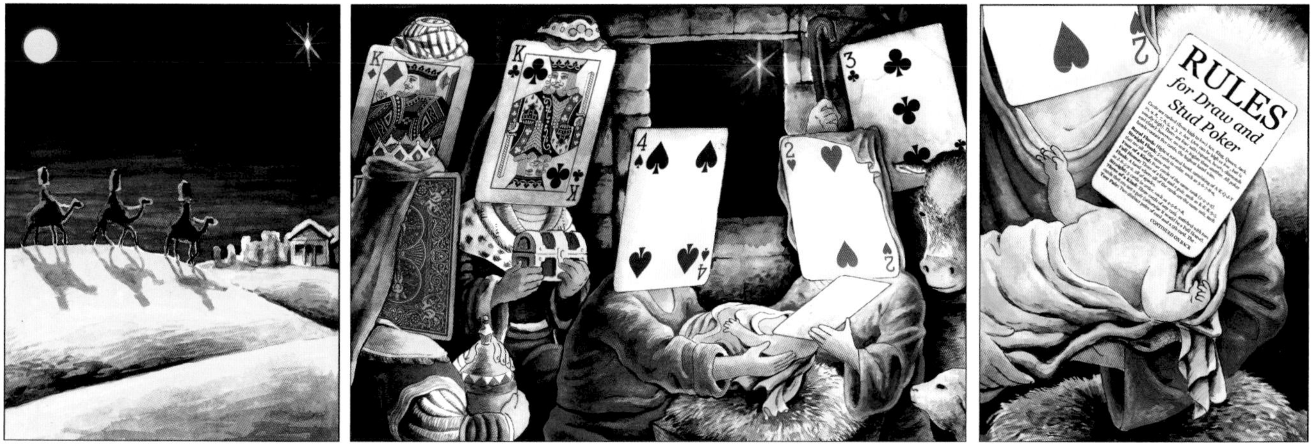
RULES
for Draw and Stud Poker

Food Fight

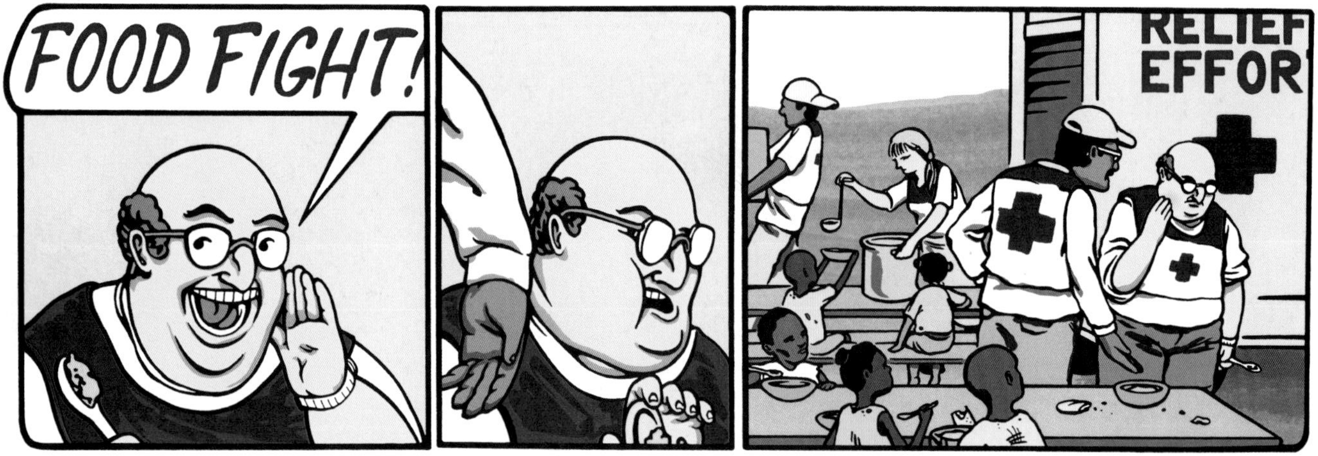
FOOD FIGHT!
RELIEF
EFFOR

Slim

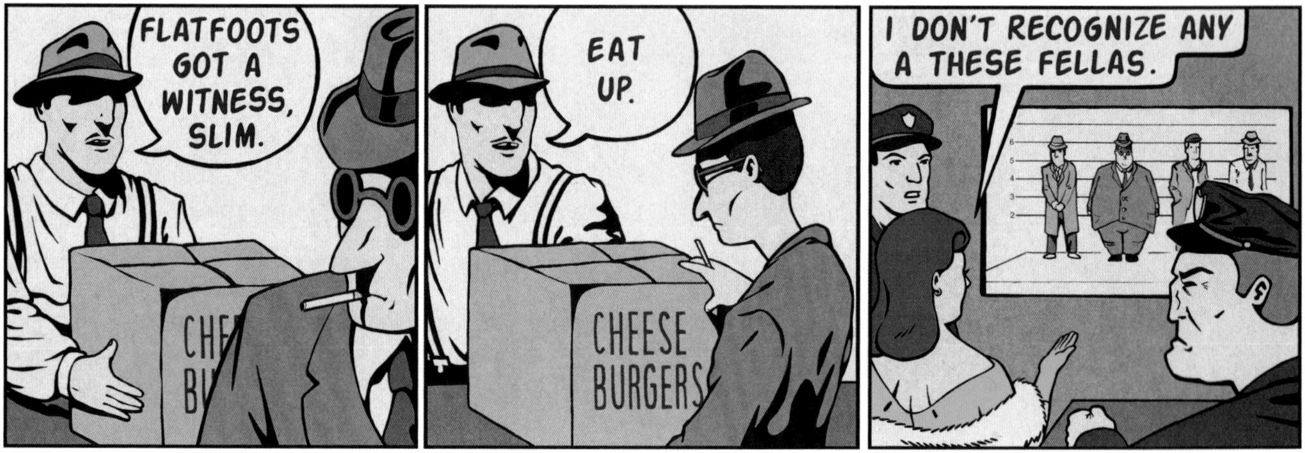
FLATFOOTS GOT A WITNESS, SLIM.
CHE
BU
EAT UP.
CHEESE BURGERS
I DON'T RECOGNIZE ANY A THESE FELLAS.

Master Yoshi

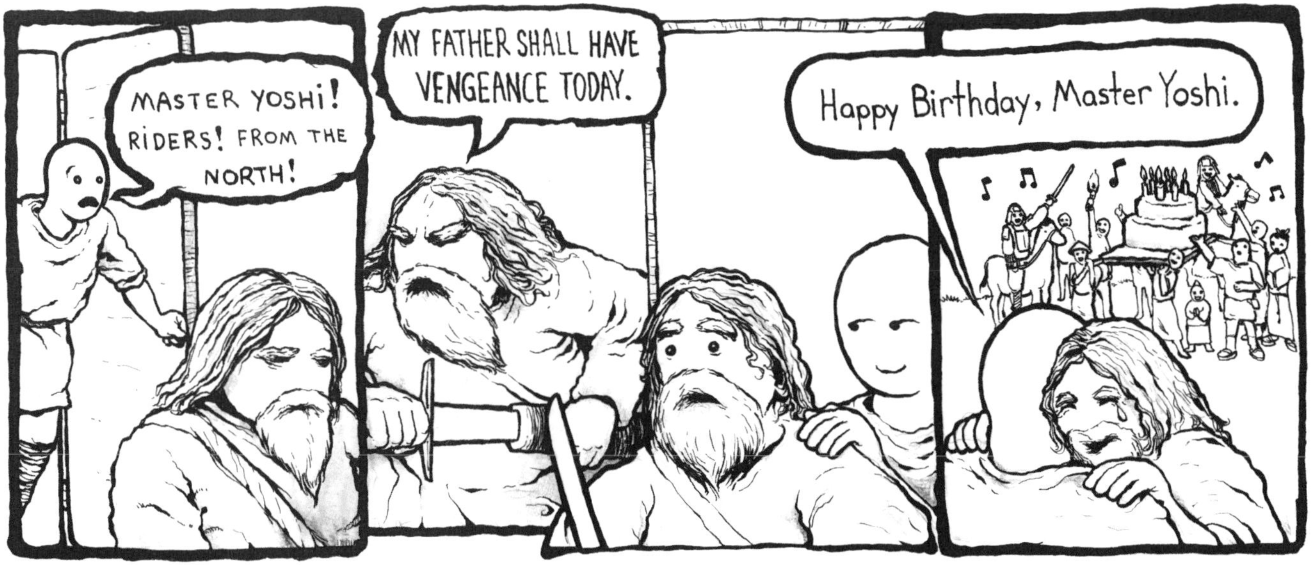
MASTER YOSHI! RIDERS! FROM THE NORTH!
MY FATHER SHALL HAVE VENGEANCE TODAY.
Happy Birthday, Master Yoshi.

Utter Pig

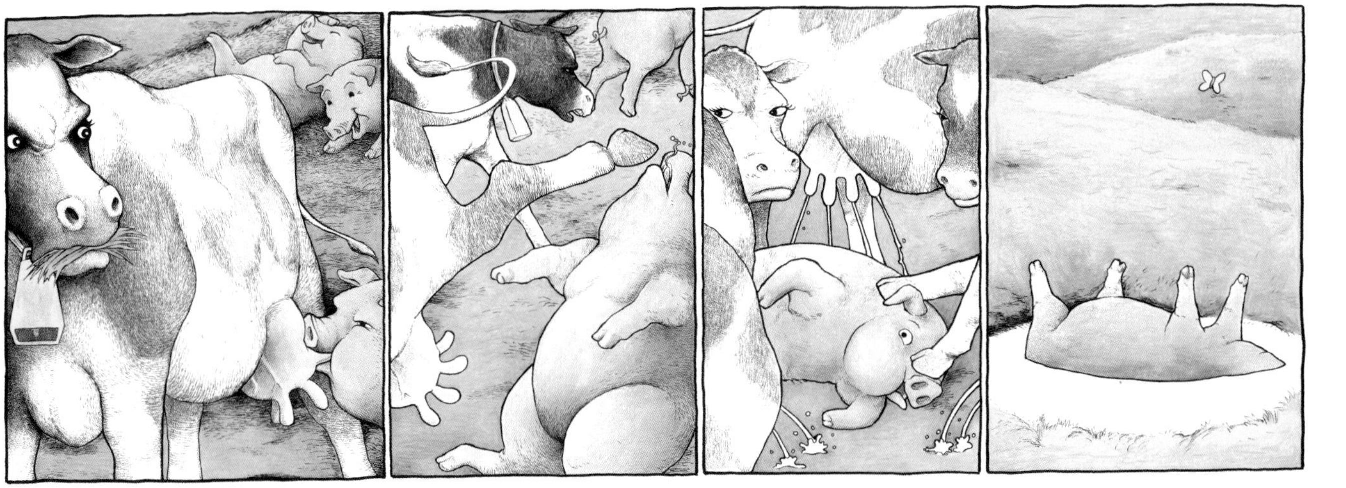

The Schlorbians Strike Again

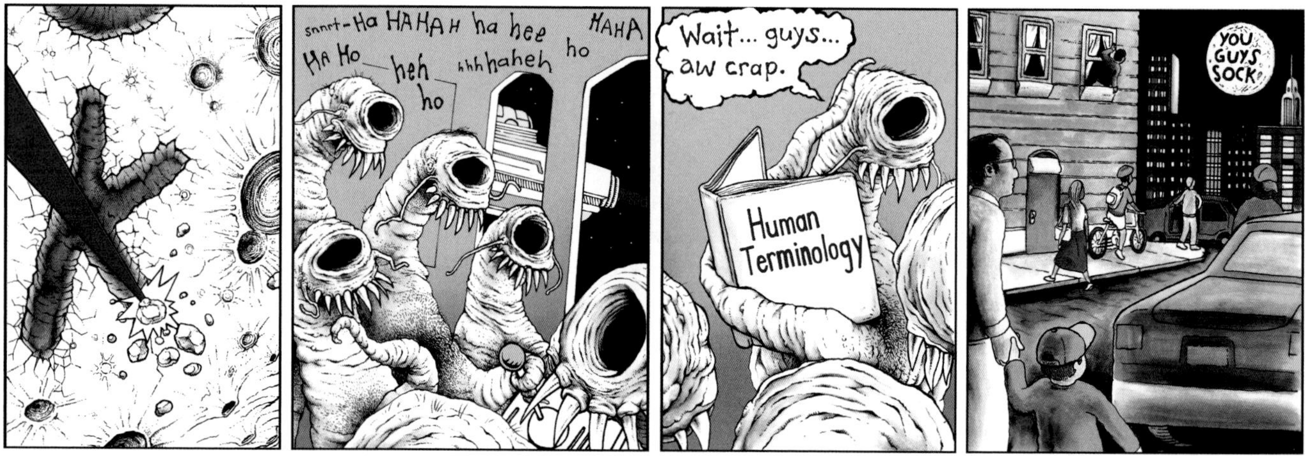
snrrt-Ha HAHAH ha hee HAHA
HA Ho heh hhh haheh ho
ho
Wait... guys... aw crap.
Human Terminology
YOU GUYS SOCK

Suck Note

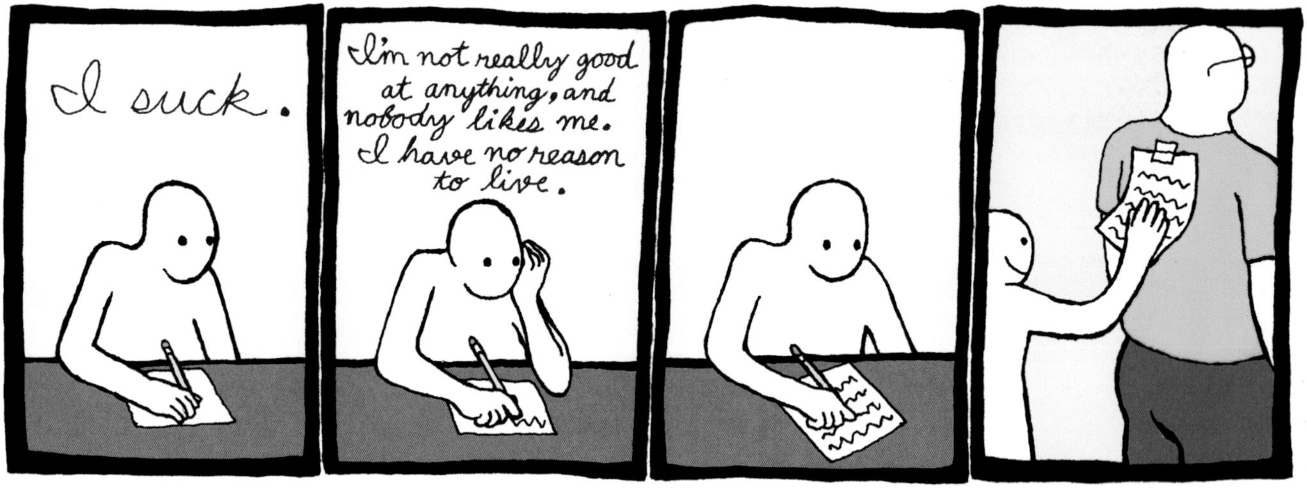
I suck.
I'm not really good at anything, and nobody likes me. I have no reason to live.

Love Wizard

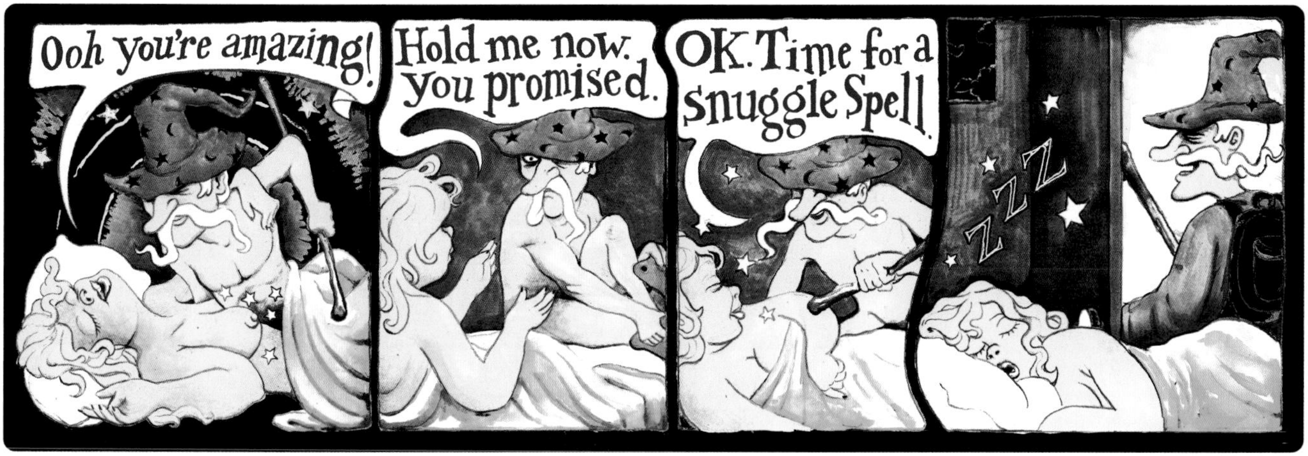

Ooh you're amazing!
Hold me now. you promised.
OK. Time for a snuggle Spell.
ZZZ

Cupid Mistake

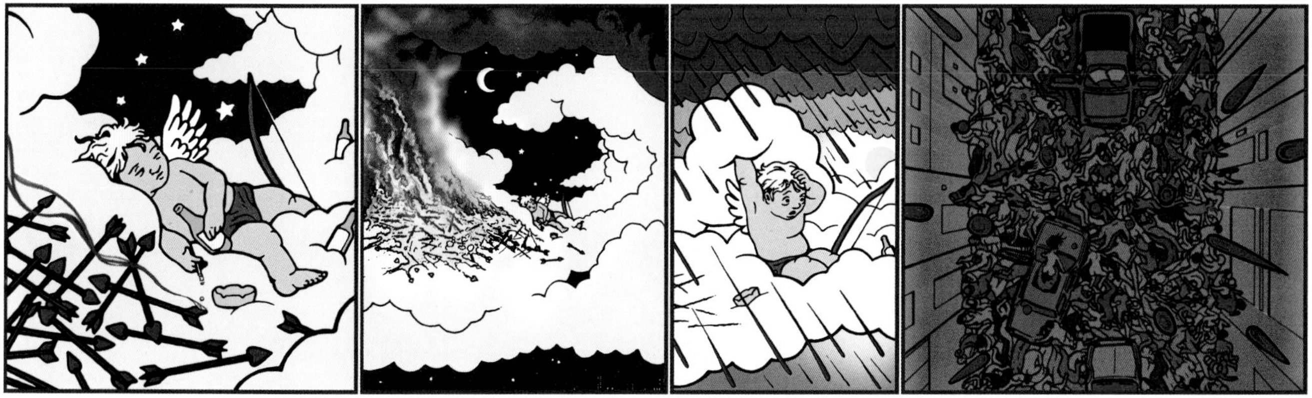

Grammar Wizard

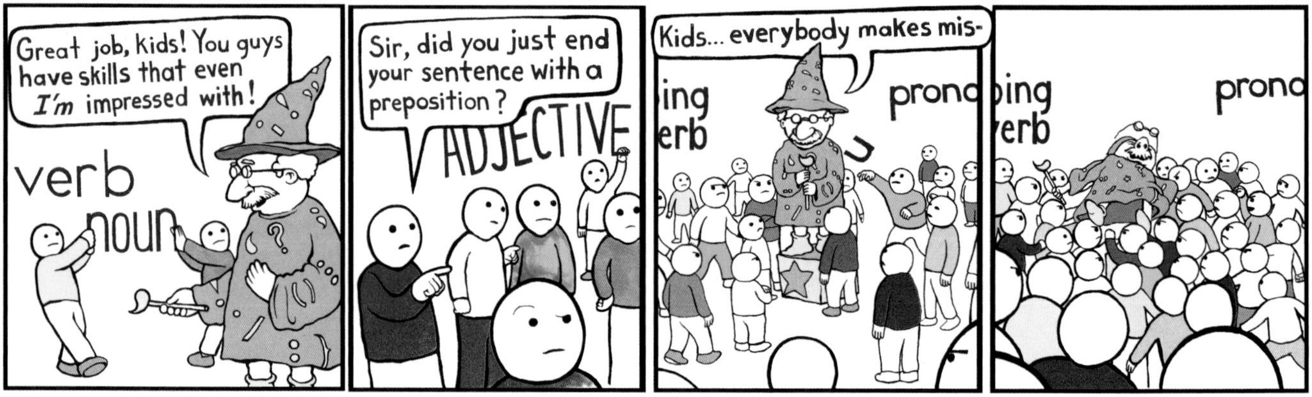
Great job, kids! You guys have skills that even *I'm* impressed with!
verb
noun
Sir, did you just end your sentence with a preposition?
ADJECTIVE
Kids... everybody makes mis-

Bed Monster

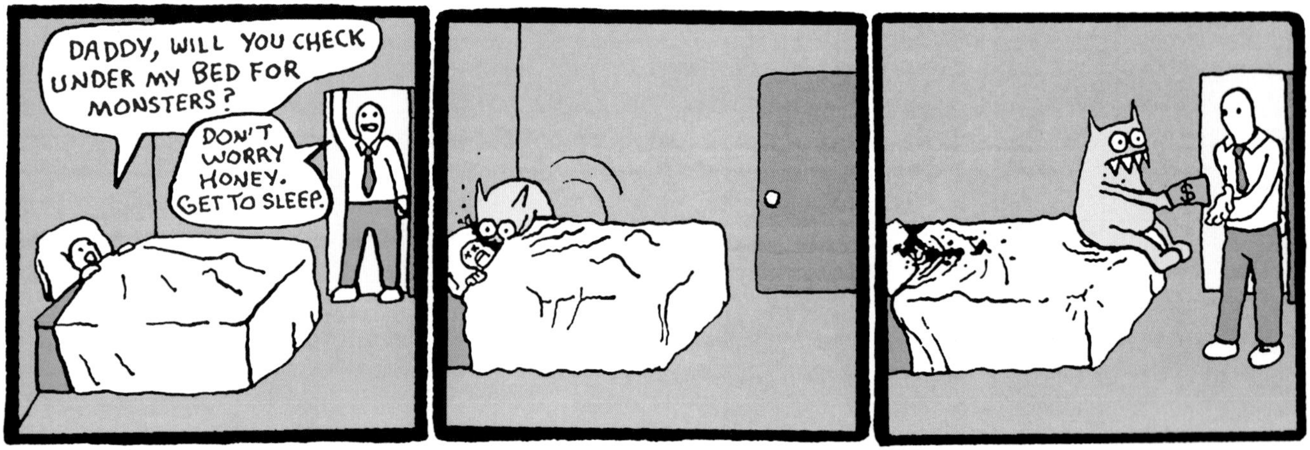
DADDY, WILL YOU CHECK UNDER MY BED FOR MONSTERS?
DON'T WORRY HONEY. GET TO SLEEP.

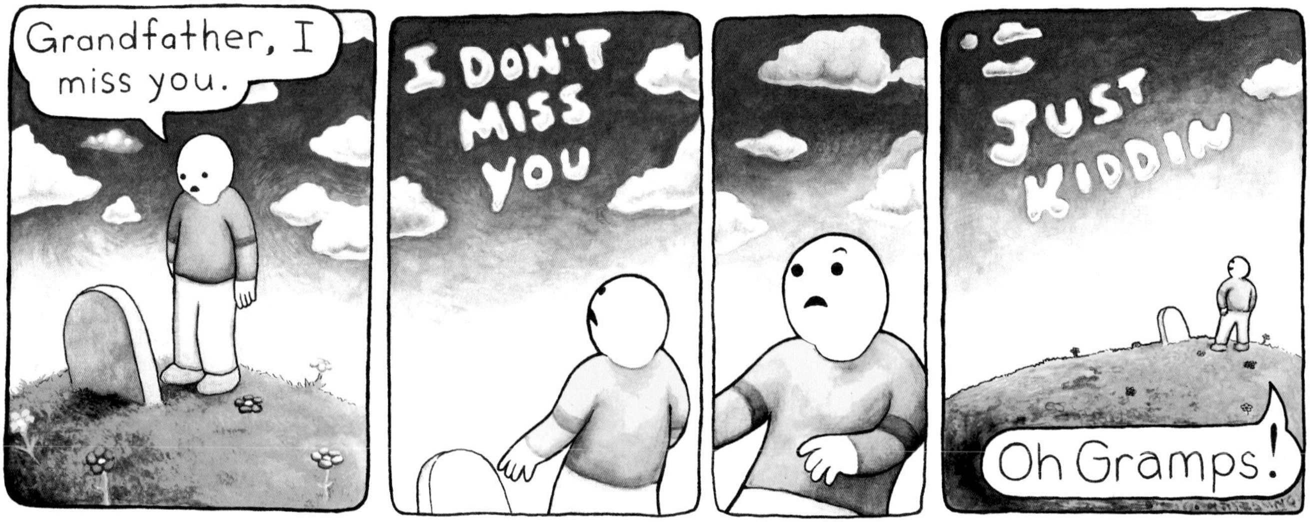
Grandfather, I miss you.
I DON'T MISS YOU
JUST KIDDIN
Oh Gramps!

Abduction

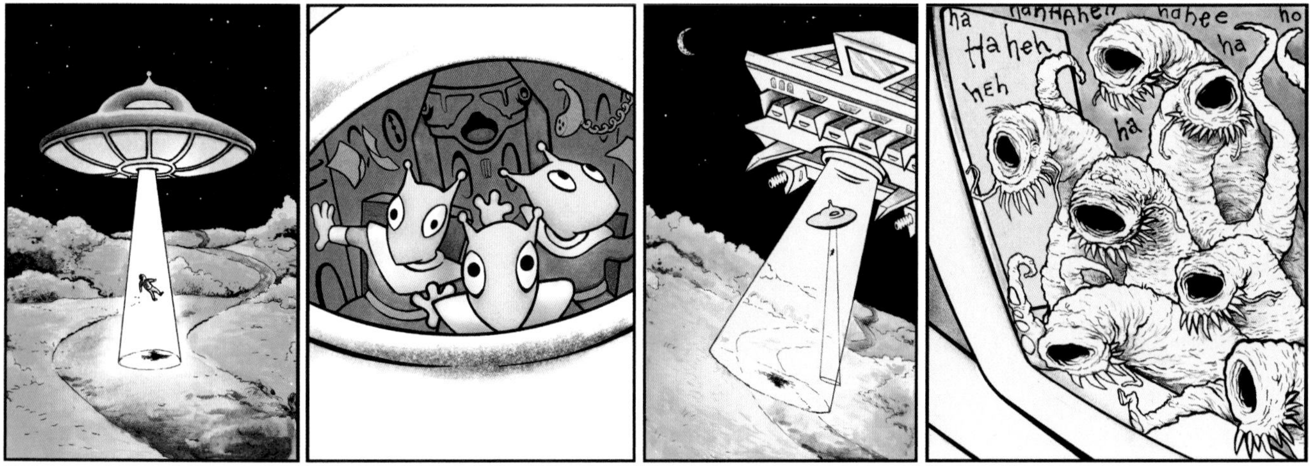
ha
Haheh
heh
hahee
ho
ha
ha

LOST STRIPS

Believe it or not, some PBF ideas exit the drawing board without ever properly finding a spot in the archive. Reservations of myself and those of my test audience often suppress the public exposure of tons of comics. Here are a few of the many "lost" strips.

—Nick

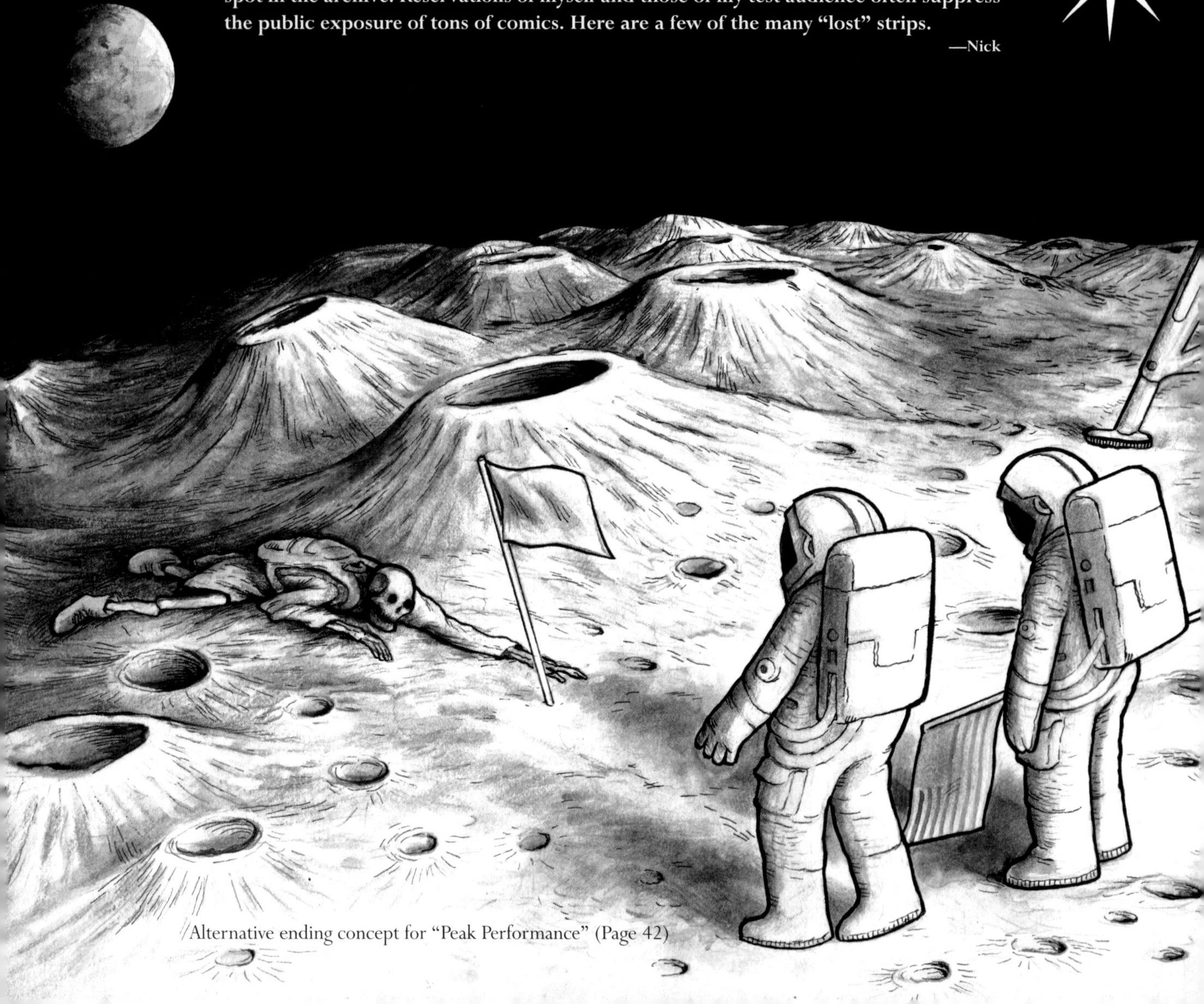

Alternative ending concept for "Peak Performance" (Page 42)

I'm not sure if it's the vast amount of text or the direct pop references, but this never really felt like a *PBF.*

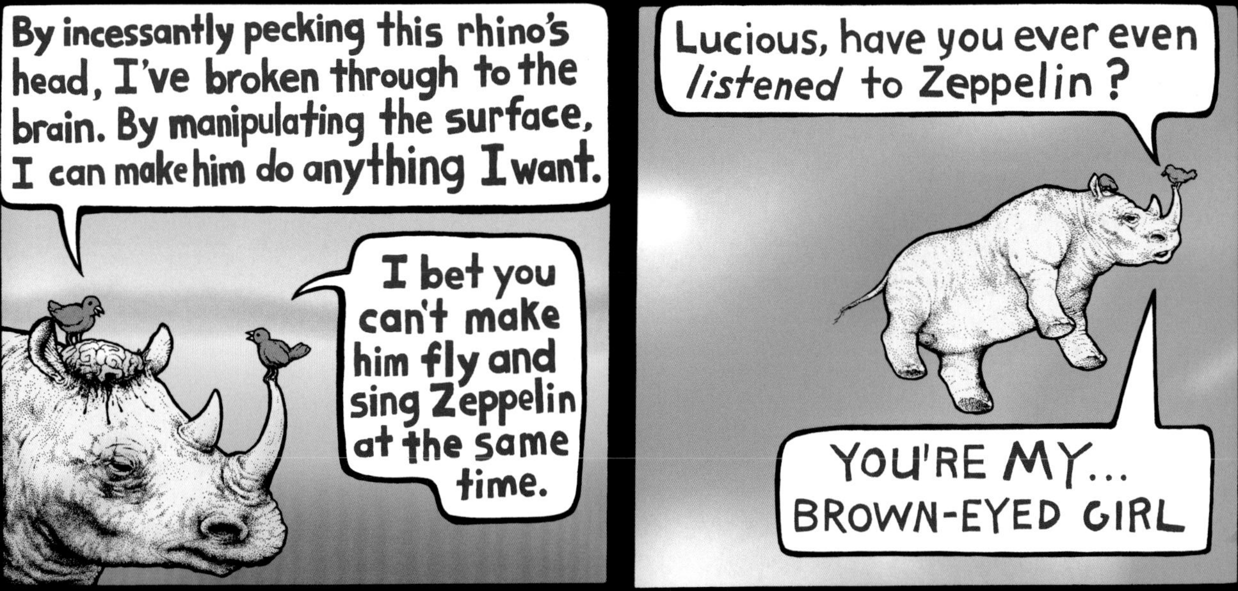
By incessantly pecking this rhino's head, I've broken through to the brain. By manipulating the surface, I can make him do anything I want.
I bet you can't make him fly and sing Zeppelin at the same time.
Lucious, have you ever even *listened* to Zeppelin?
YOU'RE MY... BROWN-EYED GIRL

This unpleasant gag wasn't appreciated by anyone, even after I explained it to them.

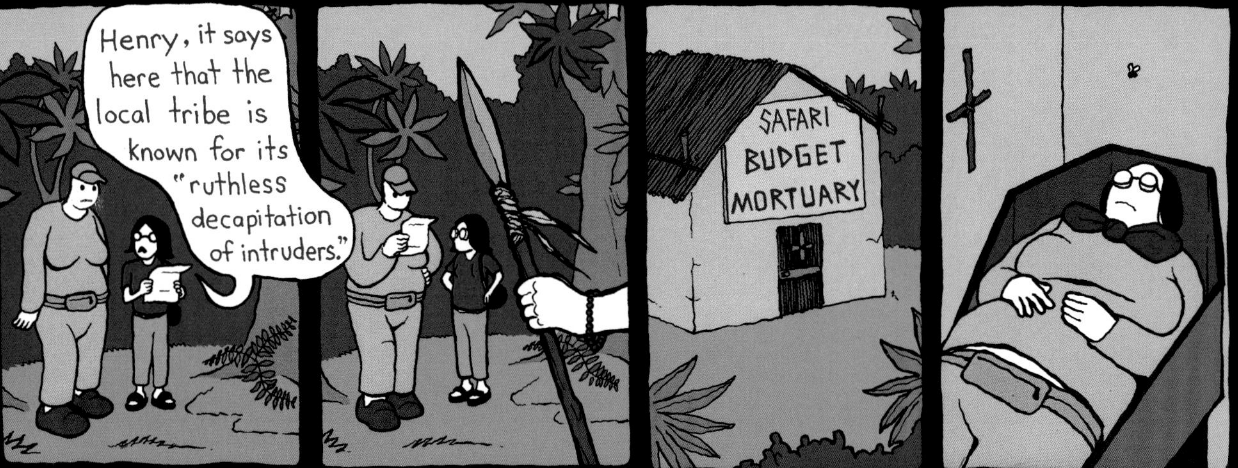
Henry, it says here that the local tribe is known for its "ruthless decapitation of intruders."
SAFARI BUDGET MORTUARY

I went through about six different versions of this comic, experimenting with the discovery of different coins (peso, game token), etc. What you see below was finally suggested by my friend Evan. It's my favorite of all the concepts considered, but impossible to appreciate if you're not familiar with the slang term for the Canadian dollar coin.

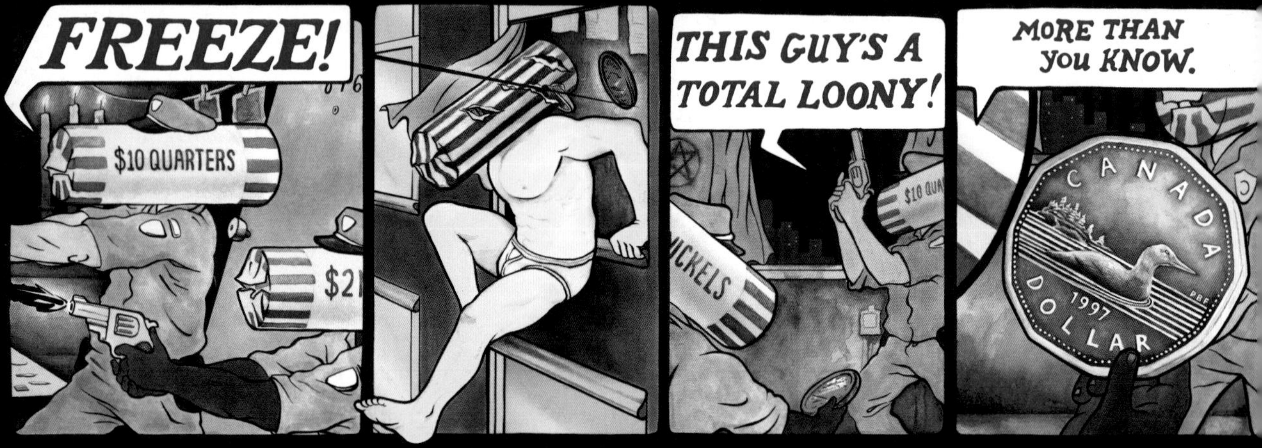
FREEZE!
$10 QUARTERS
THIS GUY'S A TOTAL LOONY!
MORE THAN YOU KNOW.
CANADA
DOLLAR
1997

I don't think I ever gave consideration to whether the boy here gave the gift maliciously, or whether he was ignorant of the girl's condition. I've never been able to defend against accusations that it's offensive.

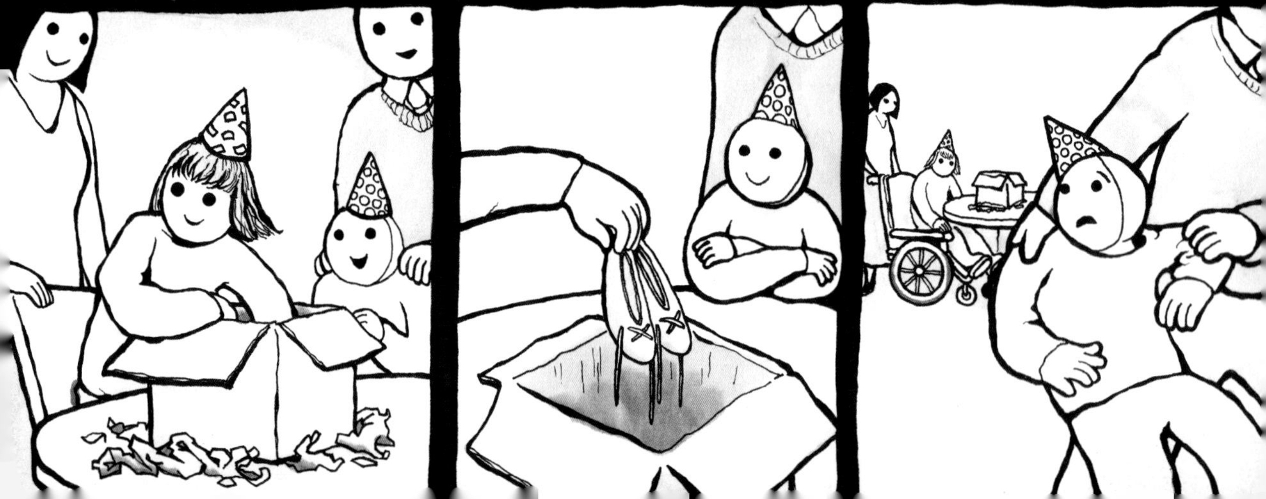

Prior to the publication of this piece, I was alerted that American stand-up comedian Dane Cook had already done a bit about a possessed Speak & Spell.

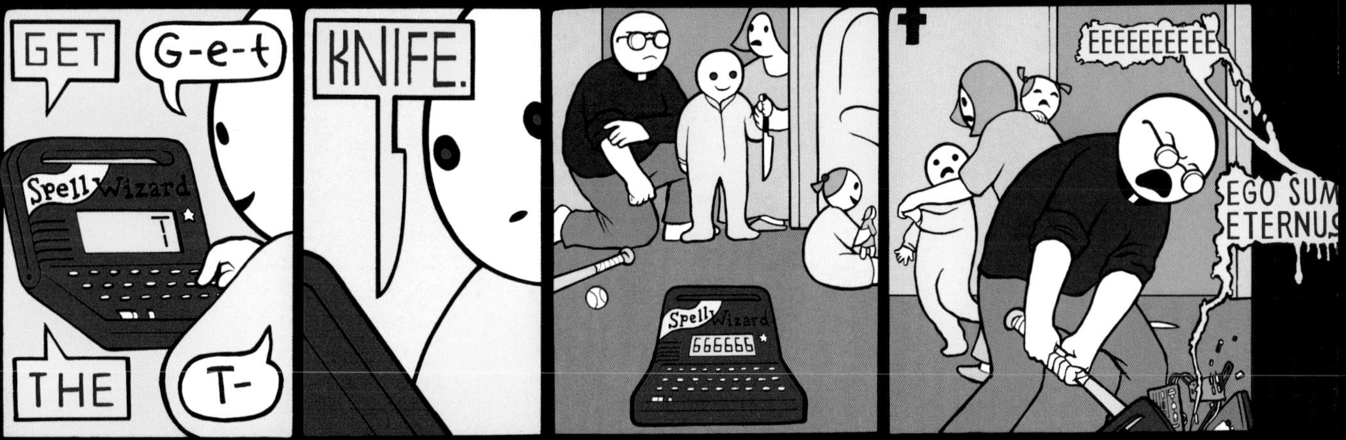
GET
G-e-t
THE
T-
KNIFE.
Spell Wizard
666666
EEEEEEEEEEE
EGO SUM ETERNUS

In a similar disappointment, I withheld the following strip from being printed because it too closely resembled a Jay Leno monologue.

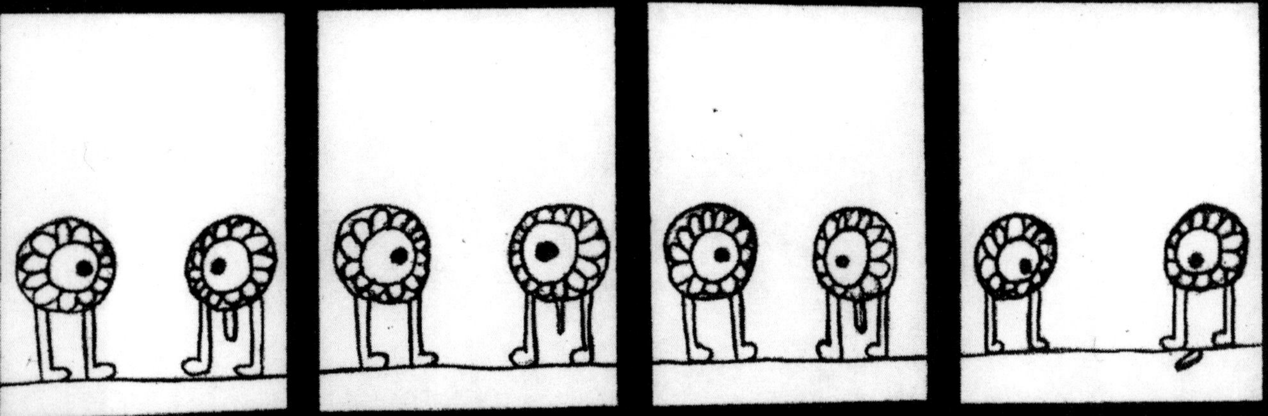

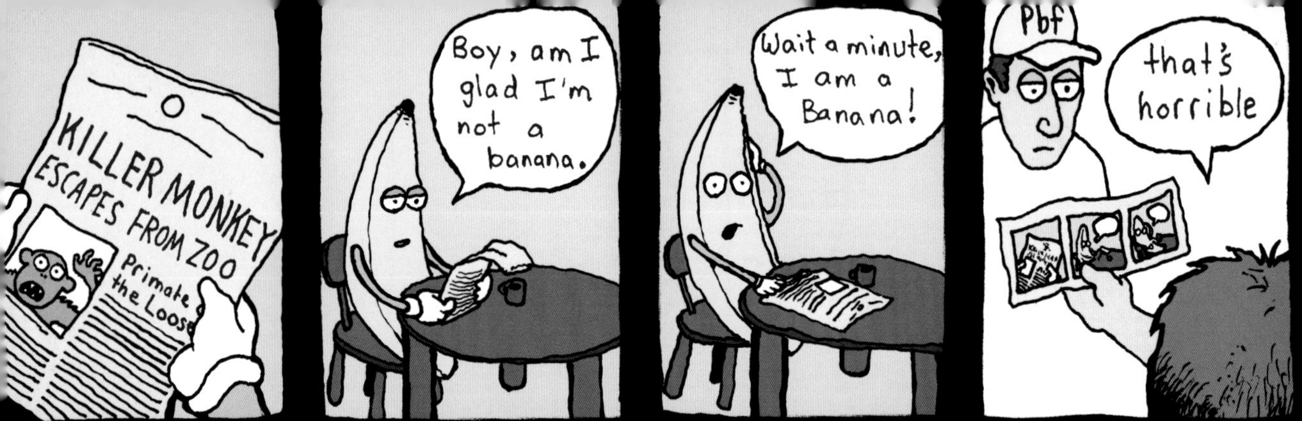
KILLER MONKEY ESCAPES FROM ZOO
Primate on the Loose
Boy, am I glad I'm not a banana.
Wait a minute, I am a Banana!
Pbf
that's horrible

These three frames work nicely as a sequel to "Check Shots" (page 59), but are a bit too uncomfortably topical otherwise.

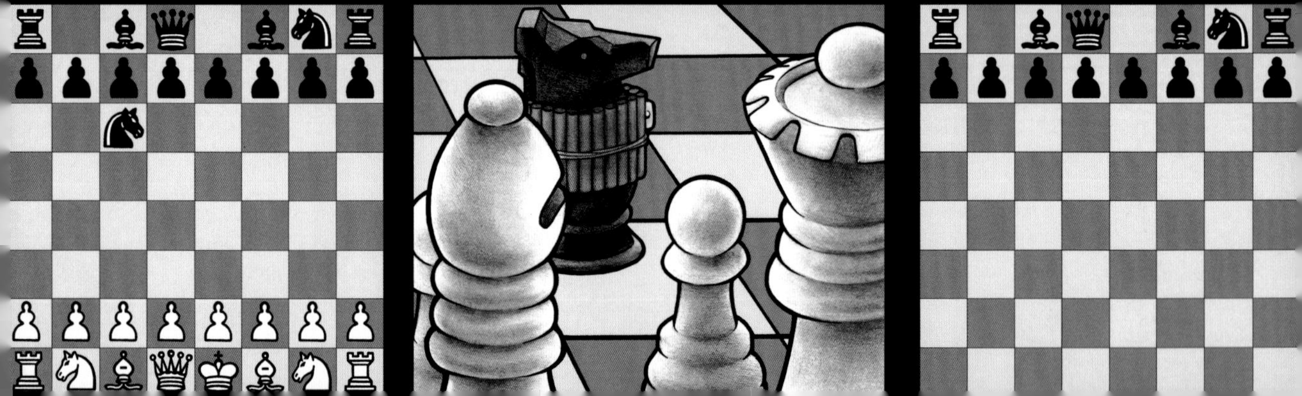

Not enough frames.

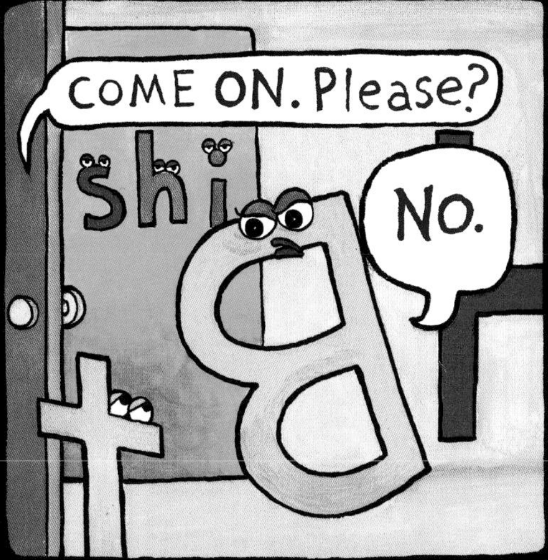
COME ON. Please?
shi
NO.

Again, this one's just a little bit too self-reflexive . . .

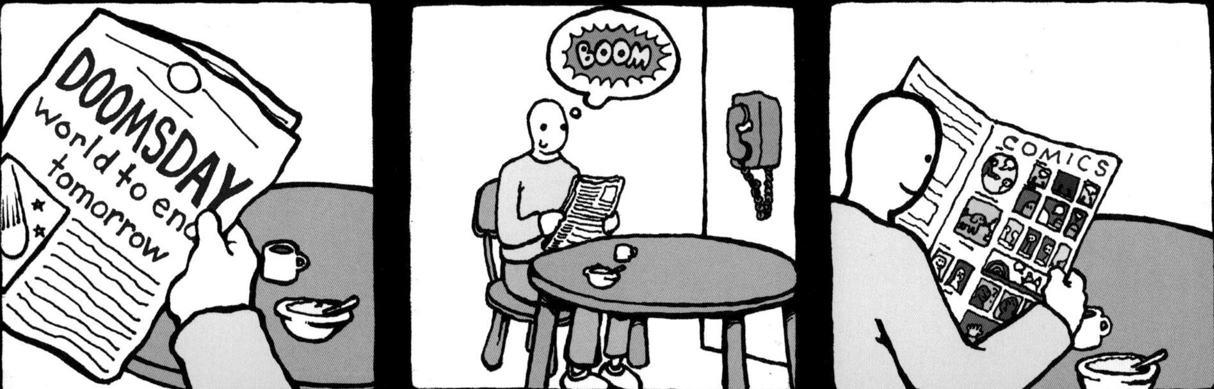
DOOMSDAY
world to en
tomorrow
BOOM
COMICS

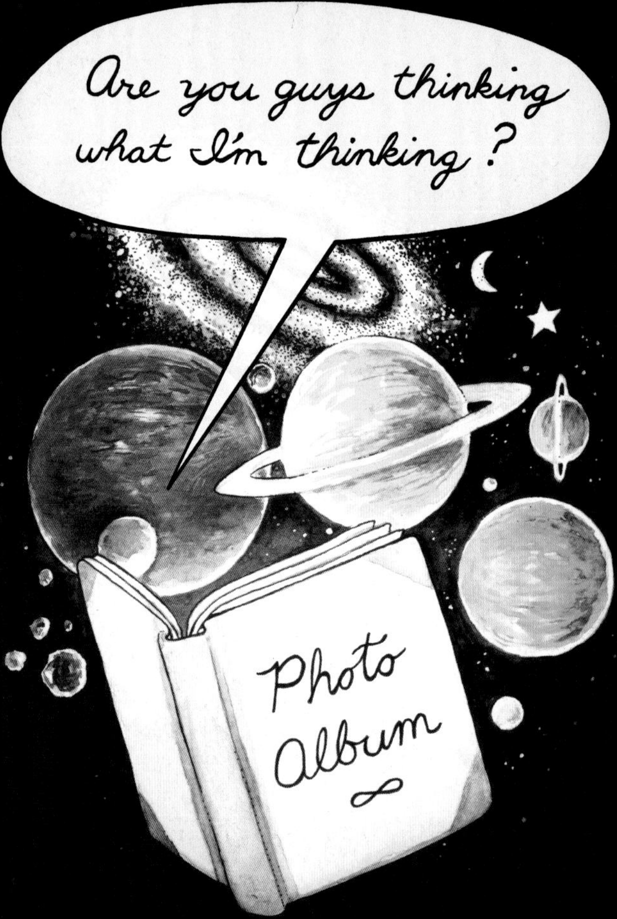
Are you guys thinking what I'm thinking?
Photo Album

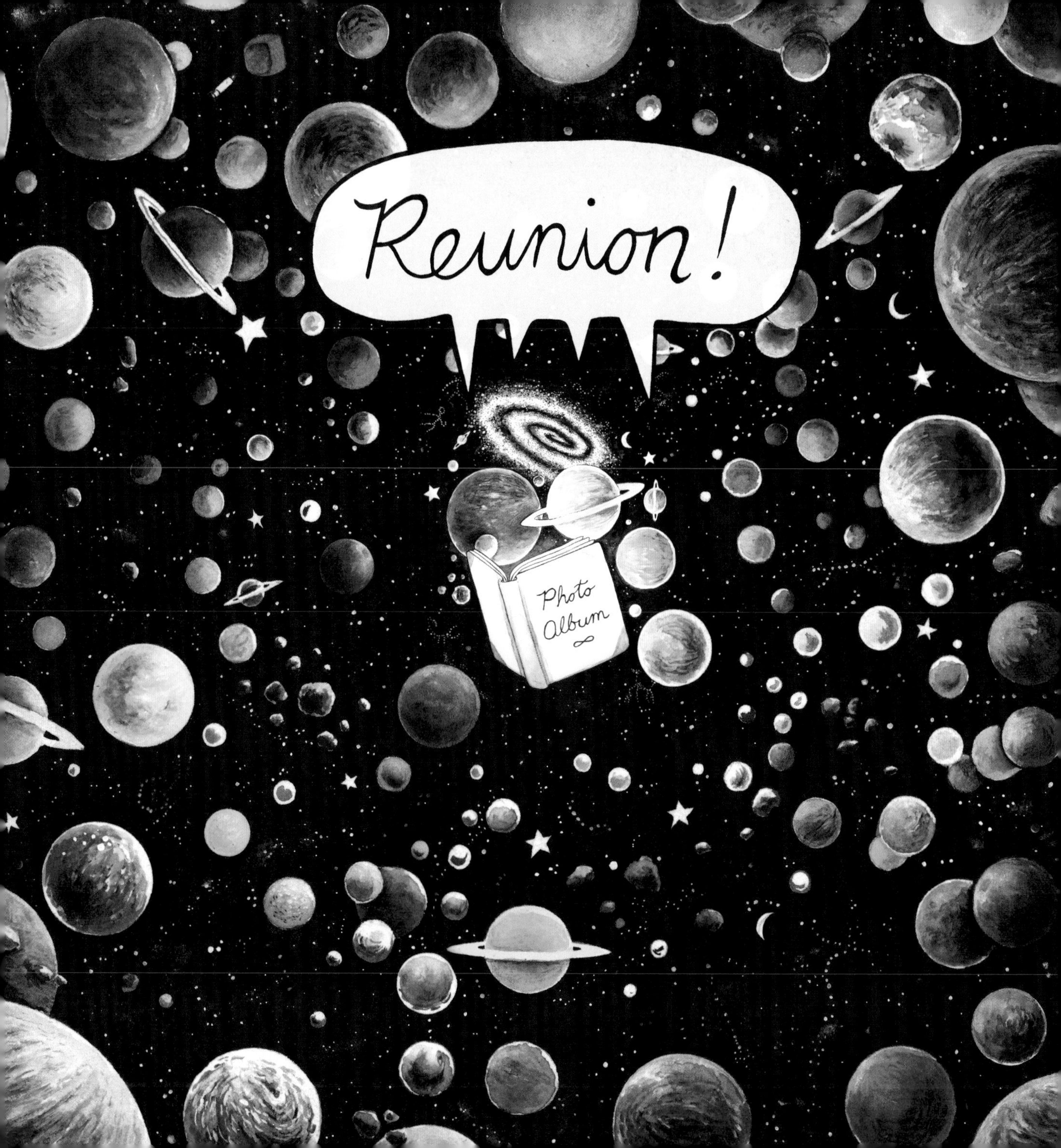
Reunion!
Photo Album

Thanks to Evan Keogh and Jordan Morris for suggesting concepts, collaborating with me, and acting as principal writers on a number of strips over the years.

Evan, your wayward sensibilities, at least as much as my own, constitute the "voice" of The *PBF*. I find it unpleasant to imagine how it might have developed had I not been sharing a room with you when I started it. If I've fathered this comic strip, you've certainly been its jolly, significantly-beloved uncle.

Jordan. I can't think of anyone whose enjoyment of a *PBF* I cherish more. Your creative contributions and scathing criticisms have really expanded the scope of the comic. Your mind, even by my standards, strikes me as a well of dark and wonderful thoughts.

I'd also like to recognize a few people who have shared an idea on which I've based a strip. They are: Eric Laplante, Matthew Roberts, Johnny Kazanjian, Alexander Gurewitch, Eric Gurewitch, and Albert Birney.

Albert Birney. Thank you for your additional contributions of a hundred different sorts, your ceaseless support, and for founding the fellowship with me. You've been there every step of the way.

Additional thanks to Jess Swazey for her photography (featured on page 77), to Rick Hock and Michael Neault for being photographed, and to the latter for returning the favor (see right). Extra thanks to Dan Reitz, Vanessa Lauria, Natalie Welsh, Dave Bour, Andrew Hussie, and Michael Elliot for various other things having to do with this book.

Finally, thanks to the innumerable friends, family members, editors, fans, and classmates who have reviewed various drafts over the years. I'd list you all, but you number in the hundreds, and I would hate to leave anyone out (except maybe Joe Macleod, who can be kind of a jerk).

Nicholas Gurewitch lives in upstate New York. He has no cats. As of this printing, his award-winning comic strip *The Perry Bible Fellowship* is published in various weekly newspapers and monthly magazines, and on Fridays in the G2 section of the *UK Guardian*.

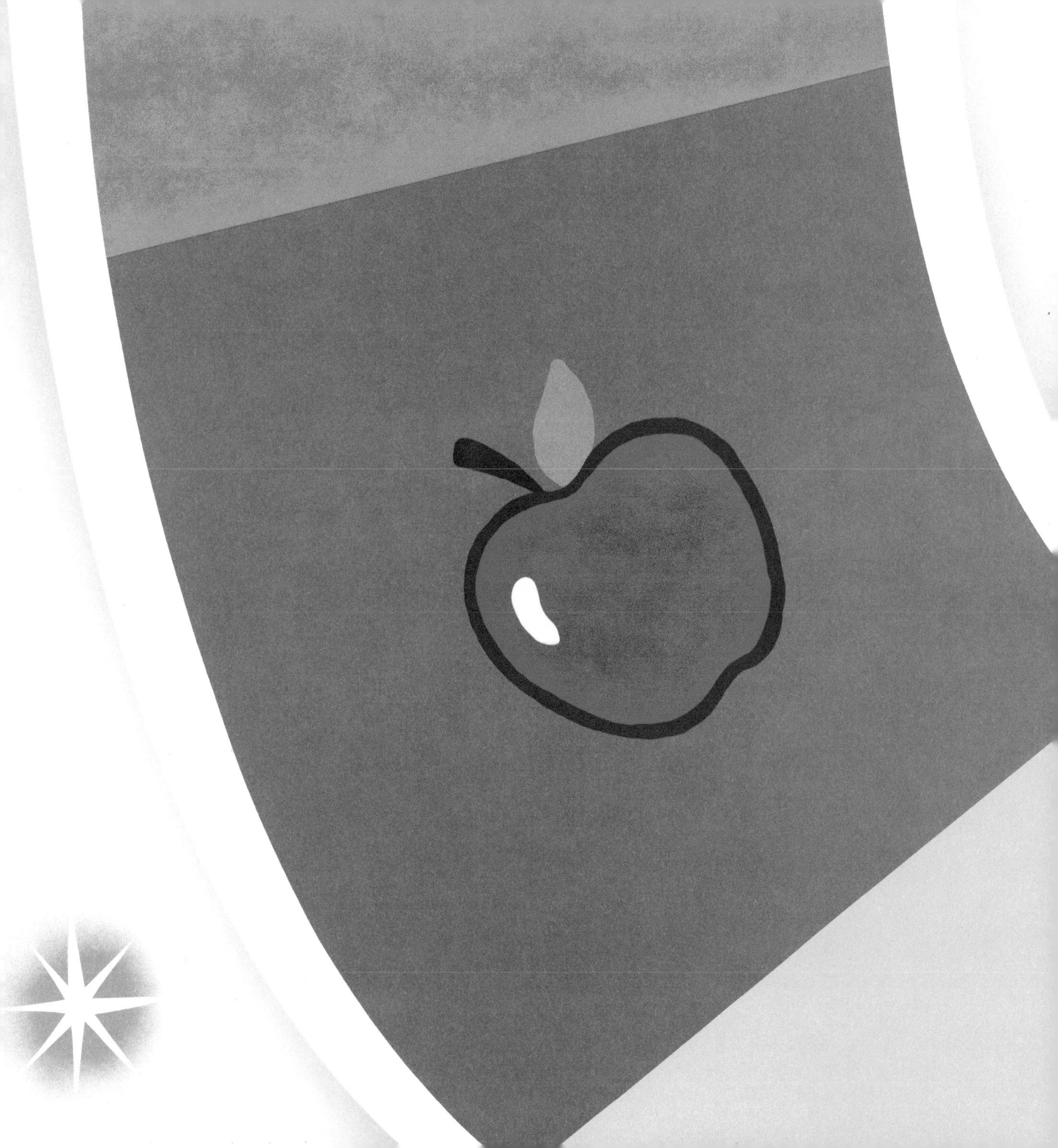

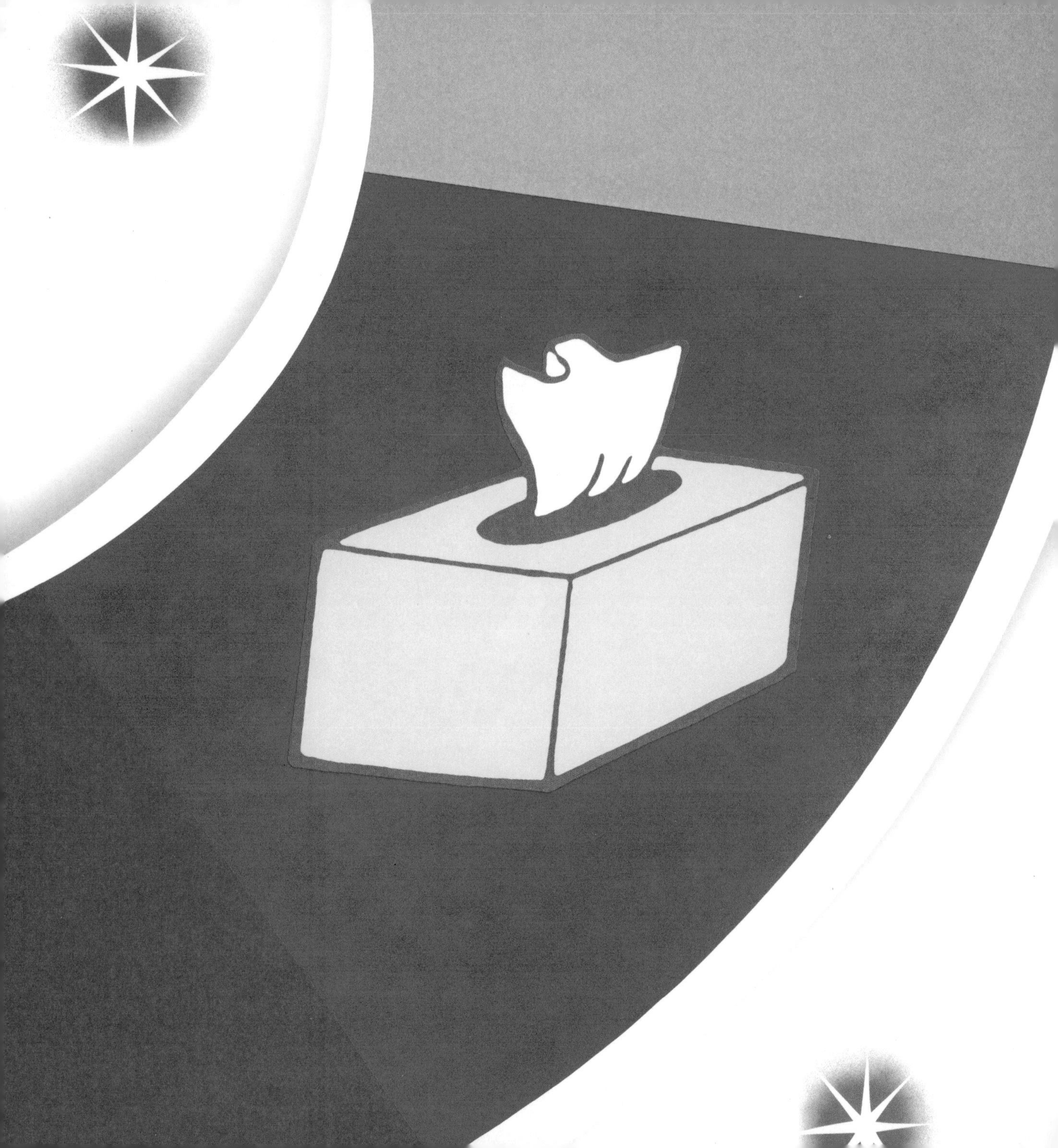